I. Going Home on the Bus. By Linda at thirteen years of age.

THE ARTIST
IN EACH OF US

Florence Cane

With 23 color plates

and 166 illustrations in black and white

ART THERAPY PUBLICATIONS

Craftsbury Common, Vermont

Revised Edition Printed in the United States of America for

Art Therapy Publications

Craftsbury Common, VT 05827

by Baker-Webster Printing Co., Washington, DC

First Edition 1951

Revised Edition 1983

Reprinted 1989

Library of Congress Cataloging in Publication Data

Cane, Florence, 1882-1952.
　The artist in each of us.

1. Art therapy.　　　2. Art—Psychology.　　I. Title.
　RC489.A7C35 1983　　615.8'5156　　　83-14347
　ISBN 0-9611462-0-6

DEDICATION

To those who long to draw or paint, but have never dared; to those who have tried but retreated, either because of some barrier of the world's circumstance or because of a blocking from within; and to the teachers and parents who are helping the young to paint—this book is dedicated.

FOREWORDS TO THE REVISED EDITION

I. BY FLORENCE CANE'S DAUGHTERS

THERE was nothing indefinite about my mother. I used to look to her face for an answer—was it "yes" or was it "no"? She was a warm, generous nurturing person of great taste, but she frightened me. Her reactions were so quick and judgmental—I wondered how she could know so much and be so right!

Florence Cane responded to everything that was beautiful in the natural world and in man and his creative expression. Her selection of furniture, colors, and paintings was a delight. Friends sought her guidance in decorating their homes. For years our house would be host to colorful swatches draped and dropped in odd places. She drank in the textures of life through her senses: the feel of moss in the woods; the sand sifting through her fingers on the beach. She gathered flowers in abundance (I would pick *one*, whereas she would gather an armful). She loved life and confronted it head-on, and so it was in regard to people—each person was a world to explore.

The world in which my twin sister and I grew up was one of experimentation in everything: new theories in education, art, music, dance, theater, morals, psychoanalysis, and so on. We were among the original guinea pigs of progressive education. We entered the Walden School at the age of three. Walden was founded by Margaret Naumburg, my mother's younger sister.

It must have been when we were about twelve years old that Walden hired an art teacher. My mother was critical of the work that came out of the art classes. Something was wrong with the approach. Creativity and individuality were being crushed.

She wanted to do something about it right away. She begged Margaret to let her experiment with one class. This led to more, including a class for the teachers who asked for after-school instruction. During this experience at Walden, Florence Cane developed her credo: keep the creative process alive and stimulate it and nurture it. Techniques were yet to be conceived, tried out, and developed. The idea of integrating the individual through the art process led to many paths of research and experimentation.

The Artist in Each of Us was published in September 1951. Many letters poured in in response to the book, asking my mother to give lectures and workshops and to teach all over the United States. In April 1952 she died of cancer.

For more than thirty years the book has been out of print. My own copies have been lent countless times. "The book should be republished" was a thought that came to me more and more insistently. I did nothing about it. (My mother would have lectured me on the evils of SLOTH.) I needed someone with authority in these matters to tell me what I already knew: that the methods and theories developed by Florence Cane were still valid and exciting. So, one particular day about a year ago, I found myself having an imaginary conversation with Elinor Ulman whom I had never met but whom I regarded with great respect. I was asking her, "Would my mother's book have merit, value—would her ideas, concepts, and practices be important in today's world? I would like to see the book republished in paperback. What was her opinion?" I wrote immediately; she replied with enthusiasm—and here is the book!

Let me acknowledge with pleasure and gratitude my indebtedness to Elinor Ulman, Claire A. Levy, and Bernard I. Levy for their expert help and unfailing support. I also want to thank Florence Cane's close associates who contributed the statements that appear at the back of the book. It occurred to me that today's readers might gain a deeper acquaintance with my mother through these people who knew her so well.

MARY CANE ROBINSON
Denver, Colorado, April 1983

WHILE I did paint when at the Walden School I knew painting was not my medium of communication. Movement was to be the means, and the body the instrument in my work. This was not as great a departure from Florence's teaching as it might seem, for to her the body and the free use of it

iii

was an important means of releasing the image to be projected by the brush on the paper or canvas.

Florence's focus on the *artist* in each of us was not for art's sake but for life's sake. She was a part of the flow of all the new forces in her time. She was a suffragette. She experienced a Jungian analysis. She belonged to a Gourdjieff group led by A.R. Orage. She studied the mind-body system of F.M. Alexander, the movement schemes of Bess M. Mensendieck, and the exercise and relaxation techniques for relieving eyestrain developed by W.H. Bates. She was open to every new wave of energy that helped free the human soul and body.

She became involved with the new art of the twenties; she knew and was vitally interested in the work of some of the leading American artists of her day: Alfred Stieglitz and Georgia O'Keefe, Arthur Dove, John Marin, and Marsden Hartley. She collected their work. She was married to poet-lawyer Melville Cane.

Later she became deeply interested in Eastern philosophy. From modern dance I turned to Yoga, so it turned out that her influence on me was from her philosophical side. Unfortunately, as so often happens between members of two generations, my interest developed years after her death and we were not able to share it. But just recently I have been acutely aware of our deep connection.

Florence Naumburg Cane was born September 28, 1882 and died April 30, 1952 in New York City. I am so happy that a new generation of teachers and students will have the opportunity to meet my mother through the reissue of her book. I join my sister, Mary, in thanking Elinor Ulman and Claire and Bernard Levy for making it possible.

KATHERINE CANE DETRE
Denver, Colorado, April 1983

II. By Two Art Therapists

IN a recent rereading of *The Artist in Each of Us* I found that time and again I had to refer back to determine whether I was reading about a person referred to Florence Cane by a psychiatrist, a person defined by her as specifically in need of "therapy," or a student being helped by means of art to deal with life's ordinary vicissitudes. Cane plainly linked two fields—art education and therapy through art. She saw that the overlap between them can be greater than any area that belongs exclusively to one or the other. As a highly effective art *teacher*—aiming to draw out the artist in each person—she directs her attention to the student's "physical, emotional, and spiritual" well-being (p. 369). As an art *therapist* her "approach," as she stated, "is not very different from that which [she uses] toward an ordinary student in art except that the emphasis is placed on expression of fantasy with a minimum of time spent on technical proficiency" (p. 318).

For most of the handful of art therapists who entered the field in the early 1950's, *The Artist in Each of Us* served as both inspiration and practical guide. In my case Florence Cane's book played a special role, since an important part of my motivation for becoming an art therapist was the hope of guiding others in a kind of art experience that my schooling in the 1920's and 1930's had failed to provide. Reading this book helped to change my vague sense of malaise into an increasingly clear realization of what I had been missing. I, too, drew no hard-and-fast line between art education and art therapy, and recognized that I was "attracted to . . . art therapy because here there is a freer opportunity to nourish genuine artistic development than in most . . . teaching jobs" (Ulman 1966). Too often art therapists forget the basis of their discipline in the healing power of art; hence the relevance of this book to the profession of art therapy today.

On the practical side, Cane tells us about her techniques with such openness and clarity that we can readily try them out. In particular her account of movement leading to scribbling restores to that series of exercises its original vitality. Nowhere else in the literature of art education or art therapy can we find such immediately applicable directives even to this day.

Cane is also more generous than most writers in giving us a full account of her verbal interpretations in addition to the student's or patient's responses and verbal initiatives. Here again the roles of teacher and therapist tend to merge.

For art educators as for art therapists *The Artist in Each of Us* maintains its relevance. Cane speaks of her belief that she stood in the forefront of a radical shift in art education. "New frontiers are opening up," she says. "The psychological approach no longer regards the art product as separate from the artist" (p. 80). But now the pendulum has swung in an unexpected direction. In education and in psychotherapy demands for measurable behavioral results outweigh concern for the inner life of human beings. It is sad that Cane's approach has not become common in general education or in schools of art—but this makes her message all the more urgent for art educators today.

I never had the privilege of meeting Florence Cane, but I feel deeply indebted to her for what her book contributed to my professional life. I am grateful for the opportunity to assist in the republication of *The Artist in Each of Us,* a classic out of print so long that few art therapists and art educators practicing today have had the chance to make it part of their personal libraries. I want to thank Mary Cane Robinson and Katherine Cane Detre for making it possible for me to repay at least a small part of my debt.

ELINOR ULMAN, D.A.T., ATR
Editor, *AMERICAN JOURNAL OF ART THERAPY*
Washington, D.C., May 1983

REFERENCE

Ulman, Elinor (1966) "Therapy Is Not Enough: The Contribution of Art to General Hospital Psychiatry." *Bulletin of Art Therapy* 6: 3-21. (Also appears in *Art Therapy in Theory and Practice.* Edited by Elinor Ulman and Penny Dachinger. New York, Schocken Books, 1975.)

In 1951, when *The Artist in Each of Us* was first published, I had already pursued studies in art and, later, in psychology. Gradually I turned from the pursuit of a career as a painter, potter, or sculptor toward a growing interest in the psychology of art. Looking back more than thirty years, I realize that I had already become fascinated with two issues: the creative or expressive aspect of art and its projective aspect. My concerns can be put in the form of two questions: (1) What purpose does the experience of making artworks serve in the life of the creator? (2) What does the completed work of art reveal about its creator?

Though some of Cane's interpretations suggest her awareness of projective elements in her students' work, her main focus was on assisting the realization of expressive art. She saw herself rightly as representing a new trend in the understanding and teaching of art. Other gifted art teachers whose published works came to my attention at almost the same time as Cane's were Viktor Lowenfeld (1947), Henry Schaefer-Simmern (1948) and Kimon Nicolaïdes (1941). Ernst Harms (1946) was the first writer I became aware of whose primary concern was with the projective power of art; Harms (1948) and Naumburg (1947) were probably the earliest writers on the use of art in a fundamentally verbal therapeutic process. Thus Cane's work belongs to a time of ferment in the worlds of art, art education, and the nascent field of art therapy.

Preparing to write this foreword, I have just reread *The Artist in Each of Us* for the first time in many years. Having meantime become a psychologist, painter, teacher of painting, and an art therapist, I brought many new insights—as well as the lessons derived from over 30 years of history—to this second reading. When Cane discusses the sources of her approach to art teaching, her language may sound romantic today, but her ideas themselves are still alive and useful. She writes of mounting the barricades to defend against the stifling of creativity by a modern industrial society. In the same vein she conveys her deep interest in Jung's ideas and her belief that there is a core of good in all of us. She eschews the panoply of psychiatric and educational language and tells us about her methods and her interactions with students and patients in helpful detail. She was generous in allowing us to look into her mind and over her shoulder— more so than most writers in art education and art therapy.

Her methods hinged on her readiness to bring out the artist in one and all. She used movement, chanting, the scribble, and the occasional perceptive and straightforward reaction to a client's art. Of greatest importance was her effort to help people reach ever more deeply inside of themselves for the sources of art and to try to formulate the graphic expression ever more effectively. This is an important set of lessons for teachers and therapists.

Yes, this book is one that should continue to live since it speaks to the mysteries of creativity and personal expression. Its approach is emotional rather than cognitive and its frequent and detailed accounts of people who worked with Cane, an art teacher/therapist, give it an enduring place in the still scant literature about the importance of art as a helping, even healing, process. (Joan Erikson [1976], Edith Kramer [1971], and Elinor Ulman [1966] are among the few authors who carry on in Cane's tradition.)

Cane's book tells us not only how to reach "the artist in each of us," but also how to use that artist to help ourselves and others deal with life.

BERNARD I. LEVY, Ph.D., ATR
The George Washington University
Washington, D.C., May 1983

REFERENCES

Erikson, Joan M., with David and Joan Loveless (1976) *Activity, Recovery, Growth: The Communal Role of Planned Activities.* New York, W.W. Norton & Co.

Harms, E. (1946) "The Psychology of Formal Creativeness. I. Six Fundamental Types of Formal Expression." *Journal of Genetic Psychology* 69: 97-120.

(1948) "Awakening into Consciousness of Subconscious Collective Symbolism as Therapeutic Procedure." *Journal of Child Psychiatry* 1: 208-38.

Kramer, Edith (1971) *Art as Therapy with Children.* New York, Schocken Books.

Lowenfeld, Viktor (1947) *Creative and Mental Growth.* New York, Macmillan Co.

Naumburg, Margaret (1973) *An Introduction to Art Therapy: Studies of the "Free" Art Expression of Behavior Problem Children and Adolescents as a Means of Diagnosis and Therapy* (Revised Edition). New York, Teachers College Press, Columbia University. (First Edition published in 1947).

Nicolaïdes, Kimon (1941) *The Natural Way To Draw.* Boston, Houghton Mifflin Co.

Schaefer-Simmern, Henry (1948) *The Unfolding of Artistic Activity: Its Basis, Processes, and Implications.* Berkeley, University of California Press.

Ulman, Elinor (1966) "Therapy Is Not Enough: The Contribution of Art to General Hospital Psychiatry." *Bulletin of Art Therapy* 6: 3-21. (Also appears in *Art Therapy in Theory and Practice.* Edited by Elinor Ulman and Penny Dachinger. New York, Schocken Books, 1975.)

FOREWORD TO THE FIRST EDITION

THIS is a story that is warm with living. It is told by a remarkable woman—an artist, not only with brush and canvas, but also with human relationships. It is a story built out of creative moments—in her life as teacher and in the lives of those whom she has taught. It is a story that will thrill all who thrill to the growth of children.

The characters in this story are, for the most part, old friends. Florence Cane has served for many years as Director of Art for the Counseling Centre for Gifted Children of the School of Education of New York University. The young artists around whose development the plot of the story is written are, in a large part, talented children whose growth it has been the Centre's privilege to watch.

Many simple but neglected truths about children's growth and the creative process are vividly highlighted in the pages that follow: the truth that all growth takes place through the creative utilization by the child of his environing experience; the truth that freedom is the very breath of the growing child, but that freedom implies support; the truth that growth is at heart an integration of the emotional life; the truth that the child's creative activities are not discrete from the rest of his living, but are the projection of his personality in its entirety; the truth that as growth achieves inner harmony, creative strength and productivity increase; the truth that children, and adults as well, particularly when troubled, seek to communicate through the medium of what they create that which they cannot put into words.

But I leave Mrs. Cane's skilful narratives and the drawings and paintings of her pupils to tell the story. All who read this book will lay it down with an excitement that demands release in experimenting with the methods she describes. Even I, to whose inhibited artistic impulse the very sight of a palette has been a source of frustration, now itch to grasp a brush in my hand.

HARVEY ZORBAUGH, Director
Counseling Centre for Gifted Children
New York University
New York, January 1951

ACKNOWLEDGMENTS

Warm thanks are given to my husband Melville Cane for his thoughtful reading of my manuscript and for his valuable suggestions; to Professor Harvey Zorbaugh, for his steady support throughout my thirteen years of work at his "Counseling Centre for Gifted Children"; to my friend Frances Gardner, for her untiring assistance in organizing the material from twenty-five years of work, and especially for her faith in the project; but most of all to the scores of children whom I have remembered as I wrote this book. Sometimes they delighted me, sometimes they tormented me, but always the children taught me more than I gave them.

F. C.

PREFACE

My work is founded on the belief that every man is born with the power to create. This power is of the spirit and through its use man awakens and grows.

Art can be the means for the rounded development of the individual. Most of the problems the student meets in his work have their parallel in life, and by facing them and solving them in his art, he grows as a human being. This growth in turn intensifies his capacity as an artist, and his work, expanding, reaches higher levels of expression. This related activity sets in motion an ever-progressing cycle of growth.

In this book, I present a modern method of teaching art. Through study of the book, the reader, it is hoped, will find ways and means of attaining to a richer art and a more integrated life; if the reader is a teacher, it is hoped he will find these ways and means transmissible to his students.

The means to achieve better results divide naturally into three parts; man's three chief functions—movement, feeling, and thought—are the pivots for this study.

Under the physical function of movement comes the use of rhythm in the body of the artist, and the transfer of the rhythm to his art.

Stimulation of feeling and thought is accomplished by several means: the training of observation, memory, and imagination; the intensification of images through closed eyes and silence; and the use of chanting. The effect of chanting is this: in that moment the student seems to unify himself miraculously, so that by the use of his three functions, he rises to a higher level of consciousness, so that the picture actually seems inspired by higher forces.

My endeavour has been to co-ordinate abstract psychological problems and their solutions with the detailed technical means of instruction. In both abstract psychology and technical means I hope that the reader will receive specific enlightenment from the study of case histories.

Another aim of this book is to clarify through the records of students' work the roles the unconscious and the conscious play in the production of art.

9

The revelations through the paintings of patients of the processes going on in the unconscious have long been recognized by psychiatrists as a valuable contribution to modern psychotherapy. There are, of course, many instances when the patient or student requires medical care, but there is proof in these pages that a great deal of healing can take place through the catharsis of art under the guidance of a teacher who understands the meanings shown in the paintings and the unexpressed needs of the child and who possesses the ability to help the child cleanse and renew himself.

F. C.

CONTENTS

PART III

Practice

The Child

The Adult

PART IV

The Healing Quality of Art

LIST OF ILLUSTRATIONS

*Roman numerals will be used for references in the text to colour plates;
black and white plates will be referred to by arabic numerals.*

Colour Plates

Black and White Plates

PART I

Theory

CHAPTER I

The Creative Process

As long as man merely senses, craves and works from desire, man is still nothing but world. That he may not be merely world, he must impart form to matter, he shall externalize all within and shape everything without.

—SCHILLER

BECAUSE of the compelling need to "shape everything without", the artist in each of us comes into being. The young artist's struggles to grow, and my efforts to help him, form the story of this book.

NATURE OF THE CREATIVE PROCESS

Naturally the first steps of the novice are to take up pencil or brush to draw or paint. Before approaching the problems which arise in this field of expression, we should understand what takes place within the young artist and what means there are by which we may accelerate his power.

Nature and art have this in common—a form comes into existence by the union of two opposites. In nature, male and female create a new life. In art, two opposite states of being within the artist are needed to create form. The active and receptive states must alternate to produce and complete a work.

The common opinion prevails that only constant effort and activity are required. This is a false notion, the cause of many failures. Take, for example, two boys, each meeting obstacles in his work, but each using a different method to overcome them.

The first boy comes into the studio and goes directly to work. He draws for an hour, but is not satisfied. He tries again and again, only to conclude that he cannot rescue the picture. In disgust, he crumples it up and throws it away. The explanation is simple. The boy was frustrated and tried to push himself past failure by continual activity.

He fought against the natural tide in the creative process. He needed rest and reflection to find the next step, but he did not know enough to satisfy that need.

Take a different case. A boy starts with an idea or an image in his mind of something he wants to paint. He picks up his sketchbook, then sits in the corner of the room quietly dreaming about the idea and letting it take shape. He makes several sketches to clarify the plan. At last he gets up, goes to the easel, and begins his picture. He may work for a long time, but he too comes to difficulties that he cannot overcome. He struggles for a while. Then, instead of forcing the issue, the boy, like a true artist, takes care of himself. He throws himself on a couch (which is there for this very purpose) and broods about the picture, letting it speak to him. During this time he may close his eyes and place his hands over them. As the darkness and quiet increase, the original images become clarified, or new ones come surging up to enrich the first plan.

The answer to the boy's problem may arise from his unconscious mind, from the sum of his past experiences, or from some outside source of wisdom. The important thing is that the solution frequently appears. The darkness, the quiet, the withdrawal, all help the boy to find the next step. Released, he can then return to work.

The idea of consciously—rhythmically—alternating the process of giving out and taking in is so simple that it seems obvious, but few people make use of it. The tendency is to work to that point of fatigue at which nothing fresh can be contributed. If the student learns to proceed in rhythm, he will find a new energy, a fresh productivity; he will, in short, be following the law of his nature.

Two photographs demonstrate these two states. The first (Ill. 1) shows Barbara preparing herself to draw. She is quiet, dreamy, receptive. The second (Ill. 2) shows her getting to work. Here she is active, having conceived what she wants to create.

There are other ways in which pairs of opposites balance each other. For example, the relation between near and distant objects creates a tension which gives a sense of space; the play between dark and light builds form; the juxtaposition of warm and cold colours intensifies their values; the use of movement into, and out of, a picture establishes living

1. Preparation: the Receptive State

form. Both the large tree trunk and the tiny leaf have their place in fine design. To be aware of the two simultaneously implies balance and understanding.

The simplest form of rhythm and the one first manifested in the creative process is repetition. It is present in the lowest form of life. Its earliest expression is the expansion and contraction of breathing. All the intricacies of form and design grow out of it. A rhythmic impulse in the child is inevitable, for it is the basis of the world of which he is a unit.

While the child is young and impulsive, his art is unconscious. As he matures and develops an active will, his art becomes conscious; and as this happens, the self becomes more integrated. Art becomes a means of developing the human being, which is its true purpose and function.

Laurence Binyon, in *Painting in the Far East*,[1] writes vividly of the place rhythm holds in the art of the Eastern world:

> A Chinese critic of the Sixth Century, who was also an artist, published a theory of aesthetic principles which became a classic and received universal acceptance, expressing as it did, the deeply rooted instincts of the race. In this theory it is rhythm that holds paramount place; not, be it observed, imitation of nature, or fidelity to nature, which the general instinct of the western races makes the root concern of art.
>
> In this theory every work of art is thought of as an incarnation of the genius of rhythm, manifesting the living spirit with a clearer beauty and intenser power than the gross impediments of complex matter allow to be transmitted to our senses in the visible world around us. A picture is conceived as a sort of apparition from a more real world of essential life.

Although many aspects of the intricate creative process will be considered throughout the text, this concept of balance and rhythm within the organism of the artist, who can then transfer these qualities to his work, provides the basic pattern of creativity.

TRACING THE CREATIVE PROCESS

Sensory and muscular activity characterize the creative process in the two- or three-year-old child. A child of this age should be left alone in a quiet, safe place, for he needs no close supervision. If he is outdoors, he should have within easy reach nature's materials, such as sand, pebbles,

[1] Longmans, Green & Co., New York, 1923.

2. WORK: THE ACTIVE STATE

sticks, leaves, or shells; if indoors, the child should have cards and blocks. These are things that he can shape or mould.

The child should be free to explore at his own pace, whether that be eager and swift or ambling and deliberate. The adult in charge should appear absorbed in his own work and should observe the child unobtrusively. Under these conditions, a healthy, unspoiled infant will explore his world, begin to order it, and eventually master it.

First, the child will touch and handle an object, try to break or bend it in order to find out its possibilities. He may taste or smell or listen to it. He is using his senses to test his material. When this natural desire for simple, sensory experience is satisfied, he will proceed to do something more with the material. If the child is playing with earth, he may dig a hole or make a mud pie; if he is playing with stones or blocks, he may pile them up and push them down. These activities are instinctive, muscular ones.

EARLY ATTEMPTS TO SHAPE THE WORLD

After a period of time, the child's desire for this simple activity becomes satisfied, and he searches for something new. A groping wish to arrange things in some sort of order arises. Instead of making one mud pie, the child makes a series; instead of piling up stones, he produces a row or a square. The row may be exceedingly irregular, and the squares lopsided, but the attempt is significant, for it represents the emergence of order out of chaos.

It is extremely interesting to note how evidences of a sense of proportion, balance, and symmetry appear. The principles of art live in everyone. They need only to be brought out by opportunity and encouragement. The child's interest in these first crude attempts is usually very serious and may hold his attention for a surprisingly long time. Care must be taken not to interrupt him during the time of discovery and execution. Something mysterious, even sacred, is happening to him. A connection is being made between the self and the universe, with the self as master. The child feels a sense of expansion, achievement, and well-being. At such a time, he may look up or call to the adult near him to share his adventure. The kind of response he receives will in a large measure influence the future. If he is met with indifference or a frown, he may feel crushed and subdued, perhaps irritable and unhappy; the new sense of achievement will be lost, and the desire to go on will be deflected. If the child wins a smile, a friendly recognition of his accomplishment, and a true valuation of it in relation to his stature, the experience will be positive and strong, likely to lead to another attempt soon after—an attempt probably a little harder and a little more complex.

The creative faculty becomes more robust through the kind of understanding illustrated in the following incident. A child of two and a half was playing on the floor making a simple border pattern out of cards. She showed deep interest and concentration on her task. Her mother, sewing near by, regretted that the supply of cards was giving out as she realized how eager the child was to continue. Then an idea occurred to the mother. She removed the cards from the beginning of the border at the farther end of the room and placed them near the child. The child was so much absorbed in her work as to be indifferent to the fate of the first part of her design. Thus the mother kept her daughter supplied with cards as long as her interest lasted. (In this instance, the interest span was half an hour.) Satisfaction was thereby completed; the child's wish and her accomplishment were balanced.

THE NURSERY SCHOOL

When a child reaches nursery-school age, simple art materials are given to him. The child proceeds very much as he did in playing with sand and stones, for the impulse to create originates in play; only later does the desire or power for sustained effort appear. It seems that energy to labour grows out of fulfilment in play.

The child begins by covering paper with bright marks of crayon or pools of paint. He does this merely for the pleasure in the movement. Next, the colour excites sensation in him; then the dabs and pools of accidental shapes arouse his imagination. These forms in turn link with his own experiences and bring his emotions into play. Thus, the whole child is functioning, and the painting becomes a simple, joyous form of self-expression.

The essential nature of a young child's drawing is fanciful to an adult. The painting may even be unintelligible to him. But any attempt at correction by imposing at this time an adult point of view may entirely cut off the child's interest in the activity. Later, instruction will have its place, but now the stream should flow on unimpeded. At this moment, the child's own world is more vivid than accurate perception. A formless pool of paint in one picture he may call a house; a similar one in the next he may call a moon. Or the pictures at this early age may have a purely subjective meaning to the child. One little girl of five was heard to say about her painting: "This looks just the way I feel inside."

This period does not last long. The child soon needs some guidance from a teacher to prevent him from tightening over his work, from getting too close to it, or from merely making muddy daubs with his paints. This assistance must be given without interfering with the child's independence. (Art experiences for teachers themselves would be most valuable at this time.) Teachers should be able to recognize the elements of primitive art in a child's drawing and encourage them, never attempting to bring sophistication into the pupil's work. The teacher should also know which materials will help or hinder the youngster. Hard crayons, for example, cause the muscles to tense and spoil the free-flowing line, whereas softer ones will permit relaxation, free expression, and a supple line.

TRENDS OF THE CREATIVE PROCESS

Throughout the first seven years of a child's life, physical growth and muscular activity are predominant. During this period the child draws chiefly in lines (one dimension). His production is characterized by quantity. He will not be interested in developing the many pictures he rapidly draws. At this stage the average child gets his chief pleasure from scribbling and revelling in colour regardless of form. A few children do develop further and begin to express their ideas more clearly.

In the next period, roughly from the ages of seven to fourteen, the child develops sensation and feeling as well as the ability to observe the world around him. He becomes interested in two-dimensional form; quality asserts itself over quantity. The pupil works more slowly and demands more of himself. Each picture must satisfy not only himself but his companions as well. The child needs the approval of others. He cares more whether he achieves what he started out to do. He wants to learn how to do better. He still has the unconsciousness of a child, but is beginning to mature. The ages ten to fourteen are a very free-flowing time before the child's conflicts begin.

The third period, roughly from fourteen to eighteen, includes adolescence. This period, initiated by the awareness of the third dimension, is coexistent with the pupil's deepening consciousness. Thought emerges and mixes with emotion. Self-criticism at this age becomes severe, and, if the right direction is not given, the boy or girl may stop work altogether because of dissatisfaction with his or her efforts.

It is the firm belief of many educators that the creative ability of children disappears at adolescence. I am convinced that the contrary is true. The changes occurring at this time enhance rather than diminish the student's ability. Feelings deepen, minds awaken; a great new hunger and thirst for life, understanding, experience, and expression take place. The desire and need to create are there; the fault lies rather in the quality of the teaching.

Most of the art teaching of adolescent pupils fails to meet these new demands for knowledge. Too often the teaching is purely mechanical and empty; too often it is without direction or inspiration. If the young student is to progress and develop in his art at this age, he must receive the most sensitive guidance. Youth deserves teachers with psychological understanding, artistic ability, and simple, direct methods of supplying the technique demanded by hungry minds and searching hearts.

Thus we trace through the growing years the continuity of the desire to "externalize all within and shape everything without". Ours is the task to nurture this desire and to clarify the difficulties as they appear so that the creative process of the pupil may be constantly flowing and self-renewing.

CHAPTER II

Conditions Favourable to Creative Work

It is not so difficult to create as it is to maintain the conditions from which one may create.

—BRANCUSI

CERTAIN conditions are favourable to the development of the creative process. I refer to those conditions which exist in the outer world and to those which exist within the child himself. If we learn to understand both, we are better able to encourage and stimulate creative work.

OUTER CONDITIONS

Children enter the classroom expectant. The room should be still and materials ready. There should be plenty of space and light; walls should be white and undecorated—this makes a fertile world for the imagination to play in. There should be plenty of good, illustrated reference books on shelves to be used when needed.

It is important *not* to have mature work of adults on the walls. These are far removed from a child's expression and may intimidate him. Preferably pictures the children have themselves made should decorate the walls and give courage to the new pupils. The fact that these pictures issue from the child's own world, his heaven and his earth, reassures him. Sometimes bright-coloured materials or fresh fruits and vegetables placed on a table will stimulate more than the presence of art itself.

THE PROPER MATERIALS

Large sheets of paper should be used. Small ones tend to cramp work. Crayons and chalks should be rich-coloured and soft enough to mark easily. Hard crayons block the intention of the artist; the softer ones encourage it. For the same reason tempera paints and large brushes are better than small, hard pans of colour and little brushes. Charcoal often responds better than pencil; lithographer's chalks and oil crayons are both extremely successful in making the work more broad, daring, and individual.

ARRANGEMENT AND CARE OF MATERIALS

The arrangement and care of materials are very important, not alone for the habits of order which are thus early established, but particularly because knowledge of where things are and of how they can best be used accelerates the creative process just as a pianist's knowledge of the position of the notes on the keyboard makes them instantaneously available to him. The materials should be placed so that they are easily accessible and they should always be in the same place. There should be boxes for the small things; there should be a table covered with oilcloth for the tempera paints and a spoon for each jar. The large paper should be arranged in a cupboard with many shelves fairly close together so that space is not wasted and so that each of the different kinds of paper may have its own shelf. The various papers used are bogus, manila (in cream and grey), block printing paper which comes in beautiful earth colours, and white paper which comes in two thicknesses. The heavier brand is better for wash and water-colour.

Each child should have his own portfolio if possible. When the cost is prohibitive, the children can make their own portfolios of cardboard tied with tape. The individual portfolio is important not only because it keeps the child's work in good condition, but also because it has a beneficial effect on the child and the progress of his art. If the child forms the habit of being careless here, he is likely to be careless in whatever else he undertakes. Carelessness breeds indifference, not respect, and the child needs to learn respect for his work in order to respect himself.

The same thing applies to materials and tools. If the child learns early that tools can serve him well only if he takes care of them, he will have laid an important foundation stone. His inclination is only to half-wash the brush and to put the chalks away dirty. He should learn that the brush will be stiff and lose its suppleness if he does not wash it well, that the right chalks will be hard to find if they become greyish from each other's dust and, in addition, that the colours they produce will be dirty. These lessons in care will help his work and his personal development. Therefore, the pupil should be painstakingly instructed in the right use of his materials as he receives them.

INNER CONDITIONS

The inner conditions favourable to creative work can be fostered by the teacher. But the teacher invites and cultivates them only if he or she is aware of their existence. By ingenuity the teacher must find ways and means of bringing them into being. When one assumes the responsibility of "teaching art", that becomes one's major task, one's opportunity. The teacher should know that the potentialities of creativeness exist in each individual, but present also are enemies of creativity: insecurity; fear of failure or of criticism; laziness and conceit; tensions and hyper-activity; and, worst of all, lack of faith in oneself. All of these the teacher must learn to understand and dispel, in order that the favourable conditions may grow.

The most important step in combating the enemies of creativeness is the attainment of a deep unenforced quiet, a real repose. This comes imperceptibly in a room where children are working with concentration, and concentration follows naturally when enjoyment of work exists. Enjoyment in turn results from the ability to achieve, which comes from control of the medium. Out of these fundamental qualities of repose, concentration, and enjoyment flow others, such as self-confidence and willingness to work until the art approximates the conception.

Thus, when we understand the needs of the spirit, we give it free space and liberating materials; we help the pupil fight the destructive forces and cultivate those states which permit the spirit to grow and to create its own form.

CHAPTER III

The Integration of the Individual through Art

THE concept of the integration of an individual includes the activation and union of all one's functions to form an effective and harmonious human being. This is an ancient ideal of many great teachers and philosophers. Fortunately, modern educators are beginning to perceive and accept the meaning of wholeness; and, to the degree that they grasp its implications and understand its processes, the effects are beneficial. They have realized the need of change in curriculum, activities, and methods of teaching and the need of incorporating in their teaching the study of a child's heredity, his social life, and his own behaviour in order to understand and help him.

THE ACT OF CREATING UNIFIES

Art may be a means of activating all one's functions; the simultaneous use of these functions assists in the integration of the personality.

Since every child is born with the power to create, that power should be released early and developed wisely. It may become the key to joy and wisdom and, possibly, to self-realization. Whether or not the child becomes an artist is immaterial.

The awakening of the creative power is often impeded because teachers put their chief interest into helping the pupil produce a good drawing or painting. This emphasis on the product makes criticism external. Definite concrete alterations are constantly suggested, but no effort is made to discover what habit of the brain or hand is at fault. If we observe the pupil, we may discover the offending trait, overcome difficulties, stir new abilities, and awaken new understanding.

Nor will the creative power be aroused by extreme moderns who turn the child loose to potter about entirely unguided and who indiscriminately admire all his immature products. Constant praise does not favour development; it is more likely to produce inflated egos and to kill creativity.

There is a third way—a middle path in which the teacher no longer desires his pupil to excel, in which he no longer wishes to impress his ideas on the child. The teacher's role becomes that of a lover and student of human beings; he or she seeks to release the essential nature of the child and to let that nature create its own forms of expression, beginning in play and growing with effort. The integrity of the child is thus preserved, and the art produced is genuine, primitive, and true.

From this point of view, we can analyse by what means an individual travels towards integration. Repressions and conflicts may split the personality, dam the emotions, waste energy, and set up all kinds of psychological and behaviour difficulties. By overcoming such conflicts, the individual releases emotional force and, with it, new energy for living. In this fashion, art can heal and make whole. Art is of first importance in education, for the adult as well as for the child, because the problem of adjustment and the full realization of one's potentialities is fundamental in all education.

We apprehend the world through three chief functions: movement, feeling, and thought. However, an individual does not begin life with all three actively employed. Usually one or two are used; the third is more or less asleep in the unconscious. Buried within the neglected capability may be the key to the development of a particular individual. The teacher's role is to find ways of activating the unused function.

An integrated individual is one who makes a well-balanced use of each of these three forms of activity. Art has three precepts which must be followed if one is to obtain its fullest expression. There is a correspondence between these functions of the human being and the underlying principles of art. The function of movement is related to the principle of rhythm; feeling, to dynamics and harmony; and thought, to balance. Since the principles of art correspond to human functions, one may therefore gradually integrate functions through the practice of art. By this fortunate relation, the teaching of art can be a valuable method for the growth and integration of the individual.

It is true that when the artist is in action, he may function in three ways simultaneously. In teaching, however, we should single out one or another aspect which at the time needs release in the pupil. We should not merely try to correct or improve the drawing or painting, but rather should use the drawing as an index of the pupil's state at the time and ask ourselves: "Does the content reveal a connection between the work and his experience? Is it vital expression? Does the line indicate free movement? Is the work organically composed? Does he understand balanced relationship throughout?" If the answers to these questions are negative, we should learn how to release and stimulate the child physically, emotionally, and mentally. When he begins to attain a rounded development, the child will be on the road towards his own integration. It is as if movement, feeling, and thought represented three dimensions, and in learning to use all three, the child were permitted to glimpse the fourth dimension, his spiritual awakening.

What is this process of integration and what does it require of the teacher? It is the process of becoming a balanced individual. Since an individual is made up of conflicting elements, integration demands the synthesis of opposites. We recognize that in electricity cathode and anode create light, that in biology male and female create life, but do we recognize in the human being that opposites have equal value and that each is needed to make the whole individual? The irrational and the rational, the mischievous and the good, the wild and the ordered are some of these pairs of opposites. Society has taught us we should only be rational, good, and ordered; perhaps it was at this point that we lost the secret of integration and forgot what the ancients knew—that life must embrace all elements.

Many educators still hold tenaciously to the idea that change can be wrought solely by what we teachers and the pupils do consciously. They fail to realize that the chief hope of change, the transcendent function, lies buried in the unconscious and that only by coaxing it up through fantasy, play, rhythmic movement, and other indirect means can it be released for union with the conscious.

Integration is of two kinds: integration within the self and integration of the self within the social unit. This should occur in the order named. The reason is clear—a city is no better than its citizens. And the character of each citizen needs some inner matrix of security before he can participate in the group. His contribution to the whole comes later. The creative process is a life process; art need not copy nature, but it must copy nature's processes. In the early stages of nature these stirrings take place in the dark—underground and unseen. The same thing goes on in the artist. That is why I believe in the necessity of individual art expression for the realization of the first steps of integration. There are processes, one active, expressive, the other receptive, dreamy, inward; they must operate alternately. Impressions are received and digested. Then they form an image and are projected outwardly. The sense of fulfilment comes as a result of the interplay of these two processes.

After many personal experiences a young artist may be ready to participate in a group project. But if some leading mind in the group has created the project and the others merely follow and participate, the experience is more limited and less rewarding than the inner, secret creation which alone develops the sense of self necessary to lift a group experience to a higher level. There are, I know, many projects which bring about certain healthy, happy states, but they are on the collective level; only rarely can they bring into activity those deeper experiences of the self necessary for the real integration of an individual.

We should, accordingly, address ourselves in the first instance to the integration of the self. Low tension, lack of fire and of intensity characterize a fairly general psychological condition in this present day. The cause is that man has lost part of himself and has buried it in the unconscious. He has lost touch with nature, with his primitive self, with his elemental needs. He has limited himself to the field of rational consciousness, to that which can be known and measured and defined. But life is made up of opposites, typified by the conscious ordered world of Apollo and the unconscious elemental world of Dionysus. Our great need is to allow for both, to admit and accept both. In their complete reconciliation lies the opportunity for integration, for transformation into a new and fuller life.

INTRODUCTION TO METHOD OF TEACHING

I did not begin teaching with any theory. I started working with little children, first my own, then my neighbours', and later those in school. I observed what the children did, perceived their needs, and

experimented continuously. Only after many years of teaching experience
did I formulate my ideas and explain my practice.

The basic aim of my method is the development of the pupil's body,
soul, and mind through art experience. Therefore, the method becomes
a series of ways and exercises to awaken and train these essential parts
of the child's being.

I begin with the release of the creative faculty through the free
rhythmic use of the body in breathing, movement, and sound. Breathing
feeds the body oxygen, increases the circulation, and produces energy.
Rhythmic movement brings order out of chaos, starts the rhythmic line
necessary to true art expression. Sound induces stronger colour vision
which evokes the desire to express "colour notes" and then, in turn, the
notes inspire form.

The release of the motor function is followed by the liberation and use
of feeling. This is done in several ways: by the pupils' own memory and
association of feeling-experiences; by the animating effect of discussion;
and by stimulation through play with colour. The power of the mind
is awakened through training the design sense, through cultivation of
imagination, observation, memory, organization, and sense of form.

When all these powers are liberated and contributing actively to the
art of the child, both he and his work progress rapidly. Through this
total activation the child may reach his essential being, and when this
occurs, his art takes on new and deeper values.

PART II

Method

A

Release of the Creative Faculty through Basic Experiences of the Body

CHAPTER IV

The Training of the Kinaesthetic Sense

ART may be inspired by feeling and conceived in thought, but it is executed through the body. Thus, the body is the instrument through which the creative process occurs. For this reason, it becomes exceedingly important to observe how the young artist uses his body and to determine whether or not he is aware of a kinaesthetic sense.

THE KINAESTHETIC SENSE AS A FORM OF PERCEPTION

The kinaesthetic sense is the sensation which accompanies, or informs us of, bodily movements. Such sensations may be complexes of muscular, tactual, joint, or allied sensations arising from the moving member. The acquisition of control over the muscles is acquired through kinaesthetic images which the teacher must convey to the student. The collection of images representing movements to the mind may be called the kinaesthetic memory. This sense is much neglected (except in specific uses, as in athletics and the dance) so that the pupil is probably unaware of how he is using his body—it may be tense and cramped or it may be drooping and flaccid. Both extremes are inadequate for drawing. If a pupil is kinaesthetically alert he will move his arms, perhaps his whole body, when expressing a line, rather than only his hands and fingers which may be doing most of the work because the child acquired the habit while writing.

The human being is so much a single organism that when one part of his make-up is functioning well, the others are quick to respond. If the senses and muscles are functioning well, for example, they will co-ordinate with reason and emotion. Therefore, in the refinement of the kinaesthetic sense, we have a starting point for the entire co-ordination of the individual.

If one's imagination is to be free, the whole muscular and nervous system must be active and alert, able to respond to the orders of the mind and to the wishes of the heart. The finger-tips, after all, are the last delicate part of the body to convey the message from brain to paper. If the whole body is awakened and electrified, the current will pass from the brain to the hand fluently, carrying new power of expression. A child sitting at his table in his accustomed slouched or cramped position may be blocked in his work—the current shut off. If he is placed before a large upright easel or board, stands in a well-balanced position, and is taught to use large swinging gestures from the shoulder, elbow, or wrist, the problem of expression immediately becomes easier to solve. Great changes take place with this kind of instruction.

Although the importance of the organic functioning of the body with mind and feeling is now being recognized, there is still much to be learned concerning the means of bringing this about. Sometimes we stumble on a truth intuitively and afterwards find the scientific explanation. For example, I discovered that valuable results were gained by drawing from the shoulder muscles. I used this technique repeatedly with my pupils. It was years later that I first learned from a physician that important nerves in the shoulder carry the message from the brain to the hand— which explains how a pupil, when released through the shoulder movement, could find expression for an idea.

There is still another reason why the pupil experiences a sense of well-being and a new power of expression under these kinaesthetic conditions. He really is discovering and utilizing the first laws of creation in himself, in his own body rather than in his drawing. These laws are rhythm and balance. By finding them in himself, the child is touching art at its source.

Rhythm governs all the universe, from atoms to human beings. If the human being is in a state of health, his heartbeat, his pulse, his breathing are rhythmic. Psychological or physical causes may upset his health. An emotional disturbance or continued nervous instability may set up a state of tension, confusion, or chaos. This affects the nerves and muscles, diminishes the blood supply, and makes a condition in which it is difficult to work. The ability to create is thus lessened. Establish a rhythmic state in the individual through balanced movement and

3. Co-ordination of the Kinaesthetic Sense and the Mind

evenness of breathing, and you make a condition favourable to creation. From this functional use of movement in the body, the student develops a strong rhythmic line in his work: the line is the product of a gesture.

Closely related to this motile power is the tactile sense. The mental imagery of an artist is often intimately associated with the sensation of touch. When drawing an object, we improve the quality of line enormously if we imagine our pencil as touching it continuously. This practice is usually called *contour drawing* and is of inestimable value in developing the ability to draw well. It has been taught thoroughly by certain important contemporary teachers in art. Nikolaides was a great exponent of this method. Instead of using contour work only with direct objective drawing, I have applied it also to imaginative work as soon as some skill has been acquired by the pupil. It is through this constant linking of skill and creative work that we strengthen the pupil's confidence and ability.

Through the training of the kinaesthetic and tactile senses, a vague and undefined image may be transformed into a clear one; thus the kinaesthetic and tactile senses become the link between conceiving and doing.

The photograph of Jody (Ill. 3), deeply absorbed in her painting, illustrates well this co-ordination of the kinaesthetic sense and the mind.

CHAPTER V

Movements to Liberate Expression

SOME years ago I had a personal experience in which large, free movements in drawing released images in my mind that I had been unable
to express on a small scale. Following this experience it occurred to me
that in a natural, primitive state man draws on as big a scale as he can
reach and that only through the intellectual influence of our educational
system is he required to draw on a diminished scale. Drawing large is
natural; drawing small requires the mental process of reduction. This
insight came to me in the following way.

I was attending the Bach festival in Bethlehem, Pennsylvania. It was
the deepest musical experience I have ever had. In that small town,
a centre of steel manufacture, with great furnaces roaring and blazing
and huge cauldrons of molten steel being turned into girders, live simple
Moravian descendants, keeping up many of their ancestors' religious
customs. To them had come the remarkable musician, Wolle, an apostle
of Bach. Wolle taught them to love Bach and to live with him in their
daily lives. He organized and developed among these people a magnificent choir. In the daytime these men and women work in the steel
mills; in the evening they sing Bach with Wolle. Every year this group
gives a Bach festival in May; people come from all over America to hear
it. The choir sings many of Bach's compositions, but they always end
the two days of music with the B Minor Mass, perhaps Bach's greatest
work. The festival is given in the church, and is sung with deep fervour.

During the intermission I left the church to wander over the hills and
under old elms. The pale green leaves and new grass shimmered in the
spring sunlight adding glory to the day. I returned to the church in a
tranquil mood.

The Mass began again with the "Credo". This builds up gradually,
with first one voice, then a second, then a third. One by one, all join

45

in a magnificent chorus of glorious affirmation. I seemed to see the music take visible form. Each voice rose from the dark earth in a slender column, then widened and spread apart to arch upward as in a Gothic cathedral, thus making an intricate and marvellous pattern. In this vision I saw myriads of columns like trees in a forest. A large one stood in the centre, seeming to divide the others into two parts. The columns grew smaller and smaller in the distance until they became infinitesimal and finally vanished. At the time I felt the impulse to stoop down and touch the ground with both hands together, then to reach up and stretch my arms wide apart, looking up as in prayer. Since I was sitting in the church among many people while the Mass was being sung, this was obviously impossible. Later, however, the idea occurred to me.

The concert was over. I left Bethlehem. I returned to my studio and tried to draw what I had seen during the music—the mysterious series of arches—but it wouldn't come. I made many efforts on ordinary size paper and canvasses. They all failed. Suddenly I remembered that during the music I had had a strong desire to stand up, raise my arms and stretch them out to the sun, then bend down to the floor with my hands touching the ground and again raise them up and outward, myself forming an arch, just as the voices seemed to be doing in the music.

PICTORIAL IMAGES AND LARGE GESTURES

Now, in the studio, I could fulfil this desire and draw with these motions on the wall of the room. I stood in front of the blank wall with a piece of charcoal in each hand. Then I bent down to my feet and drew the central arch of the picture as large as myself and as far as my arm could stretch on either side. This formed the centre framework for the rest which followed rapidly. Later, having found my plan, I used a smaller canvas.

As I worked on the painting, things developed which I had not planned. Under the arches on the left, mounds of earth arose; under the arches on the right a rhythmic sea appeared, and over all, above the topmost arch, sky and clouds developed.

The point of interest to me was that the painting followed the words of the "Credo" without my being aware of it. I was moved by the music and guided by its rhythm. It was two months later when, finding the programme, I read the words:

> I believe in one God, the Almighty Father, Creator of Heaven and Earth, and of all things visible and invisible.

Another version of the "Credo", given elsewhere, was:

> I believe in one God; the Earth, the Sea, and the Sky unite in worshipping his glory.

The very forms that I used in painting resided in the text which had inspired Bach in the medium of music. There seems to be an inner connection in these experiences; they were brought into pictorial expression through the large gestures which had come to me instinctively—first while listening to the music and later in the studio.

Following my own experience of release through large movements, I studied the cave drawings of primitives and found that most of their drawings of animals were large also—some were six or seven feet long. I then tried experimenting with my pupils. That was the beginning of my work with large papers, heavy chalks, and rhythmic movement to release expression. I added one more factor to these exercises: re-education in breathing. It is well known that when a person is very happy, he breathes deeply and evenly. As most people are somewhat constrained and not radiantly happy, the breathing is restricted; accordingly, vitality is lowered and tension increases.

When anyone suggests deep breathing, the first impulse is to make an effort and suck in air. This is a mistake. We should first breathe out to empty the lungs, then pause, and lastly let the air filter in of its own pressure. The empty lungs are a vacuum; new air will flow in by itself. As we breathe in, the cells of the lungs fill with oxygen. As we breathe out, we energize the cells. Try drawing a line when your lungs are filled with air, and, as you finish the line, let the air out. See whether the experiment does not give your work new life and new strength.

Using these ideas as a basis for my work, I have experimented with many movements. A few liberating exercises are necessary. When the student makes the line he wishes to convey, he will be able to express it with confidence, fitness, and beauty through the movement of the body.

In the following pages I have given a few examples of the kinds of exercises I use with pupils. Photograph (Ill. 4) illustrates a few of these exercises.

In all instances, be sure to keep the child interested. Don't do more of this sort of work than the span of interest will allow. Usually one exercise in the air and then the same one on paper is enough for one session. Some students may be ready for two, but don't force them. Try to keep the exercise a game, and as soon as the child has gained something —a little more courage, a little more freedom—let him apply this to some imaginary drawing, rather than drill on mere movements too long.

EXERCISE I

Exercise: Let the pupil stand with feet about twelve inches apart, bend down from the hips, and touch the ground. Then rise slowly and let the arms go gradually wide apart. Suggest to the pupil that he is touching the ground and then reaching up towards the sky or that he has a tree trunk between his hands, that he feels the trunk as he goes up, and that at the end he reaches out to the tips of the branches.

Purpose: To loosen and stretch the pupil's muscles and give him a realization of the wide expansion of his body.

EXERCISE II

Exercise: Pupil faces the teacher. Stands in an erect position. Breathes in, lifting the right arm forward and up from the shoulder joint without bending the elbow and wrist; continues until the arm is perpendicular and the fingers are as high as they can reach. Then let the arm come down in the same way. Breathe out as the arm comes down slowly. Keep the elbow and wrist stiff, as if the arm were one piece without joints. The movement, which is entirely from the shoulder, should be firm, fairly slow, and rhythmic. You can tell the child to imagine he is drawing on a flat rock on the side of a mountain, in order to give him the idea of immensity and strength in his movement. Then let him repeat the exercise with his left arm.

Purpose: To develop the use of the shoulder action. This is the most important thing in preparing to draw. I have used it with many pupils with very good results. The interesting discovery is that there is a physiological corroboration of what I came upon intuitively. There are two

4. LIBERATING EXERCISES

very important nerves in the shoulder which help to carry the message from the brain to the hands, and when the shoulder movement is used, the passage of this message is accelerated. Therefore, a person drawing in a standing position and swinging the arm from the shoulder has a greater chance of projecting his image than when he is seated and using only the finger muscles.

EXERCISE III

Exercise: Similar to No. II, only done horizontally across the body instead of vertically. Be sure to have the arm start at the side. The hand starts to stretch out at the side and crosses the body, without bending the elbow, as far as it can reach and back again. Be sure to do both arms.

Purpose: To give a balanced movement, using the muscle on either side of the upper arm, the biceps coming in and the triceps going out.

EXERCISE IV

Exercise: Similar to Nos. II and III, a shoulder movement, but the student makes circles in the air, first with one arm and then the other.

EXERCISE V

Exercise: Have the pupil draw a horizontal figure eight in the air at right angles to the body, first one arm and then the other. Then use both arms together.

EXERCISE VI

Exercise: Let the pupil go to the easel and draw on paper all the exercises he has first done in the air. In addition to the use of the arm swinging, he must now use the whole body, including knee-bending. Place the pupil with feet apart, one foot ahead of the other in relation to the easel. Have him practise passing the weight from one leg to the other, bending first the front knee and then the back knee, so that when he starts a line high up on the paper, his weight is on the forward leg with knee bent. As the hand passes gradually down the paper, his weight should go to the back leg and the front leg should straighten out.

Purpose: To co-ordinate the body so that the line drawn is the result of complete body balance and is rhythmic in its swing. The pupil should breathe in before he begins to draw and breathe out as his hand travels down the page. The line will be the result of the gesture. You can judge how well co-ordinated the body and movement were by the kind of line and series of lines produced.

EXERCISE VII

Exercise: Similar exercise, only horizontal lines are drawn and the pupil must find a balanced position of the legs and torso in relation to drawing a horizontal line.

EXERCISE VIII

Exercise: Similar exercise in drawing a circle. As there is not room enough on even a large paper to draw a full circle, only an arc can be made. However, you can take the pupil to a blackboard and let him swing full circles as large as he can make them.

Purpose: To generate energy (through the repetition of the arc movement which becomes a pendulum-like curved swing) and to give dynamic power which may go over into the next drawing.

EXERCISE IX

Exercise: Let the pupil stand a little farther away from the paper and reduce the size of movement. He can then draw a complete circle. This is especially useful in producing a rhythmic state.

EXERCISE X

Exercise: Let the pupil draw on the paper as in Exercise VIII, but on a smaller scale. Bring both hands together at the bottom of the page and start upward, going out and spreading apart.

EXERCISE XI

Exercise: Let the pupil practise movements from the elbow joint similar to all of the shoulder exercises—vertical, horizontal, and curved.

EXERCISE XII

Exercise: Wrist movement. Let the pupil, keeping his wrist as flexible as possible, make short vertical, horizontal, and circular movements with the wrist.

Purpose: To get a small free curve, helpful in drawing something like the cheek of a child or the petal of a flower.

EXERCISE XIII

Exercise: Return to large gestures with arm. Practise making a spiral in two different ways—one starting with a large movement and going in and getting smaller—the other, the reverse, starting small in the centre and growing larger and larger.

EXERCISE XIV

Exercise: The last six exercises have been related to curves. Here is one which produces straight lines like a series of pointed mountains. Let the pupil stand facing the easel, feet placed apart equally distant from the easel. In each hand hold a piece of chalk which you rest on the paper. Then bend the knees up and down. The arms will go with the body and register pointed forms.

Purpose: To acquire a new flexibility in the body and produce new gestures: the forms stimulate the imagination later.

EXERCISE XV

Exercise: Let the pupil run along the length of the blackboard, touching it with his chalk as he runs. As he moves his arm up and down, he will leave a wavy line on the blackboard. (Many other exercises which will increase freedom of movement can be devised for use on the blackboard.)

Purpose: To free the body, delight the child, make him playful, and let him discover that certain movements and gestures produce certain kinds of lines and patterns.

I usually do not attempt to explain to very young children (those from three to five) the purposes of these exercises. I merely take them by the hand and swing their arms to and fro. This gives the children a sense of the freedom in the movement without their having consciously to think about it. Sometimes I try to make a game out of the movements, saying, "Let's make great big trees (or great big balloons)—so big." For the running line at the blackboard I sometimes suggest that the children pretend they are butterflies and that their arms are wings.

5. THE FAMILY OUTING. By Nancy at eight years of age.

When the children are seven and eight, I begin to give the exercises as described, taking care to watch for any lagging of interest.

One result of rhythmic work has frequently been to make it possible for the pupil to express himself whereas before he was inhibited. In addition, rhythmic work has very often released unconscious and elemental forces that lay buried beneath the surface. This physical liberation, which has led to an emotional one, may later lead to a deeper mental and spiritual liberation. A further effect of the freely moving body is the transference of this physical condition of freedom to the work of art. The following three paintings are a demonstration of movement in the picture which has been brought alive gradually through the relaxation of rhythm in each pupil. These three pictures were all painted directly without making a drawing.

6. BRONCHOS. By Susie at nine years of age.

7. SAILING. By Mark at twelve years of age.

The first, "The Family Outing" (Ill. 5), was painted by Nancy, a lively, intense little girl of eight years. Her former style was cramped and conventional. This painting was accomplished in her third year of work and shows how she has been freed. The second painting is called "Bronchos" (Ill. 6) and was painted by Susie, aged nine. The movement is dynamic. The third of the group, "Sailing" (Ill. 7), was painted in poster colour by Mark, aged twelve. It expresses well the work and movement.

In an earlier chapter I spoke of rhythm and balance as the basic pattern of creativity. We now add movement, and in the same way develop it in the body, and subsequently movement will find its expression in the art.

CHAPTER VI

The Significance of the Scribble

TRANSITION FROM EXERCISES IN MOVEMENT TO CHILD'S DRAWINGS

THE scribble is a kind of play with a freely flowing continuous line. It is made without plan or design, and occurs as a result of the easy movement of the arm while letting the chalk trail along on the paper in any direction. The line may intertwine or it may be clear and simple.

The making of this rhythmic pattern is the first step of the scribble. A scribble may be made with the eyes open or closed. The value of closing the eye is that it prevents the mind from directing the hand to represent some familiar object. The intention here is to get away from conscious drawing and, instead, to let the hand make an unconscious rhythmic pattern. The use of the left hand instead of the right also facilitates this intention. The reason for this is that the left hand is less habituated to obey the conscious mind than the right hand.

The scribble reflects the state and nature of the person drawing it much as his handwriting does. The pattern thus made may appear meaningless to the average onlooker, but it is not so; it contains something very precious, as the next step will show.

A CHILD'S PASSPORT TO THE WORLD OF IMAGINATION

Having made the scribble, the student now should be asked to sit down quietly at a distance and contemplate it. If he gazes at the lines a while, he will begin to perceive some pictures in them, much as one may find some form in the clouds. After he has discovered a definite pattern in the scribble, the pupil should emphasize the lines that will bring out what he has seen.

This second step is the stirring of the imagination. Through this stirring, material is awakened in the unconscious of which the student may be quite unaware and in which he may see no meaning. It is not necessary that he should, but he will probably enjoy representing in drawing or colour the things he finds. The objects a little child finds in his scribbles will be simple and part of his young child life—animals, or mother, or other children or flowers, and sometimes the sun or earth. The objects seen by older people very often reveal deep inner problems, conflicts, or aspirations. Sometimes no objects are seen, but design is found. That also may be useful. When the design is developed, it serves the purpose of freeing the individual from the inhibition against getting started. The mere play with form and colour frees energy and imagination.

Recently I found corroboration of my use of the scribble in a passage from Leonardo da Vinci's Notebooks, *Precepts of the Painter: A Way to Stimulate and Arouse the Mind to Various Inventions:*

"I will not refrain from setting among these precepts a new device for consideration which, although it appears trivial and almost ludicrous, is nevertheless of great utility in arousing the mind to various inventions. And that is that if you look at any walls spotted with various stains or with a mixture of different kinds of stones, if you are about to invent some scene, you will be able to see in it a resemblance to various different landscapes adorned with mountains, rivers, rocks, trees, plains, wide valleys, and various groups of hills. You will also be able to see divers faces, and outlandish costumes, and an infinite number of things which you can then reduce into separate and well-conceived forms. With such walls and blends of different stones it comes about as it does with the sounds of bells, in whose clanging you may discover every name and word that you can imagine."

There is a resemblance between Leonardo's use of the mottled wall and my use of a scribble to "arouse the mind to new inventions". They both demonstrate the power to stimulate through suggestion.

This initial release through the scribble is demonstrated by the following cases.

The first is a boy of seven, Stanton. When he began studying art at my school, he was shy and clung to his mother; in fact, he would not stay in the class unless she remained in the room. I proceeded as usual by giving him materials and letting him make his first picture entirely alone. I offered no comments or suggestions of any kind.

This first picture is "The Two Deer" (Ill. 8). Using it as a means of judging the child's state, I made these observations:

8. The Two Deer
First drawing, revealing insecurity and adult
influences. By Stanton at seven years of age.

The line is shaky, indicating insecurity and fear. The picture is placed in the upper half of the paper. This shows a lack of awareness of his whole paper. His use of the upper half also suggests that he lives in a fantasy world or tries to escape from reality. The lower part of a picture may be analogous to common reality, the upper part to the wish or dream world. The whole subject and composition seem to be inspired by pictures he has seen rather than by his own observation and impressions. It indicates too much adult influence and the wish to please adults.

My first desire was to help Stanton overcome his insecurity and fear. I used some of the co-ordinated movements described in the last chapter.

These brought rhythm and liberation into his drawing. I next let him play with the scribble which freed his imagination. Following these two experiences, I let him return to drawing pictures of his own choosing. Through this process he learned to overcome his fears and to express his own thoughts and feelings. As his ability to express himself in his art grew, he unconsciously gained similar power in his life.

In his first scribble he perceived a seal (Ill. 9). He brought it out by darkening those lines which suggested the seal to him. The way he has drawn the seal shows a new assurance. In another scribble he saw trees and hills; these he brought out by using colour, thus gaining experience in the use of chalks and in the making of strong colour contrasts. See "Landscape" (Ill. 10).

The boy continued these scribbles for several weeks, apparently enjoying each one as he discovered something new in it. All the while he was acquiring skill and courage. An indication of a change taking

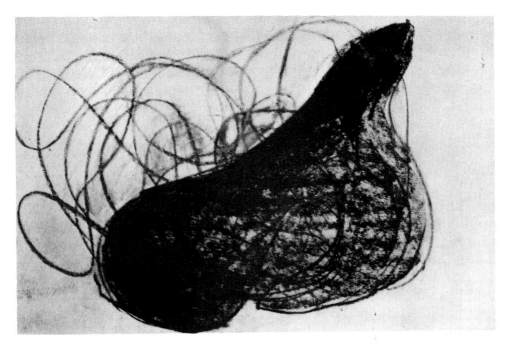

9. THE SEAL. Drawn from first scribble. Shows new security, rhythmic line, and natural childlike expression.

10. LANDSCAPE. Second scribble, beginning of design.

place in him was that he no longer demanded that his mother stay in the room with him. He was satisfied to remain in class while she went home.

One day Stanton said, "I've made all the scribble pictures I want. Now I want to make a real picture."

"Very well," I said, "go ahead."

The picture he did was "A Mare and Foal" (Ill. 11), in which a horse and her colt are running together in the open field. Contrast this picture with Stanton's drawing of the two deer. The latter is static and timidly drawn, badly placed, and unchildlike in conception. The former is well composed, shows movement and freedom of line. The subject matter and handling are natural to a child of his age. The foal and mare may be himself and his mother unconsciously expressed in this fashion. He made progress.

Later on he drew a battle scene. The healthy thing about the drawing is that it is an expression of Stanton's aggressive side, a further

11. MARE AND FOAL. Shows gain in power to express form and movement,
also shows qualities characteristic of his age.

development away from fear, insecurity, and babyhood. It is executed
with strength, action, and humour.

This boy is now several years older and has developed well. He is
editing and illustrating a school paper and taking a leading role in his class.

CASE HISTORY OF GORDON L.

Another example of rapid unfolding through the use of the scribble
is found in the work of Gordon L. Born of Catholic parents who died
young, leaving him in the care of relatives, he moved from one family
to another several times and probably was mishandled by them. He grew
up to be a problem. He threw over the Catholic Church. This act made
him a great sinner. The cousin with whom he was living at the time he
came to me was trying to help him; he had consulted a priest whom he
considered wise in experience and the priest had said to let the boy be
and let him live through this period—he would probably return of his
own free will, later on.

12. NUDE. Conventional drawing made in Art School.
By Gordon at twenty years of age.

This cousin noticed a great change in Gordon after his first lesson with me, and in talking with him was sure that I had touched him and could help him. When the cousin saw the pictures he was amazed and said they showed the whole history of Gordon's conflict—his need of prayer, his fears, his sense of guilt and the feeling of being lost. The cousin referred to some philosophy or cult that the young man had become interested in, but he would not tell me about it.

Then Gordon enlisted in the Navy and here his talent for drawing was noticed. He came to New York and studied drawing at the Art Students League under Arthur Lee. Gordon told me that he received

13. MAN PRAYING I. First scribble revealing an image from the unconscious.

no helpful instruction, only generalities such as "You must work harder, observe more, use a finer pencil, etc." He found the work dry and dull.

One day he came to a lecture I gave. He stayed afterwards and told me that my ideas of art teaching, particularly the idea of what could be done if we tapped the sources of the unconscious, were new and strange to him and that he would like to study with me. We arranged for lessons.

Gordon brought his portfolio of the work he had done at the regular art school. One of these sketches, "A Nude" (Ill. 12), is included to show Gordon's ability to draw—but in a manner entirely academic and unimaginative. He was in a confused and unhappy state about many issues. His drawing, though clever, was not in any sense used as a vehicle for the expression of his own being. He was crowding feeling back and drawing only with his hand and eye because, he confessed, feeling to him was very closely associated with suffering. By arousing the functions of thought and feeling I helped Gordon to integrate his work and then himself. This is demonstrated in the lessons which follow.

FIRST LESSON

During this period I began showing Gordon my method of release through rhythmic movements. He responded with understanding and seemed to enjoy finding this new use of his body.

First, he made several sheets of rhythmic lines. Then I told him that the next step was to make what I call a "scribble", explaining that this was a continuous line without any plan, a line going in and out and roundabout with an instinctive movement of the arm and hand. I suggested that this line would contain an individual characteristic rhythm just as definitely his own as his posture, walk, tone of voice, and facial expression. I told him that after he had made the scribble he was to sit comfortably and gaze at it, letting his imagination find some form in it. The form discovered, I said, will inevitably express a content which is in the life and the unconscious of the person seeing it. In other words, it becomes psychic material very similar to dreams.

Gordon swiftly grasped the suggestions and immediately made his first scribble with a fine, powerful, rhythmic line. When he stood back and gazed at his handiwork, an idea flashed to his mind and he drew without hesitation a tragic figure of a man on his knees, his head buried

14. MAN PRAYING II. Second study. Same subject drawn consciously after realizing the mood of prayer from the unconscious.

in his hands. He wrote across the bottom of the page in large letters, "A Man Praying—I" (Ill. 13). He showed relief and satisfaction and confessed, "This is the first thing of my own I've ever drawn. I didn't know what I would be able to do when I came here. Now I'm glad I did come. What shall I do next?"

I explained that this theme had come through the freeing of his unconscious thoughts and from a state of feeling which indicated a need for help. Since this was his first spontaneous statement of emotion, I suggested that he try to carry it further by making a conscious endeavour to plan and compose a drawing based on his initial effort. This interested him very much. Thereupon he drew a second study, also entitled "A Man Praying—II" (Ill. 14). In this we can note the maintenance of the original concept and a decided development of form.

Gordon then made a succession of scribbles, finding each one a fertile source of inspiration.

In his third scribble he discovered a tremendous head suggesting an evil force. He called this "Fear" (Ill. 15), and commented, "I thought of the fear that lies in every man's heart, in you and in me. It seems to be the biggest part of me—fear of myself."

In the drawing inspired by this fourth scribble he depicted, standing on a beach by the sea, a strong young man who seemed in great distress. He named this one "Man Lost" (Ill. 16), and said about it, "He has strength, but it all goes down through him. He is sluggish and can't put his strength to any use. I don't know how this happened to come out of me. I never did anything like this before."

When I said to him, "Perhaps you are contacting your own soul as the source of this material," he answered, "That's the thing. But it's something outside of yourself, too." "Yes," I told him, "but you reach the forces outside of yourself through your own soul; you must reach that first." Before he left, he thanked me with deep feeling and said again, "I'm glad I came."

SECOND LESSON

Gordon immediately began work with his big black chalk on the white paper. Without performing any preliminary rhythmic movements, he made a circular scribble. The drawing which he made from the

15. FEAR

scribble was very jumbled and unsatisfactory. He said it was meant to be a man in chains struggling to free himself. Then he made a second scribble and sat back to look at it. In this Gordon saw a picture of a man who feels beautiful things. The abstract form in front of the man is crushing him, is stronger than he. The action of the legs and feet indicates a desire to run away from this force. But this picture also was somewhat jumbled, and again the young man was dissatisfied.

"Gordon," I said, "both of these pictures have failed to come through as well as the ones last time. I think it's because you skipped the rhythmic movements first. You probably don't realize that it is because of them that you are able to draw from the unconscious. Go back now, take a fresh sheet of paper, stand in a good, easy, well-balanced position; and begin swinging your arm. Make your circle just as long as you wish."

He did as I suggested and kept on swinging and making lines as he struck the paper for several minutes. I waited without speaking, realizing that something of value was going on because he was very definitely living the experience.

The beneficial effect of his rhythmic work was immediately demonstrated in his next drawing, "In Dreams" (Ill. 17). This picture shows a man's head with a woman coming out of the top. She is seated on the crown of his head, one arm dipped into the head, the other turned back and resting on her own shoulder. As an indication of Gordon's inner state, the drawing is remarkable. The boy began talking about it.

"The woman is part of me and yet separate. She was trying to bring out something. She is definitely helping. In fact, she is the only one who can help. She is a dream come true and at the same time a reality. It couldn't be otherwise. It was very strange the way I drew this picture. I was looking at the scribble upside down and I saw this form. The woman coming out of his head is trying to arrange his thoughts—she's trying to move them about to help him. When I drew the arm back of her head it was meant to show that even she was in doubt as to what this man was capable of."

He looked at me and smiled. "You are an old friend, aren't you? I think it took me a long time to find you. Ever since I was seven I knew such a person who would guide me existed. Do you believe that possible?"

16. A Man Lost

I encouraged Gordon's train of thought and told him that I believed some of us might have such foreknowledge.

He continued, "I do think we have it—tomorrow, tomorrow, to-morrow—well, who knows? We have to try to make the best of tomorrow. Strange she should have come out of the circular motion. This motion represents time to me, a wheel going around. Ever so often comes a hitch that will make a bump. You pause a bit. In that pause something happens way back in my head—then the wheel clicks with me. It is difficult to speak of these matters. I am very conscious of that. To someone other than myself the picture would seem like the morning after. But it is not like that; the picture means much to me. It is as if I held a sacred jewel in my hand. What does it all signify? I am almost afraid to think."

I answered him as best I could. "If you cannot think out the answer, let the woman, who is a symbol of wisdom for you at this moment, communicate with you. She communicates with you through these circular rhythms you are drawing. Had you ever thought that the curve and the circle are the symbols of woman just as the straight line and the square are the symbols of man? They have been used through the ages in art, and now they are appearing in your own work. Next time we will take the straight line and the angle for a rhythm for you to play with, but today as long as you have started working with the circle, why not try it again?"

Gordon proceeded to make another circular scribble. He called the drawing he made from the scribble, "The Help in You", and spoke about it in this manner: "This is an abstraction about what is taking place, please don't mind it, this is what happened. I began again with the circular motion. The first result was that I saw a hand. I continued to run the charcoal over the paper and found the form of a sleeping woman. I thought of the tremendous power in that sleeping woman, of her being able to go and put herself in the hand—she was a hand—even though she was asleep. There was a door in the ground. The person's hand vainly trying to open it. Useless, you see, the person's effort to open the door, alone, useless. There's a trapdoor in the earth. She can help him to open it. He wants to get out. He is in the earth trying to get out. The sleeping woman will open the door for him. I'm puzzled

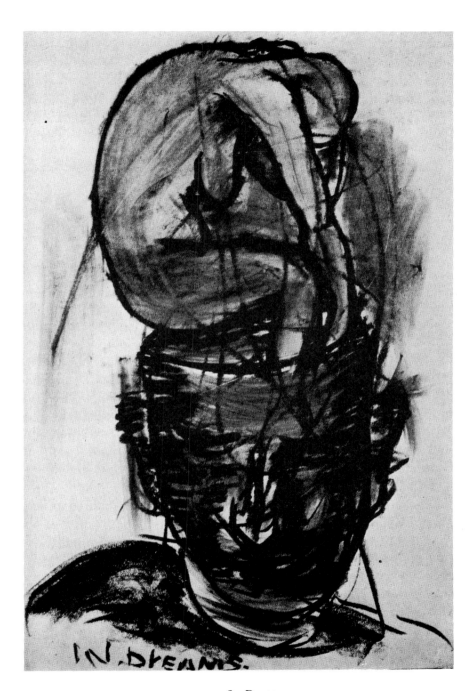

17. In Dreams

why I should do these things and say these things that I say. It's almost beyond me."

And I assured him, "It is strange to you because it is new. But it's not strange to me because I see a newly awakened part of you opening a door to a world that is new to you. It is like the fourth dimension, a world where things are not measured and limited by what you can touch and see and hear with the senses. You are entering into a greater world."

He showed by the light in his face that he was understanding what I said, and he continued, "You know I've thought of these things often and have thought of having lived in other times before. For instance, when I saw the picture *Ben Hur* I felt sure I was living at that time. The conviction was so strong that I thought perhaps I was insane. I felt sick with confusion. But now when I think of these things, it seems different."

There followed some discussion about the idea of reincarnation and the progress of the human soul through eternity, and thus ended another lesson.

THIRD LESSON

He came in promptly at five o'clock, went into the studio, and got his materials ready quickly, showing real eagerness to get to the job. I said to him, "I'll let you get started alone today and just remember how much some rhythmic movement at the beginning helps you." So I closed the door and left him. I looked in several times and saw he was busy, so I did not speak to him until he called me over. The drawing was finished. He had written in large letters, "Ashamed" (Ill. 18).

I asked, "What is this?"

He pointed to the title and said, "Something I did from a scribble."

"What is he ashamed of?"

Silence, and a slow, long, sly smile.

"What is in his hand?" I asked.

He answered my first question. "What strikes me is that he is ashamed to do a thing he wants to do and ashamed after he does it."

"Why should he be ashamed?"

A long silence.

"What are the things he has done?"

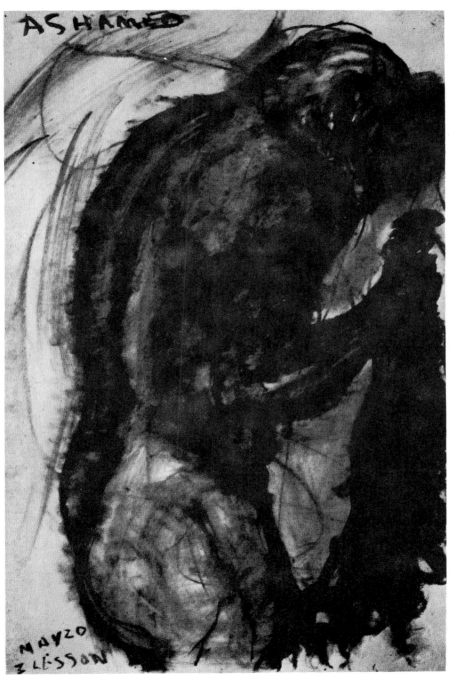

18. ASHAMED

He answered, "Why is anyone ashamed? They're afraid of what they may think of themselves, don't you think?"

"Could you tell me the kind of thing you have in mind?" Then, noticing his hesitation and silence, I guessed what was troubling him and decided to ask a direct question. "Is it the sexual act?"

"Yes—I feel ashamed before and after."

"But it is a natural experience—a form of energy expression—and belongs to a normal life."

"But if it is ingrained in you from the time you are a little child that it is evil, it is hard to get rid of that idea and sex has never been satisfactory for me. It has never meant more than the moment's satisfaction. It has just been the need of a sudden something—a barrier always comes up between the two—a wall—I tried to climb over it, but it is always there."

"You may be hungry for more of the spirit in this relation."

"That's it! You think you're going to meet someone who can give you that and they may seem wonderful, but when it comes to it, it's always a disappointment—it's always empty—there's always a wall."

"I think you haven't found yourself yet. When you find yourself you will be a different kind of person and you will attract a different sort to yourself, or you will be able to bring out the deeper side of the people you contact."

He expressed doubt, scepticism.

At this point, the discussion became so intense I could not take note of the words, but when I described further how a person may evolve and change, he said, "Aw, that's bunk, damn nonsense! I'm afraid of it all. I don't know—you either are, or you are not."

"When you say *are*—what do you mean? What *are* you?"

"You either are on my side of the fence, or your side of the fence. You can't change like that."

"You're wrong about that. Human beings on this earth are in a state of *becoming*. Think of the growth of the spirit as similar to the growth of physical life. A seed is not a tree at once, nor is a human being a man when he is born. What you refer to is a state of being which does not alter. If such a thing exists it belongs to a higher order of beings than exists on this earth. It is the acceptance and knowledge of our fallibility and our potentiality of growth which form the key to life." Then I brought out a photograph of a painting I had made which contained this very idea, of the tiny creature on earth kneeling in prayer before a great cosmic entity. The painting was named "Immanence and Becoming".

(This painting is developed from the idea of the small self in the state of Becoming, and the greater self, or universal being, as in the state of Immanence, eternally the same. The little figure is in a lotus flower which is opened through great tenderness received from the spirit. The upper part of the painting is treated in reds and yellows and represents sunlight, and the lower part night, or the moon and the darkness of night. The central triangle of light symbolizes a state of peace, and the smaller triangles to the left and right represent the terrifying force of the everyday world.)

I referred to his drawing again. "What is the thing the man is holding in his hand?"

"It's a cloth. He feels the need to cover himself. It's queer how this drawing came. I sat here quietly until my mind became vacant, until every material thought was gone so that nothing would interfere, so that I could actually bring something out. After a long blank time I made a scribble and I saw part of a head with a hand in front of it and then this long line trying to bring up a covering. He was ashamed."

We then had a discussion in which I brought forth the idea that the reason his experiences had been so unsatisfactory to him was because he was really seeking to find his own soul and to do that he would have to find the woman in himself, the feminine aspect in his soul, the anima figure of Jung's psychology, and that was what he was doing in this work; if he could find and develop this aspect of himself he would be strengthened, the power in himself could be channelled. "Then when you mate," I said, "you mate from strength, not from weakness. Those drawings that you've made of the woman coming out of the man's head and the sleeping woman opening the trapdoor are symbols of the feminine aspect in yourself."

He looked at me with a strange smile and made a funny little sound like "Hmph", then added, "That clicks—that's going to be something new for me, finding the woman in myself. God, what a joke!"

"Why a joke?"

19. COMFORT

"First time I've ever thought of anything like that. A woman in me. Holy God! I don't know how to use it—yes, I do. After this discussion, you can see where it hinges on the truth, which it does. Do you know what we are going to do? We're going to harness that woman like a horse and make her do our work for us. It's strange how she influences us. Whenever I thought of nice things, I'm sure it was she—nice things for me, I mean."

"What kind of things?"

"Such as—I don't know—you see, I like beautiful things—women— many beautiful things. Anything that has a little beauty. So it's not me that likes beautiful things but it's she."

He laughed happily.

"How does that idea strike you now?"

"It spoke the truth in myself."

"What did you mean by harnessing her, and how are you going to do it?"

"I expect to know her and who the devil she is and what she's actually capable of. You know what I—today—what I was thinking over—just how far I have gone in knowing myself—all the steps in the past, where I learned this and that, where I saw this thing and that thing—a sort of zigzag course, the final thing is finding you who—— First, I have to tell you a story in order to explain what I have in my mind. Way back on the other side of the continent lived a woman in a beautiful house. She was a beautiful woman and besides that had a Ph.D. and what have you. I used to go for a week-end about once a month to see her. She was past middle age, was nice to me. I didn't misunderstand it, of course —like a neurotic morbid person. I decided I would like to know her, she knew so much and did so much—I thought I would like to know her, which I did.

"That was the first person who struck the first blow on the concrete. It stunned my thinking power. I really got to know her after which she told me several things that interested me very much. They mean more to me now—gave one idea connected with what we are talking about today. Once when I was talking, she said, 'Those thoughts don't belong to you alone, they come from several people inside of you. You don't know them yet'—and now I understand there is a woman in me." He

20. SLEEPY MAN. Indicating introversion after these experiences.

said this last part very dreamily as if he hardly knew what he was saying. Then he went on, "When you were talking at first, I almost got mad, then something inside of me said, 'Now, wait and listen, maybe she's adding up—two and two make four'—and they did."

"Yes, I admit I was a little frightened when I saw you getting angry. I thought perhaps I was undertaking to do something more than I could handle."

"You needn't be afraid of me. I'm all right——" He smiled. "Well, we got over that hump."

FOURTH LESSON

He spent most of the time on a picture which he called "Comfort" (Ill. 19). The subject was an older woman giving sympathy to a boy, and he said it was a presentation of his recent experience.

FIFTH LESSON

The picture he drew at this lesson he called "Sleepy Man" (Ill. 20). It was the last one he did with me, although I did not know it was going to be so when he drew it. I think it is an unconscious presentation of his state at that time. Much had been opened up to him; he had been put in contact with the great forces within himself. Now he needed time to be alone, to go through a period of introversion in which to draw from his own strength and to rebuild himself. He went away. I have not seen him since, but I have heard of his progress. He is finding himself both as a human being and as an artist. He has become a successful teacher of art and has made a fruitful marriage.

B

Release of the Creative Faculty through Basic Experiences of Feeling

CHAPTER VII

Psychological Approach

THE teaching of art is changing. New frontiers are opening up. The psychological approach no longer regards the art product as separate from the artist. The work of art is recognized as a psychic chart of the state of the creator, showing his attitude, direction, and pattern. All the problems the young artist confronts must be realized by the teacher in terms of psyche.

A remarkable parallel exists between this new outlook in art and in the recent direction of scientific exploration. Science until now has largely dealt with matter which can be analysed and measured. The concept is limited, good as far as it goes, but leaving vast areas unexplained. The new frontier includes the hidden life in the world of minerals, plants, animals, and human beings. They all have these psychic and physical parallels. The laws in the universe which apply to one domain can be discovered in the others. That is why mathematicians, scientists, and artists use symbols; these can be transferred from one realm to another and still maintain their meaning.

The recognition of the meaning of symbols in art is an important factor in the psychological approach to art teaching. As the teacher grasps the hidden meaning in the child's work, she can penetrate his problem and his needs. As she studies his needs, she will find in most cases something which keeps him from the complete expression of himself. I have found that inertia, fear, and pride are the most common difficulties which block creative expression. These are usually symptoms of underlying psychological attitudes which vary in individual cases. Psychologists have formulated certain generalizations that are helpful to the teacher in understanding these mechanisms or attitudes.

INERTIA

One of the most common blocks to creative activity, one of the great interferences to individual growth, inertia, is frequently caused by a lack of psychic energy, the energy having been spent in conflicts or inhibitions. In such cases there just isn't enough vitality left to go into expression.

If we examine the laws of physics, we may perceive in them an analogy to the pull of gravity towards the earth. When we are at rest, we may be like an inert mass held there by the pull of gravity. To lift ourselves out of inertia, to fight this pull of gravity, we must use a counterforce. The counterforce can be the elevating power of spirit, channelled to us through imagination and perception. It is one thing to know this, another to put it into practice. The approach used will vary with each situation.

How often the artist, young or old, cannot get started! He postpones the beginning over and over again—lies in bed, looks out of the window, reads the paper or a current magazine, and generally fools himself into thinking he is not ready or inspired. If he could by some means force himself into action, he would begin to cut through this weight, then formulate a project, and be on the way.

Suppose a child is in a somewhat dull or listless state and that we have tried in vain to stimulate him by all the physical methods suggested in earlier chapters. Then we must find other means. One way is to ask him to take out some unfinished drawing in his portfolio and complete it. This often arouses him to action, stimulates his imagination, and from that motion his energy will carry him on to a new piece of work.

I remember reading an account of an interview with Van Wyck Brooks. The reporter had asked Mr. Brooks, "How do you work? Have you any routine?"

The author replied, "Yes, I have. When I go to my desk, I take out yesterday's work, go over it, make changes and corrections. By the time that is finished, I am warmed up to my work and full of ideas for the next chapter." This routine can be applied to painting as well.

Sometimes a child is blocked because he cannot decide which subject to choose. The making of a choice presupposes several things: some acquaintance with the various objects or acts from which we are about

6

to choose, some awareness of our desires and what would satisfy us, the ability to weigh and judge these matters, and the power to come to a conclusion and act thereon. If the child cannot decide, he will be thrown into conflict, unable to move. The teacher must make him aware of his needs and help him learn to make decisions based on them—in subject matter, choice of colour treatment, and so on—because it is in the practice of making clear, conscious, rapid decisions that the individual grows.

Sometimes inertia overtakes the pupil when the work seems spoiled beyond recall. Then he sits unwilling to do anything, unable to make an effort, caught by gravity. I try to make it clear that such dissatisfaction is the common lot of the artist and that it is caused by the discrepancy between what he conceived and what he has produced. The creator's task is to labour and lessen the difference by making his work more nearly approach his vision.

There are, of course, many ways to improve a drawing. Sometimes I suggest turning the picture upside down, for seeing it in a fresh aspect often shows up the defects and helps the student become aware of just what he wants to do. Working "upside down" also gives a certain freedom from fear of spoiling what one has done, emphasizes values and forms rather than facts, and acts generally as a liberating force. Changing from the right to the left hand, or even using both hands, frequently produces the same results. It is my opinion that the right hand, because of its almost constant use, automatically expresses conscious thought and that the left hand, though more awkward, can sometimes reveal deeper sources of rhythm and form.

On the purely technical side, I spend quite a little time showing children how many ways there are of retrieving work. If, after using these techniques, the painter is still not satisfied with his work, I suggest that he make a new picture of the same subject, and for this reason: the original image still remains in the mind and can be recalled. The second painting may be better, because the artist learns from his failures. It is wise for the child to try to master the difficulties which frustrated him, for if he doesn't master them in the study in which they first occur, he will soon meet the same problems over again.

This presentation of the way to meet a spoiled picture has had happy results many times. I remember a child who wanted to discard a half-finished picture because she could not make it look the way she wanted. I said, "Very well, but you will come up against the same difficulty, or one like it, in the next painting. If you meet it here and let me help you work through it, you will know what to do in the next one." The argument evidently appealed; she was willing to stick it out and did a good piece of work.

Giovanni Gentile, the Italian philosopher, writes eloquently in *The Reform of Education:*

> Work may sometimes appear irksome because freedom of its movement is checked by certain resistances which have to be overcome and removed. But in such cases it is not work which vexes us, but rather its opposite, sloth, against which we must combat. It follows then that the more intensely we occupy ourselves, the less heavily we are burdened by pain. For as our efforts redouble and the resistance is proportionately reduced, the spirit, which perishes in enthrallment, is enabled to live a richer life.

FEAR

Fear makes a child shrivel. Something which threatens his security, his enjoyment, or his very existence. makes a heavy weight on his heart and brings about an attitude of hostility and a feeling of guilt. The child may have strong aggressive or negative feelings which he represses. When they come near the surface, he has anxiety reactions and tries to hold them back. The expression of these unhealthy emotions may help to banish them.

Mario's story, related in detail in Chapter XVII, shows how one boy was helped through the expression of his fears. But in many cases children's problems are simpler, easier to reach and to dispel. Often there is a fear of failure caused by insecurity. Or the child's efforts may have been mocked, or perhaps some stronger and more capable brother or sister has caused the child to become timid through a feeling of inadequacy. These are a few of the most common causes of fear.

How can we meet the monster, fear, and conquer him through art? First, by making the initial artistic attempt so natural that no matter how young or how unskilled the child, he may derive some satisfaction from it, however slight. If the problem is too difficult, he will immediately be afraid of failure and start feeling inhibited and tense. This is a time when making a scribble is useful. It will be the child's own design, and he can believe in it. There will be no comparison with adult standards to intimidate him.

A timid boy of ten was trying to paint a mountain scene which he remembered from the summer. He laboured over it haltingly for days. No suggestion helped. He had bogged down among his fears of incompetence, was weighted down with conventional ideas of how a landscape should be painted. I said, "You are working too hard and are afraid you cannot succeed. Why not play at painting? A horse sometimes has to pull an ice wagon, but other times he just gallops in a field. Why don't you take a clean board and fresh paint and play that you are galloping in a field, just having a good time?" The boy made a joyous and fantastic abstraction of shapes with a beautiful full flower blooming out of it. The colours were fresh; the design, delightful. The play spirit banishes fear. Pictures made after such an experience are always more positively done.

We can get rid of fear in another way, by using this little exercise. Put two dots on the blackboard or on a piece of paper, as far apart as possible. Ask the pupil to connect these two dots. He will probably proceed carefully and make a shaky timid line. If so, you know he is bound by fear of failure. If, however, you show him the pendulum movement from the shoulder (as described earlier) he will draw the line with delight and confidence. The line will then be guided by an unconscious faith that his arm can be depended on to do what he wants when rightly used.

When the child says he does not know what to paint, he may be deterred by fear. Say to him, "If you were a great artist and could paint well anything you wanted, what would you paint?" He usually will look surprised and pleased at such a possibility and flash back an answer telling what he would paint. The spontaneity of his answer reveals the hidden idea he was reluctant to express.

One day a student was sitting disconsolately in front of a blank canvas. She said:

"I can't paint!"

"What would you paint if you could paint very well?" I asked.

The girl's face lit up as she began describing rapidly and vividly a scene she had recently observed—a grey sea and sky, a sandy beach, and a little old woman in black on the beach alone, looking out to sea. I said:

"Well, where would you put the edge of the beach?"

Her hand made a quick line.

"And where would the sky and sea meet?"

Another quick line.

"And the old woman?"

She stopped. "I can't draw an old woman with a shawl!"

So I volunteered to pose, drew a sweater over my head and shoulders like a shawl, and turned my back. She roughly sketched the woman and thanked me. Without any further help she finished the painting, and an extremely fine thing it was—full of the sense of sea, its greyness and its loneliness. It was only her second painting, but her intense feeling for the scene carried her beyond all immediate problems.

One new girl was so inhibited that even questions such as those just given brought no response. I did something I rarely do: I suggested things to her. She shook her head "No" to flowers, fruit, landscape, people. Then I asked, "Could you imagine yourself under the sea?"

That caught her. She dismissed me with a wave of the hand; she knew what she wanted to do. Her foreground was the floor of the sea, a pinkish-brown colour growing out of it; swaying in the water were all kinds of water plants—short-stemmed coral-like forms, long lily pods floating upward, seaweeds, and so on—in vari-coloured greens from palest yellow-green to darker blue-green. It had an "under-the-sea" quality, the sensation of plants moving under water in cool dim light.

Once she called in distress: "I can't draw coral; I don't know how it looks."

My first impulse was to tell her how or to draw a little sketch of it, but I decided not to; this was an imaginary thing and her freedom would be strengthened if she relied on herself. So I told her, "This canvas is your world. There is no right or wrong in it but of your own making. If you want it like coral, close your eyes and try to remember it, or look up coral in a book or museum. However, unless you especially want it like coral, you can imagine any sea life, as this is an imaginary picture."

My comments set her free, and she finished without asking for further advice. As it turned out, the plant was exactly like coral, showing that the girl really had a good idea of it but was merely timid.

In reviewing these cases where fear inhibits or corrupts, we can fairly say that the key to ridding our children—as well as ourselves—of fear is to engender belief in ourselves. It's as simple as that. We must teach children to go on doing their own work according to their desire, to disregard the quips of playmates and the criticism of elders, and to have faith in themselves.

PRIDE

Pride is like a swollen, tender shoulder; it smarts to the touch. Two conditions involve pride—in one, the pupil is conceited; in the other, he feels inferior. When the child's ego has become inflated by too much praise, he becomes conceited. Then he has lost his balance, does not want any suggestion or criticism, and no longer does good work. His main interest is to make pictures that will be noticed and praised. With this motive, his work will naturally deteriorate.

One way of changing this condition is by replacing the child's desire for praise with a new concept. I remember one pupil, a girl of about twelve, who brought to the studio some drawings which she had made at home. As soon as she arrived, she opened her portfolio to display her work, expecting praise—but I could not give it. The sketches were drawn with a very hard outline and filled in with colour as in the old-fashioned drawing-books. When I pointed this out, she pouted and said, "This is the way I want them; I like them like that."

I was a bit stumped at the finality of her answer and had to search for a way to reach her. I said, "Think of your life as a continuous line. You are only twelve years old. If you look back on that line, it is fair to say, 'I can draw better now than when I was two or three, and so I may feel I've accomplished something. But if I look ahead and see how much more the great painters of the world have achieved, then I can think I have done very little compared to that, so I must work hard and learn a great deal before I can be at all satisfied.'" The remarks gave her a fair picture of herself. They did not stab her by a sharp rebuke, but let her down gradually in her own eyes. Seeing that she had understood my meaning and was willing to rejudge herself, I said, "Let's look at your work, and you tell me how you could make it better." This was the beginning of a fresh attitude towards her work.

It is in ways like these that we can reach the over-sensitive ego and bring the child into a new balance where he is again ready to create for the pleasure of creating, not for the praise he receives.

The other condition of pride is related to the problem of inferiority. Another girl I remember was proud but suffered from dissatisfaction with her accomplishment. She preferred to do nothing rather than produce something below her ideal of perfection. She preened herself on this idea, thinking it showed fine character. "I have such a high idea of perfection," she insisted, "that I don't want to do the kind of crude, splashy things the others are doing."

"Well," I countered, "perhaps you have a mistaken idea of the road to perfection. That road is similar to the one nature takes in the development of its plants and animals. The beginning is from a seed and is quite shapeless with no detail; only gradually does life develop and the parts become visible and take form until all the plan hidden in the seed or embryo becomes perfect. In art the way to progress is to be willing to do crude and imperfect drawings first. It is through practice, through trial and error, that the artist grows. The imperfect works are stepping stones towards the fulfilment of your ideal of perfection. If you continue to think of the ideal as something you can have without effort, you are completely mistaken. Better to make a drawing of what you want to do, no matter how poor you may think it is. Then call me over and let me show you a way to improve it; bit by bit you will be on the road towards your concept of perfection."

I have found that the understanding of the law of growth as applied to creative art excites the imagination and reveals to students these problems of the ego in a fresh way. This new outlook in the study of art is a challenge to us, both as artists and teachers. It demands that we look below the surface to learn to analyse and understand the forces and influences at work. These forces create the attitude, direction, and pattern of the individual. If the direction is healthy and leads to growth, encourage it; if it doesn't, learn how to change it. If the individual pattern begins to take form, cherish it and cultivate it, for in that lies the essence of the artist.

Another way of relating the student's work to his psychology is to analyse the design of his picture. Suppose we divide a painting into three horizontal parts—foreground, middle ground, and distance. The way the student handles or avoids handling the problem in each section is significant. The foreground is that part in the picture and in life that is nearest to him, the concrete reality very difficult for some types to meet. If the child's foreground is empty and undeveloped, you may be sure he passes by his immediate and concrete problems and looks at the central part of his picture.

The middle distance is usually the easiest to paint, the eye falls on it naturally. Out there are the dream city, or the dream hills, where the artistic type naturally dwells without much exertion on his part, and it is the most frequently well painted.

The upper third of the picture is the high distant sky, analogous to the great vision the child may be too frail or too small even to aspire to.

The middle distance is symbolic of the dream or wish, expressive of the passive state of the student; the lower and higher parts of the picture require exertion of both the physical eye and the willing spirit to see them and to incorporate them actively in the painting and in life. This idea sometimes startles the student into observing both himself and nature afresh. He may commence his canvas in a totally different way. Before, he was passive and put down just what he liked instinctively, but now he is more aware, more active, and able to work from deeper levels. It gives him understanding about himself, and a new perception concerning his art. This analysis is based on observation of a great number of pictures of both children and artists, and it is very interesting to go to a museum and apply this test.

The harmonization of earth and sky, symbolizing man and God, was one of the great goals of Chinese painting. Young children nearly always place a big sun in their landscapes. It is as if in their naïve efforts they feel unconsciously the need of harmonizing earth and sky. In the older students this deep mystical expression is usually lost, and they become aware only of the sections of the world they look at; but when the larger outlook that shows them the symbolic values in the development of all parts of the picture is brought to their minds, it frequently opens new horizons and brings about work of a deeper nature.

CHAPTER VIII

The Awakening and Education of Feeling

THROUGH FEELING ASSOCIATION TO THE UNCONSCIOUS MIND

IF you touch real feeling in a pupil you generate energy without measure. Therefore, it is important that the subject matter of a pupil's work mean something to him, to his whole self—not just his thinking mind, but his whole being.

Feeling is a spade with which we can dig deep into the content of a child's mind; he will reveal his relation to life and his judgment of it. By means of feeling we can reach his memory and imagination, the two great tools of the artist.

A reporter once visited my group to pick up a "story" for his paper. He began by saying he had to get something of the moment which would line up with the news. His first suggestion was: "How would America look if Hitler came over and took possession?"

There was a chorus of protest at once.

"Aw, that's nothing to draw," exclaimed one child. "Everything he could do here has been done in all the other countries. We've seen pictures of it all in the newspapers and magazines for a long time."

"Yes," said another, "we couldn't give anything new; we would be copying all the other reports."

"It's no idea for a picture anyway," a third child complained. "It's just a thought. You have to have more than a thought."

In short, the children booed the idea out. It had not touched their feeling, nor had they an individual approach to it. It was mass horror, already made trite.

The reporter made other suggestions, all negated by the children because they were equally disconnected from their interests. Then the children themselves began making suggestions. They wanted to do New York. They liked the crowds, the different kinds of people, the activities, the news-stands, the subways, the parks, the theatres. But the reporter said, "No, that's too mild; it has no news interest."

However, he was quick to see what these children needed, and he said: "How about Harlem, the Negroes, their problems, the crime wave?"

"Oh, yes," they responded.

"I could do something with that," one said.

"We could do their crowded tenements and the children who have to play on the streets," said another.

"I'd do scenes of fighting and robbing and killing," cried a little boy.

Another boy said, "I'd do a picture showing how it would look with new playgrounds and the children playing there."

"I can see the Negro children from my school window. I know how they look," a little girl remarked.

From this variety of comment we can read the interests and character of each child. Through it all runs the thread of their sympathy, their feeling for the Negro. He is near enough for them to have a personal reaction. The Hitler problem was so far away from their lives that they could not envisage the material from which it was constructed.

The students undertook the new adventure immediately. During the following week they visited Harlem and upper Central Park, took either mental or pencil notes, then came after school and at odd extra hours to the studio to launch and further the work. They soon produced a vivid and varied collection of drawings, some of which are reproduced here.

Bobby, a boy of seven, had heard his parents talk about the lack of playgrounds for children in the coloured districts. That seemed strange to him, and he pondered over what the children could do with no place to play. He has drawn three little boys gazing out into the world, swinging their legs, with nothing to do. "This," he said, "is the way they get into trouble. They are sitting in front of the grocery store, thinking what to do. The man comes out to chase them away." He called his drawing "No Place to Play" (Ill. 21).

Vera, a girl of thirteen, had seen Negro children playing in a court-yard from her schoolroom window. She remembered that and used it for her picture. She depicted tumbledown houses and space too restricted for so many children to play and called her drawing "Crowded Court-yards".

21. No Place to Play, Trouble Brewing. By Robert at seven years of age.

David, a boy of fourteen, planned a more complex picture, designed somewhat like a mural. This is what he said about it: "In the foreground there is a crime taking place. The background shows the causes—poor houses, lack of playgrounds, discrimination against Negroes, and crowded schools." He named his picture "Causes of Crime" (Ill. 22).

Harold, a sixteen-year-old who had already developed a very strong social consciousness and a passionate sympathy for the oppressed, produced a whole book of wash drawings for this project. He said he was not going to draw any particular scene of crime, but wanted to picture life in Harlem and to show the unfortunate living conditions which inevitably result in crime. All his pictures showed a poignant sympathy for the Negro. "Boys in the Back Alley" (Ill. 23) is one of them.

Having seen from this group demonstration how children were unproductive when feeling was omitted but were actively creative when feeling moved them, we should next analyse what causes feeling to be buried and then discover ways of reaching and stirring it into action.

22. CAUSES FOR CRIME. Sketch for mural. Background shows the causes of crime.
By David at fourteen years of age.

Everyone is endowed with the capacity to feel. If this capacity is limited or negated, it may be due to several causes. Three are especially important: first, the child has retreated away from feeling because he has been hurt; second, the child is predominantly of the intellectual type and thus tries to rule emotion out; third, the child's interest is diverted to other subjects and the work becomes a mere casual performance.

When feeling is dormant how can one summon it to consciousness? What techniques can we use for so subtle an undertaking? I have found inspiration in the Socratic method of questioning and drawing out from the pupil his strongest feeling memories. In what seems casual talk I often discover some memory or symbol which is for the child the key to a newer form of expression. The memory or fantasy will evoke an image which will be subject matter for his picture.[1] As the child works, his imagination will assist in developing the subject which memory has evoked. In the process he will encounter difficulties of expression or execution, problems in technique; it is in these that I am of use to him. Simultaneously I serve as a guide who reminds him how he can help himself become a better instrument for his work by returning to the original image in his mind which can be recalled and will aid him when he feels confused, or by refreshing and stimulating himself by rest, deep breathing, free movement, or humming.

The first and perhaps commonest negation of feeling is due to early association of it with pain. In some way the child reaches out for affection and is denied the full satisfaction of his need. The frustration may be due to unawareness, indifference, or callousness on the part of the parent. The unconscious reaction to these rebuffs is withdrawal. In order to avoid fresh pain, the child avoids all feeling. Thus the soul retreats, refusing to know or show emotion. The result is a timid or perhaps a closed personality. This introversion can be gradually lessened and the emotion made articulate.

Danny, a little boy who was definitely a sensitive, feeling type, did not know what subject to choose. He fluttered and hovered around the room disturbing everybody and rejecting any suggestions. Although this made him a difficult pupil to work with, I felt sure that he was an extremely emotional child, deeply hurt and upset, and in need of help.

For a while I tried to be kind and sympathetic, but finally I took a firmer tone. "Danny," I said, "you have been here a month and have made no progress. You do not seem able to admit that I might help you. When I leave you alone, you do not find what you want to do; when you start something, you don't complete it; and when I make suggestions, you reject them. There is really no use your continuing here unless you change your attitude. This is the situation: you have some ability, you have a good mind and your own opinions about many things. You are not a very strong and robust child; a great deal of your fidgetiness and inability to settle down to work is due to your physical state. Now,

---

[1] It may be quite unknown to him why he chose the particular subject (and it is unimportant for him to know), but the choice is not accidental. It is expressive of his interest, his difficulty, his need, or his wish.

23. BOYS IN THE BACK ALLEY
Gangs threatening younger boys. By Harold at sixteen years of age.

if you want to stay and work here, I want you to go out in the hall with me and do a few simple exercises willingly, as all the other children do."

Taken aback at my severity, his cocky resistance collapsed. We went out into the hall together. I explained the value of deep breathing and moving. Then I left him, saying, "Stay quietly by yourself and close your eyes. You will see colours better when you are alone."

I returned to the studio without much hope of a change, but a little something actually did happen. He came running into the room. His eyes were brighter and wider open than I had ever seen them. He called to me, "I did see a ship on the sea."

I replied, "Go ahead and make it."

He completed the drawing in about half an hour. Though not remarkable, the picture was, at least, a beginning. However, as time went on, no great change took place. Danny reverted to his short trivial sketches.

I thought a good deal about him, wondering just what to do. His bringing-up had made him egocentric. I decided to try to appeal to this great self-interest. "How would you like to try a self-portrait?" I asked. "You could stand over here by the mirror and study yourself. First draw a sketch; then, when you get a good one, you can use coloured chalks."

At first he resisted, but after a while he said he'd try. I set up his easel near a window, placing a mirror near by. Naturally the drawings were not very satisfactory, but they did contain some quality of himself —enough to keep him interested an hour or more. Then he became restless and moved about the room watching the other children. However, from whatever place he was, he would glance back at his easel with, I thought, a sense of pride. He returned to his picture. We talked over the many things he could do to improve it, and, much to my surprise, he had sufficient desire to go on. For several weeks he continued to make studies of himself, some in black and white and some in colour. They grew better in form and likeness.

Then, after about three weeks, he said, "I want to do something else—my house with my dog in front of it and the bare trees." He was able to express this scene with more feeling than he had shown before. Next he did his mother before her mirror and dressing-table. This gave him great satisfaction.

Danny went on to many other subjects, gradually achieving a longer span of concentration and reaching out to subjects farther away from himself. Although the progress was slow, I felt I had learned something about handling a child spoiled and flattered into an unnatural state of self-importance. Giving him a big dose of himself was a bit like vaccination.

When the intellect is dominant, feeling is frequently repressed. Clarity, exactness, and thoroughness hold first place in the pupil's conception of art. Cold hard drawing, with emphasis on correctness or on minute detail, characterize the intellectual type of person. Such was the case with Leonard.

When he first came, all his pictures were firmly outlined, rather like illustrations. I had no success in several attempts to find some interest which would lead him to discover feeling. One day I asked, "Have you ever thought of doing scenes from home?" He showed interest and in short order produced a sketch of his father reading a newspaper. It was the first thing that showed sensitivity and his own approach to expression. I had touched a spring which opened the door to feeling. True, the door may swing closed again, and a new approach be necessary.

One day Leonard had a subject he was particularly eager to interpret —the problem of the oppressed minorities in Europe. The idea was to make a picture of a simple workman with a government police-officer arresting him. The workman would reach his arms out towards America. On the other shore was to be an American boy with arms outstretched to welcome him. Of course, this concept was so motivated by idea and so difficult to execute with any plastic sense that it soon sent the boy beyond his depth. However, I believe in letting pupils try to express any idea in which they show enthusiasm, no matter how unsuitable the idea may be. No one can tell how the painting may turn out and interference at this point would make for harmful censorship.

Leonard made a preliminary sketch of his idea, "Escape—I" (Ill. 24), which proved quite unsatisfactory. The workman and the policeman were fairly well done, but the American boy was very stiff and stilted. To help Leonard realize what the natural action and movement in the figure would be like, I asked him to act the role by closing his eyes (so that he would not be self-conscious) and then imagining himself as the

24. THE ESCAPE I. Feeling covered, awkward expression.
By Leonard at twelve years of age.

25. THE ESCAPE II. Feeling released, freer expression.

figure stretching out his arms to rescue the foreigner. Gradually the boy forgot himself and was able to express the intended action. In acting the role of the American boy he unconsciously revealed to himself how the boy felt and thus discovered the appropriate gestures and posture. Then, with deeper meaning, he approached a second sketch, "Escape—II" (Ill. 25). Here, the same idea flows forth with freedom of movement and at least the beginning of a translation of the idea into plastic form emerges from dramatizing the idea.

A later example shows Leonard's further development. One day I read to the group from the Bible. Most of the children became interested at once, but Leonard said, "I don't want to draw from the Bible; I don't see why I should."

I replied, "You don't have to if you don't want to, but why not take a pad and pencil and sketch a few things to see whether you don't find it more interesting than you think?"

He took a pad and red and black "conte" crayons. He started with the idea of creation—God creating Man. The drawing showed a new strength in his work.

A few days later he commented, "You know it's really fun. I thought I didn't want to do pictures out of the Bible, but now I don't want to do anything else. There's everything in it." He went on, drawing not only what was read to him, but also what he had read by himself. The difference in scope, quality, and technique of these Biblical sketches compared with his pictures of sports and everyday subjects was astounding and shows the inspirational quality of great thoughts for the artist.

Another boy was also inspired by the Bible stories. His painting, "God Blessing Adam and Eve" (Ill. 26), was a fine example of how his feeling of reverence guided him to expression.

The next example, "A Boy and Girl Dancing" (Ill. 27), is by Robert F. at fourteen years. It tells of a very tender love between two young people. It is most unusual for a young artist to be able to express a personal experience so poignantly.

In some cases lack of feeling may be temporary. The interest of the pupil may be focused on something else, and, for the time being, the art becomes trivial or commonplace. The pupil can be recalled to a deeper interest through feeling.

26. GOD BLESSING ADAM AND EVE

When she was sixteen years old, Jane Dudley had an experience in which feeling helped her regain her power to express an idea. She had been working on a large painting for several weeks and was extremely discouraged with her slow progress. In fact, she wept and said, "I can't paint. I'm going to quit and never paint again."

"Let's talk it over together," I said, taking her into another room, where we sat down. "Forget about this picture for the moment. This particular picture may be spoiled, but the image in your mind is still there and you can make another picture if you wish. In the new one you can overcome some of the mistakes you made in this. Before you attempt that, however, I have a suggestion. Take a fresh piece of paper and some coloured chalks and paint your tears, your very mood of despair, and we shall see what happens."

Although sceptical, Jane wiped the tears from her face and returned to the studio. The results were extremely valuable as an indication of what may take place when emotion is thus used. Her first picture expressed her dark mood. The flowers are drooping and done in dull red, olive, and dark green, with a dark brown and black background. The completion of this picture acted as a catharsis for her sorrow. She called the drawing "Despair" (Ill. 28).

I was busy with other pupils, and when I next stopped beside her, she had already done a second picture. This depicted the new mood which followed after the other one had been dispelled. It represents a bowl of flowers near an open window with the curtain blown by fresh air. The colours are light and gay. This is named "Hope" (Ill. 29).

Immediately afterwards, she did a third picture.

"What is this?" I asked.

"Oh," she replied, "that's a picture of myself thinking it over. Something very strange happened to me. When I painted the broken flowers, I suddenly became very light and happy inside, and I felt I could paint anything. So I did the flowers at the window all upright and gay, except one little bud drooping over the edge, reminding me a little of the other picture. Then I stopped and said to myself, 'It's queer how just saying a thing in a picture changes everything inside.' And then I thought I would make a picture of that and call it 'Contemplation'" (Pl. II, facing p. 104).

27. BOY AND GIRL DANCING. By Robert F. at fourteen years of age.

29. Hope. By Jane at sixteen years of age.

28. Despair. By Jane at sixteen years of age.

Thus Jane contemplated the mystery of creation and its effect on one human being.

If we pause to reflect why art expression is so valuable to our development, we may arrive at this conclusion: Self-knowledge is the basis of clarity and growth. Most of us do not know ourselves, but live in a beclouded state, hesitant about making choices, postponing decisions, and insecure generally as to our direction. How does art expression affect this? If the condition within ourselves is vague, comparable to vapour, then, when we make the effort to create, we project this state outside ourselves, crystallized into form. We objectify it, and subject becomes object. Whether the art product is a poem, a statue, music, or a painting, the effect is the same. The self has become separated into two parts, actor and spectator. The spectator sees the actor, judges him, and so is beginning to know him. When the artist has objectified his state into a form, he has emptied himself. A catharsis has taken place, leaving the individual free, clean, and ready for a new work.

Jane was confused and her state was, like vapour, unformed. She drew her dark mood in the first picture and became cleansed; then she drew the second picture of the light flowers at the window; finally she became truly spectator, and, in the third drawing, actually observed herself. This is a fine example of the process. We have traced the acts of creation through the beginning of self-awareness.

These short case histories show the tremendous importance of feeling in the creative process and how a teacher may help to liberate emotion when it is repressed or buried.

CHAPTER IX

Colour and Sound

COLOUR

THE world as perceived through the sense of sight is a world of colour. Children are born into this world with a highly sensitive perception. They see colour flowing through everything. Their reception of colour is true, clear, and brilliant. But as they grow older their colour sense is frequently dulled or lost.

The dulling of the colour sense may arise from lack of use, unawareness, or lack of training in perception. It may arise also from a psychological cause, such as fear of full perception and full expression, for a certain daring is necessary really to see colour and to be true to our vision. But the main cause of the child's loss of his colour sense is our ignorance of his needs. Each child has his own colour chemistry and his own affinities in colour. If these are ignored or distorted by the imposition of other tastes on him, his own colour world may be lost to him for ever. If the child's outlook becomes drab, it is because we negate colour and his vision fades to our dullness.

It is important, therefore, to let a child use the colours he loves, to surround him with colour, and to give him colour to play with while he is still young. Black-and-white drawing is an abstraction of the forms we see. It is an intellectual concept and belongs to later years.

An important concept relating colour to form has evolved out of the work of modern artists. Beginning with Turner, form was conceived as being created from the relationship of planes of colour. The perception of their differences and their qualities and of how they built up form and space opened up new horizons in the understanding and use of colour. Turner is supposed to have received his new ideas from the reading of Goethe's book *Farbenlehre*, which was translated about the middle of the nineteenth century just when Turner began those

II. CONTEMPLATION. Thinking over the change of moods.
By Jane at sixteen years of age.

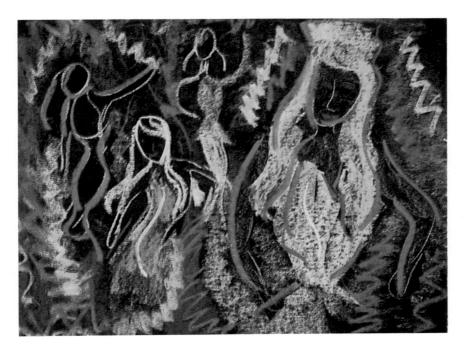

III. FAIRIES DANCING ON THE MOON. Drawn after chanting.
By Nancy at nine years of age.

IV. Play with Limited Colour. Blue, yellow, black and white. By Naomi at eleven years of age.

V. The Family. Making use of the colour mixtures discovered in Play. By Naomi at eleven years of age.

VI. PLAY WITH LIMITED COLOUR
Red, yellow, black and white. By Mark at twelve years of age.

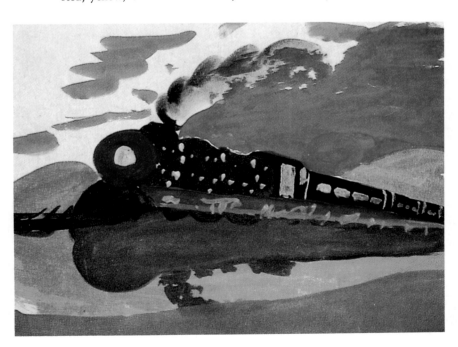

VII. THE SPEEDING TRAIN. Making use of colour combinations in previous "Play in Colour". By Mark at twelve years of age.

VIII. Cat Prowling. By Noel at seven years of age.

IX. The House. By Noel at seven years of age.

explorations with colour that shocked and startled his contemporaries so much.

Cézanne carried these ideas much further. He demonstrated how each colour moves forward or back according to its quality and its vibration. The yellow and orange expand and come forward, red is in the middle, and blue and violet contract and recede, so that colour used in this manner creates form. A further development is that each colour contains the ones next to it in the spectrum. For example, a blue object may contain yellow in one part and thus form a greenish blue on that section of its surface; another part of the object may have some red in it and here reflect a warm purplish blue. Thus, a vibrant blue will contain the whole spectrum, even if only by suggestion. A living exponent of this concept of colour is Abraham Rattner. He is bolder than Cézanne and uses his colour much more daringly and brilliantly. Another great difference between these two artists is a fundamental one. Cézanne was a great intellectual while Rattner is moved by deep feeling and sensation.

This modern interpretation of colour is realized only through mature experience. The young child sees brilliant, simple planes of colour in two dimensions. Sensation and feeling in the child are satisfied with drawing or painting in one and two dimensions. The capacity to see and understand three dimensions rarely appears before adolescence; it comes simultaneously with the awakening of thought.

There are several ways of using colour. First, merely through sensory reaction—colours being chosen to create harmony, dissonance, or balance. This is the basis of abstract design in painting. Second, the selection of the colour may be guided by the feeling associated with the subject of the painting. Third, the choice may be directed by a combination of these two, plus the work of the mind which may introduce colour arrangement based on scientific colour knowledge, colour chemistry, and resulting effects.

Colour sense is individual. Each person according to his cultural background or temperament or chemistry likes or dislikes certain combinations. While it is important to express fully individual affinities for these first natural colours, there is no need to keep the colour perceptions in the instinctive state. There are ways of training the eyes to more varied vision, as I shall describe later.

COLOUR SYMBOLISM IS A KEY TO UNDERSTANDING A CHILD'S NEEDS

The symbolism of colour may be used as a basis for understanding a child's needs. Colour symbolism has been interpreted in various ways by different peoples in different ages, but certain interpretations have been generally accepted from the ancients and passed on to us. I have experimented with them and found so many verifications that these interpretations have become valid for me.

In my experience, for instance, red, the colour of blood, usually denotes vitality. Red has a masculine overtone; it is associated with aggressiveness, anger, and power, and frequently expresses itself in angular forms. Rose colour has, of course, different meanings. It is apt to be used in expression of tenderness or love.

Blue is usually used in a more feminine interpretation. It suggests water and sky, and frequently appears in rounded, wavy, or spiral forms. It is the colour of emotion and sometimes of the soul. The use of blues and browns, without reds, often indicates some lack of force.

Yellow is the colour of the mind and spirit. If a child is inclined to use yellow predominantly, he is most probably a "thinking type". Yellow should never be used as a means of design; it is really an expression of light and should merely illumine design already created through other colours. Religious painters employ it to indicate divinity.

If a child is strong and extroverted, he is likely to choose complementary colours, such as green and red, or blue and yellow. The selection of colours nearer to each other in the spectrum, such as blue and green, indicates a kind of passivity. The child who chooses these needs to be stirred up. In such a situation a teacher may help by talking to the child about the characteristic meanings and use of colour and thus tempt him to experiment with stronger ones.

THE TEACHING OF COLOUR

In teaching colour, I begin with chalks. They are the simplest, most direct medium and require the least skill. I use rich colours and a soft quality chalk. The soft chalk responds well and will express what the child intends more easily than a hard chalk or crayon. These chalks are spread out on a table, each box containing only one colour. Thus the children see each colour in a mass, and it makes a more vivid impression than when they see one box with eight colours packed closely together. From this bright display the children can make their choices more readily. Ill. 30 shows a boy choosing his colours thoughtfully.

A girl approaches the chalks and looks at them. I say to her, "Choose one you like." I don't hurry her, but wait until she has made a selection. She looks the colours over and takes one with decision, as if she knew at once which she preferred. Her choice is blue. She is more comfortable with this basic colour than any other. It is this particular child's key colour, and the use of it leads her to the understanding of all colours. This is similar to finding her own pitch in music. Once she has done that she can sing all notes harmoniously. Asking her to choose the colour she liked best was a way of saying: "What is the vibration of your own body? What colour will heal you? Take the colour you respond to."

The child has instinctively chosen her key colour—a colour which we recognize as fundamental to her body and spirit. She is now ready to go on. I say to her, "You have chosen blue. Keep it in your hand and hold it near the other colours. What colour is the blue asking for? It probably wants one colour more than any other. Wait until you know what that is."

The girl looks at the boxes thoughtfully a moment. The idea that the colour in her hand is active and has a preference rather pleases her. She soon makes a second choice, a soft yellow. This she doesn't do haphazardly or carelessly, but really out of desire. The first colour demanded the second. It is a marriage of colour. It draws the creative force to her. The first choice, blue, is the child's key colour; the second, a soft yellow, is her stimulus. One colour was not enough; it would have been monotonous. But now she has acquired a basis for creative form. At this point, she is likely to look up with a smile of contentment. She is ready to begin her picture. She is also permitted to add black and white to these colours to give her the range in values as well as colours.

Some children may ask for more colours, just because they have been used to helping themselves promiscuously. Usually it is not difficult to dissuade them by saying, "Some other day, but now we're going to play a game with just two colours and see what may happen. You will discover lots of things for yourselves."

As the child uses and mixes the colours, he finds for himself what the combinations will form. For example, the girl's blue and yellow will give green; other combinations will ensue as one predominates over another. She thus begins forming her own colour vocabulary. By limiting the number of colours to two, she finds the colour process for herself, and does not waste energy in dissipation with many colours.

After the child has become thoroughly familiar with the possibilities of these two colours, I add a second step to the colour experience. I ask the child to compose a whole picture using just the two colours he has been experimenting with. Thus the child makes use of his new-found colour vocabulary.

From chalks the children go on to paints. "Play with Limited Colour" (Pl. IV) was done in water-colours by Naomi, a girl of eleven, who also chose blue and yellow and who added to them black. After making many combinations of the colours in both hues and values, she painted "The Family" (Pl. V) in which she applied her new colour experience to a picture.

A second example of this experience with limited colours was done by Mark, a boy of twelve years. He used red, yellow, black and white. These are again two illustrations. The first (Pl. VI) is the play with colour, trying to make as many combinations in the arrangement as possible; the second is the painting called "The Speeding Train" (Pl. VII), in which he makes use of this experience. There is a simplicity about the harmony which would have been difficult to achieve with a great variety of colours.

It is interesting to observe that the girl first selected a blue harmony. Blue is a colour expressive of feeling, and she unconsciously selected a fitting subject, "The Family" In a similar fashion, the boy selected red as his natural theme of action colour, using "The Speeding Train" to carry out the harmony.

Too free choice robs the child of necessary creative effort. The teacher must be on guard not to invite the child too soon to the wider combinations. The child should be protected from becoming complex before he has fully learned to be simple.

There is another approach to this method of teaching colour. The aim in these techniques in colour training is to clarify any confusion the

30. Boy Choosing Colours Thoughtfully

child may have about colour. If we can aid him in this way, he can carry out his subsequent intentions with fewer difficulties, disappointments, and failures.

In this approach to teaching colour we omit the preparatory play with limited colour and proceed directly to a picture. The child chooses one colour and is given black and white in addition. With these he paints the first picture of a series. In this composition he will be able to express simply colour and dark and light. For his second picture he selects an additional colour and paints the same subject again with this richer combination. He then selects a third colour and paints the subject a third time. The progressive use of additional colours gives the child an opportunity to make rich and subtle combinations and usually develops the spatial sense to a greater degree. In the experience he learns the possibilities of combinations and permutations of these colours. Children seem to enjoy this exercise and almost always gain a new confidence in their ability to use and understand colour.

If the pupil's interest still continues after the third painting, a fourth picture may be composed with an entirely fresh subject, but with the same colour. In the fourth picture, we can usually judge quite accurately how much new power of expression the child has gained. The new subject brings fresh interest and freedom from any sense of the pictures being a lesson, and the child exploits his newly gained knowledge without being aware of it.

Johnnie, aged nine, selected a dinosaur for his subject. The colours he chose for his paintings significantly changed the animal in each successive picture. In the first, done with purple, the animal is fairly small, not very vigorous, and faces to the right. In the second picture Johnnie added orange and got beautiful tones of grey and brown through the mixture of the orange with his purple. At the same time the dinosaur grew larger and stronger and was moved diagonally to the left. The addition of yellow in the third picture gave light, strength, and movement to the whole. The animal, now luminously painted, was placed in an almost upright position and thus became much more powerful and striking. The child's ideas seem to have grown and expanded as much as the pictures themselves did through the successive building up of colour in them.

Fourteen-year-old Judy painted a series of dancers which exhibits an unusual degree of strength and rhythm. The girl's first selection was green. With the addition of black and white, she produced an extremely dynamic picture. In a second painting she combined red with her green, white, and black and thus created the warmth and neutral tones needed to give her work plastic form and variety. Her third colour choice was yellow ochre, which gave a sense of light.

This colour experience means much to the children. They realize they have learned something new and exciting. They can't put their knowledge into words—but they show their awareness by the satisfaction they get from the completed series, by the eagerness with which they show their paintings to the parent who calls for them, and also by the way they look at their pictures on the wall or in their portfolio. They examine the other children's work to see what each one has discovered.

SOUND AND COLOUR

In an earlier chapter we discovered how rhythm and simple design came out of movement. Now we are to find how colour emerges from sound. No one can teach colour to another; each must find colour through the functions of his own chemistry and his own nervous system. But the close *relationship* between sound and colour we *can* teach.

By sound I do not mean completed music already made by others. I mean vocal sounds that issue from the sounding board of one's own body. This kind of sound produces the sea on which the whole process of colours sails forth.

I have discovered the effectiveness of sound in relation to colour through my own experiments in painting. I first noticed that crooning or humming made the work go more to my liking, that the painting became clearer and richer in colour, that the form frequently was influenced, becoming simplified and integrated. Later I tried making up simple chants merely on the sound of a single vowel. The various vowels suggested their own colours and forms. In this primitive procedure we can, I think, find real relationship between sound and colour.

In contrast to this, the method of playing completed musical compositions for children to paint by seems artificial, and much too complicated for an honest interpretation. I have therefore rejected this method as a means of relating sound to colour and prefer to continue experimenting with the more elementary sounds.

I have condensed many experiences of my own and of the children into a simple routine by which to evoke the emergence of colour from sound. I begin by telling the pupils that we are going to play a sort of singing game. "It helps us to see colours and gives us ideas for pictures. First, stand up and stretch, even yawn if you can; that will relax you. Now close your eyes, breathe out completely. Then as you lift your arms above your head, breathe in and try to breathe in on a sound. For instance, the "AH" sound. Having breathed in on "AH", bend over from the hips as far as you can, and when you are near the ground, breathe out the "AH" as deep and bell-like as possible. Try and let the breath out slowly, making the tones last as long as you can, and gradually as you lift your body, let the sounds become a chant on a few notes, and let the body sway or swing as you do it. During this exercise, keep the eyes closed all the time, because the images in the mind are more active when the physical eye is at rest."

This exercise can be repeated with the same sounds until the child sees something or wants to go back to draw or paint or chooses to play with another sound. The sounds can be combined with movements— sometimes swinging curved movements, at other times sharp and angular ones. The different sounds and movements bring forth a great variety of material, as these following examples of the children's experiences will demonstrate.

I use black paper in these experiments because I find it acts as a stimulus to colour; the children see colour in black more easily than in white. Creating in nature takes place in darkness, so creation in art functions best under the same circumstances.

A further aspect of sound is its cleansing property. It will do for the body what water will do for a vessel you are cleansing. You shake the water up, it seeks out the corners and rinses them. So sound, chanted, clears the lungs, decarbonizes them of half-used air, lets in fresh oxygen, increases the circulation of the blood which stimulates the body, and, in turn, the mind. The strange fact is that simple exercises in breathing, moving, and chanting, intensify and purify the capacity for seeing colour to a degree that may seem incredible. Only demonstration can prove it.

A good example is found in the experience of ten-year-old Joyce, a happy child with only average ability, and, for that reason a good choice to show the unifying and enriching power of sound. If chanting can thus transform the work of the average child, we may look forward to immeasurable benefits to the mass of children as well as to artists.

When Joyce first started lessons, her work was only fair. It showed sensibility, but on a shallow level. At the time I am writing of, it had even deteriorated. I had been ill and had missed classes for ten days. When I returned to the studio, I found that Joyce had made a picture of a skating scene. It was stiff, badly drawn, and rather poor in colour. I felt discouraged. I told the girl I thought the work showed a troubled state and observed that her arm must have been stiff when she drew her picture, for it showed such a lack of freedom and confidence.

Then Joyce and I discussed the principle of sound, breath, and movement, and its possibilities of freeing her. I asked her whether she would like to go out into the hall and practise it a little, all alone. She was quite responsive. As I left her, I said, "When you have something you want to paint, come back."

After a little while she returned and told me she had been chanting the "OU" sound, that it had appealed to her and had made her think of the wind. She made a delightful little sketch on black paper of grass and trees being blown by the wind. The drawing had rhythm and the beauty of simple colour—it was just a clear brown tree with green leaves and a different shade of green for the tufts of grass.

She said, "I sort of got the curve movement from the sound. Now it is finished, and I want to make it just the opposite. I want to make the sunshine and the stillness of trees and see the difference in colour I would use. I will make the same tree, but this time it will be in bloom with flowers along the walk and someone jumping rope."

This child's experience proves, I feel, that the old way of teaching is obsolete. It is not enough to help the child construct her skating figures better, she herself must be revitalized and filled with the force, the power, and the imagery needed to carry her through to the creation she desires to make. When Joyce made the sound of the wind, all these things happened, and consequently there was true expression.

8

Susie, a girl of twelve years, had been doing fairly conventional work depicting girls of her own age in their usual activities such as swimming or dancing. An extremely important change took place with her first experience in chanting. It showed deepening of her consciousness. I quote from what she wrote about it:

> I saw a door or a window which was part very dark and part in the light. The rim around its dark corner was a brilliant beautiful colour, given light by a beautiful object which was a pearly white—right in the middle of the rim. The beautiful colour of the rim receded as it got farther away from the pearly white sphere. The part of the window that was in the light gradually disappeared into the blackness.
>
> As a whole, it seemed that the window was sort of the turning point in someone's life; showing that the person was leaving the bright, day part of their life, and entering a blackness, nightlike part. But this person was to reach the pearl—which might have been Hope or Happiness or something good, relaxing. This pearl was to spread its goodness through the person's life—or maybe this was significant of not just one person's life, but of all the people in the world. Maybe it was the lives of the masses, and the pearl was Freedom, Liberty, Equality.

Another example of a different type imagination resulting from an exercise in chanting is the illustration "Fairies Dancing on the Moon" (Pl. III). It brought out greater freedom and beauty of colour than the pupil had ever shown.

Not all pupils are ready to respond to these colour suggestions. They are given individually and only to those pupils who have indicated their receptivity to such experiments by an alertness and sensitivity above the average. These examples have all dealt with definite experiences in the method of developing colour sensitivity. It is well, however, to see how these students make use of their training in their later expressions.

"Cat Prowling" (Pl. VIII) was done after making the sound "Meow", which suggested the colours and the subject. The cat has a terrifying quality as it slinks along with tail erect, one eye round and one eye square. There are queer bits of design to be seen which Noel always introduced in his pictures. The overall blue-and-black design is very satisfying.

"The House" (Pl. IX) was done after chanting to the sound of "EE". The child saw gay colours and children playing. The strong colours and clear design came from his having seen the image vividly.

More mature work in colour derived from chanting has been done by those pupils about whom there are separate studies in later chapters. A full discussion of this colour work will be found in the story of each individual child. (See Chapter XVI, Linda; Chapter XVII, Miriam; Chapter XVIII, Steven; Chapter XIX, Harold; and Chapter XXV, Mario.)

We have observed the possibility of stimulating the colour process in various ways and have seen how the fuller comprehension of colour has transformed the art and influenced the life of a few young people.

These examples make us realize what great unexplored possibilities exist in the extension of colour perceptions. We are coming into an age of colour, and its possible effect on the race is incalculable.

We see the beginnings now in the use of colour in factories, hospitals, schools, and homes. Formerly work in factories and offices was done in small, dark cubicles, often painted in browns and greys; now rooms are wide, with big windows and light colour on walls and furniture. Hospitals paint their walls for the therapeutic effect of the colours used—cool green or blue for excitable patients to induce calm, pale yellow or pink for depressed patients who need stimulation and hope. In the school and home fresher hues and more subtle colour relations are contributing to an inner harmony.

Nature uses colour for her various purposes. The plumage of the male bird is brilliant to attract the female; many animals and insects have protective colouring against destructive attack. Now, as man awakens to the possibilities of colour and discovers the value of colour in his life, he accelerates his own evolutionary process.

CHAPTER X

The Significance of Distortion

DISTORTION is emphasis; it is a means by which a plastic artist expresses his interpretation of life. Often the type of distortion shifts during a child's development. While he is seeking to express a need, an idea, or a desire in a certain direction, he must distort that part. When he has resolved that phase, he drops it and draws normally, but may later distort something else. The distortion, if sincere, gives character, style, and significance to the work.

An example proves this clearly. In the country, a girl was painting three heads of young women emerging from a background of leaves. The leaves had the definite rhythm of a serpentine curve. Two of the heads were straight—one vertical, one slightly diagonal; the third head was distorted with a curve in its axis. My first criticism was to draw the girl's attention to the head which was askew. She was silent for a time.

"Do you disagree with me?" I asked.

She paused and then replied, "I think I wanted to distort her away from the human and make her link with the leaves."

Now there was meaning in her distortion which I had missed. After what she said, I could see it. It expressed the kinship between vegetative and human nature—something the child was feeling in those days she was spending among the leaves and grasses.

Another example is found in the experience of Harold, whose development is discussed in detail in Chapter XX. I mention it here, as it gives further insight into this problem. Harold has always distorted hands, making them huge in proportion to the figure. See "The Strikers" (Pl. XX). He says he cannot help this, for he feels them that way. His answer indicates that he is deeply impressed with the power of hands. He senses that they are his means of survival in a terribly strained and difficult world. It is a projection of his dependence on his hands that makes him distort and over-emphasize them to satisfy his need.

From the study of such examples we see that distortion is one way for the artist to express his personal interpretation of life and that it is important for a teacher to understand and encourage such expression when it is the desire of the pupil. Blind criticism of irregular form may reduce the pupil's work to the commonplace and prevent his natural development.

C

Release of the Creative Faculty through Basic Experiences of the Mind and Spirit

CHAPTER XI

The Role of the Power of the Mind

LITTLE is known of the areas in which the creative mind functions, but a few general ideas of its nature are generally accepted. We know that the mind can be divided into the unconscious and conscious realms. We know that the unconscious is the great primordial source of the higher imagination, the locus of the creative impulse; it includes in its scope everything which is above and below our average intellect. We know that the conscious mind contains the knowledge of principles and techniques we have acquired through study and experience.

The highest power of the mind is vision, which extends from its first flash to the clear and steady illumination of its fulfilment. The artist is stimulated to begin his work by the feeling which co-ordinates his senses, accelerating the magic with which his vision invests the world. Through it he sees within and beyond the commonplace, as Blake did, who glimpsed "a universe in a grain of sand". This vision, or imagination, is the source, the fountain-head of art. It exists deep in the core of the artist and in each of us—we all have this potential force, though we scarcely use it. The artist, however, serves his vision, gives it time and opportunity; for him it grows strong, and, in turn, the vision serves the artist. Thus, we see imagination as the power which conceives the form and starts its projection into a space-time world—creation is then born. But in the process of creation, other powers of the mind are needed. They are observation and memory, which respectively note and store images from the sense world. Perception follows from the exercise of these two. It discerns the essence hidden beneath the surface of objective forms and discovers the fundamental principles of dimension, proportion, and relationship.

Thus far, the artist has shown us his sources—the subjective one of imagination and the objective one of observation. Now comes the welding of these sources into design. Design is the flower of a third great power of the mind—the power of organization.

The fourth power is understanding, which is not a mere process of the intellect but the operation of a maturer and more comprehensive intelligence. This higher wisdom, which flows from the unconscious and grows through experience, enables the artist to conceive form in its relation to space and time. The ability to express one's vision in true form is the supreme spiritual achievement of the artist.

CHAPTER XII

The Awakening of the Imagination

*Imagination is the Faculty of Forming Images Whereby the Soul
Beholdeth the Likeness of Things that be Absent.*

—TREVISA (*15th century*)

Too many people think lightly or casually of the imagination, not pausing to realize its significance or to value its power. Occasionally they confuse imagination and fancy. Imagination, the word of higher import, connotes especially the exercise of plastic or creative power; fancy suggests the play of associations more remote, arbitrary, or capricious; but the imagination remains conscious of an indestructible domain.

Unfortunately, many art students rely almost wholly on models or some form of nature. It is of fundamental importance to interest such students in the possibilities of imaginative conception. A little later in this chapter I shall describe the practice of imagination among my pupils, with exercises to stimulate it, and examples. But before doing this, let us search the minds of great thinkers, artists, and poets that we may read their elevated conception of imagination.

From Plato: "Imagination is the faculty of representing thoughts under the form of images." This is distinctly a philosopher's viewpoint.

In contrast, Aristotle has defined imagination as "the movement which results upon an actual sensation, i.e. the continued presence of an impression after the object which first excited it has been removed from actual experience".

Plotinus was a true mystic; that is, one who was conscious of the immanence of the divine in the human, and of the spiritual in the material. He deals with imagination in the first and fourth Enneads, and says, "Imagination transforms into images both the form of sensible objects and our thoughts about them."

With Chaucer a broader meaning starts and develops, beginning with the notion of mental imaging of things suggested but not previously experienced; thence it expands, first to fantastic representation or fancy and later to the idea of mental creation and poetic idealization—the productive, constructive, or creative imagination of the psychologist:

> Men may dye of imaginacioun
> So depe may impresioun by take.

In the time of Shakespeare imagination and fancy were used interchangeably, but since Wordsworth's time the words have been commonly discriminated. Fancy deals with the superficial resemblances and imagination with the deeper truths which underlie them. Wordsworth speaks thus of imagination: "When imagination frames a comparison the resemblance depends less upon the outline of form and feature than upon expression and effect; less upon casual and outstanding than upon inherent and internal properties: moreover the images invariably modify each other. The law under which the processes of Fancy are carried on is as capricious as the accidents of things . . . but the Imagination is conscious of an indestructible dominion." These words, especially the last sentence, should be of true assurance to the student who hesitates to use this latent capacity and to investigate for himself its unlimited potentialities.

In *The Defence of Poetry*, Shelley states a fresh point of view about imagination. He says: "The great instrument of moral good is the imagination. Poetry enlarges the circumference of the imagination and strengthens the faculty which is the organ of the moral nature of man, in the same manner as exercise strengthens the limb." What a responsibility this conception of imagination places on administrators of education! They would need to reapportion time in the curriculum and assign a place of major importance to art, giving sufficient opportunity to expand and cultivate the power of imagination in order that it may be not only the chief creative faculty of the mind, but also the instrument of moral good.

Another viewpoint is voiced by J. C. Shairp, nineteenth-century educator,[1] from whose analysis of imagination the following excerpts have

[1] J. C. Shairp, *Aspects of Poetry*, Houghton, Mifflin & Co., no date.

been condensed: "To our ordinary perception of things imagination adds force, clearness, and distinctness. It seems to be a power intermediate between intellect and emotion. In its highest form, it would seem to be based upon moral intensity. The emotional and intellectual in it act and react on each other. In its highest form it is that intense intuition which goes straight to the core of an object and lays hold of the essential life of a scene. It is that by which Shakespeare read the inmost heart of man, and Wordsworth of nature. It is also the combining and harmonizing power, and it is the power which clothes intellectual and spiritual conceptions in appropriate form. Shakespeare says, 'it bodies forth the forms of things unknown'. But it can also spiritualize what is visible and corporeal, filling it with higher meaning. It is a truth-sensing faculty, perceiving aspects of truth which can find no entrance by any other inlet. It is accompanied by a delight in the object or truth beheld, a thrill which is one of the most exquisite moods that man ever experiences."

It remains, however, for William Blake to give us the most elevated and inspiring words on the subject: "A spirit and a Vision are not, as modern philosophy supposes, a cloudy vapour or a nothing, they are organized and minutely articulated beyond all that the mortal and perishing nature can produce. He who does not imagine in stronger and better lineaments, and in stronger and better light, than his perishing and mortal eye can see, does not imagine at all."[1]

In another place he says: "I know of no other Christianity and of no other Gospel than the liberty both of body and mind to exercise the Divine Arts of the Imagination. Imagination is the real and eternal World of which the Vegetable Universe is but a faint shadow."[2]

And again: "God is the poet's inward vision of outward things. He is in short the Poetic Genius or Imagination, sustainer of this mighty universe of ours that has its roots in outward facts, but is in soul a fourfold chorus of joy and praise. . . . I question not my corporeal eye any more than I would question a window concerning a sight. I look through it, not with it."[3]

In the course of his development, an artist sometimes changes from

---

[1] *A Vision of the Last Judgment*, transcript in Gilchrist, Descriptive Cat. No. IV, Gilchrist, ii, p. 153.
[2] *Jerusalem*, p. 77. The Emanation of the Giant Albion, 1804. Wickstead, p. 217.
[3] *A Vision of the Last Judgment*, Gilchrist, ii, p. 200.

a representative style of art to a deeper style. Van Gogh was such a man. He was in conflict between fact and feeling, between realistic and imaginative vision. In his letters to his brother Theo, he reveals his struggle. In 1888 Van Gogh, who had been a devout impressionist, began to respond to the liberating influence of his more imaginative friends, Gauguin and Bernard. This influence was countered by Theo Van Gogh who was loyal to impressionism and wanted his brother Vincent to stick to fact. The conflict is revealed by the two paintings reproduced here and the following quotations from Van Gogh's letters to Emil Bernard and Theo Van Gogh:[1]

April 11, 1888, to Bernard: "The imagination is certainly a faculty we must develop and it alone can bring us to creation of a more exalting and consoling nature than we are shown in a solitary glance at reality —which we perceive. A star-spangled sky, for instance, that's a thing I would like to try to do. . . . But how can I manage unless I make up my mind to work from imagination?"

September 1888, in a letter to Theo, defending the idea that a painting, especially of the sky, can be both an expression and a symbol of deep human feeling: "To express hope by a star, the eagerness of the soul by a sunset radiance—Certainly there is nothing in that of—realism, but is it not something that exists?"

September 1888, to Theo: "The problem of painting night scenes . . . on the spot and actually by night interests me enormously." Then at the end of September he writes of a canvas: "The Starry Sky Painted Actually at Night Under a Gas Jet" (Ill. 31). This first realistic starry night painted in September 1888, he describes with aesthetic detachment: "On the blue-green field of the sky the Great Bear sparkles, its discreet pallor contrasting with the brutal gold of the gas light."

The influence of Gauguin and Bernard is at work. Later in 1888 he writes to Theo: "Gauguin gives me courage to imagine things."

Finally, with this courage, he painted the "Second Starry Night" (Ill. 32), which is a masterpiece of imaginative form. On June 19, 1889, he wrote to Theo announcing the new picture: "I have a new study of the starry night. Though I have not seen Gauguin's or Bernard's recent

[1] *The Letters of Vincent Van Gogh to His Brother.* Constable & Co., London. Houghton, Mifflin & Co., 1927.

31. THE STARRY SKY, Van Gogh. Painted from nature.
By Courtesy of the Museum of Modern Art.

canvas, I am pretty well convinced that this study is parallel in feeling
to their work."

When this painting was being exhibited in the Museum of Modern
Art, A. H. Barnes, Jr., wrote this description of it: "The starry night
goes further, it is fundamentally an imaginative invention—the sky, the
sunbright moon, the milky way turned to comets, the stars like bursting
bombshells—this is the unique and overwhelming vision of a mystic, a
man in ecstatic communion with heavenly power."

These two paintings and Van Gogh's letters concerning them give
us an intimate glimpse into the working of an artist's mind on this subject.

There are two aspects of the imagination. The one embodies things unknown. The other "spiritualizes what is visible and corporeal, filling it with higher meaning. It is a truth-sensing faculty, perceiving aspects of truth which can find no entrance by any other inlet."

Imagination is also an extensor faculty which leads man beyond where he is. Through imagination and the act of creation which follows it, man realizes the highest aspect of himself. As a creator, he functions in the image of God.

This same extensor quality is used by the artist when he imagines the plastic reality of the inner image and projects that form out and beyond himself. The problem of the artist is to make a correspondence between the inner experience and the outer expression which will satisfy

32. THE STARRY NIGHT, Van Gogh. Painted from imagination.
By Courtesy of the Museum of Modern Art.

him. There are conditions tending to promote this effort. Stillness, relaxation, darkness, and leisure time are all conducive to intensifying the image in the mind because, if activity and brightness are closed out, the inner eye is strengthened and the mind enabled to find its focus. The artist's mind is selective, and when he uses his imagination, the work of art will express greater truth; it will place the emphasis on the spirit rather than the semblance.

The value of conditions which promote effort was mentioned in Chapter II. Now I wish to describe these conditions in detail, explaining how to do preparatory work in ways I have found effective.

The first thing to consider is the position of the body—it must be comfortable. Lying down flat on a couch or on the floor is good if there is sufficient space. If not, a relaxed, seated position will do. One very convenient position is to sit before a table, resting the elbows on it and placing one hand over each eye to shut out the light. There are several ways of proceeding from this point. Sometimes I ask the pupil to imagine himself in a quiet place, an orchard or meadow, perhaps lying face down in the deep grass, and to recall all the sights and smells. This induces rest. The pupil might also imagine himself on a country road on a starless night, sensing the blackness around him, or he might even imagine going out into space with the stars and planets, to be one with the vast darkness of the universe. Another suggestion is to think in the darkness of a point of light like a star; however, in order to gain quiet, one must not stare at the imaginary point of light. The gaze should pass over it from side to side. This gives a slight swing, which puts the student into the rhythm of the world. These various exercises towards achieving inner vision bring about stillness and prepare the way. The stream of active consciousness is subdued; the depths of the unconscious or the radiance of the superconscious images take form and inspire the young artist. This withdrawal from the outer world, this shutting out of confusion and overcrowding from the mind, lets the pure thought or image shine through. This practice of introversion teaches the pupil to find within himself the source for fresh inspiration.

There are, of course, other ways of stimulating the imagination. Next I wish to emphasize the value of play and enjoyment as stimuli to imagination in contrast to the sense of work and obligation to learn,

33. THE ORIGIN OF LIFE. By Jane at fifteen years of age.

34. FIGHT ON A WALL. Battle in Ancient Greece. By Barbara at ten years of age.

which should come as a second step. If the pupil starts with play and enjoys this expression, he will out of his own need for perfection wish to work on it and arrive at the stage of work naturally and in its own sequence. So, for a young child, or even a timid adult, the simple device of removing a strained and over-anxious need for external resemblances and substituting the relaxed attitude of play and fun will accomplish the desired result of freeing the imagination. Following are illustrations of how some children have used their imagination effectively.

Robert, a boy of seven, was excited by the story of Adam and Eve. He made two coloured chalk drawings. The first, "Garden of Eden— Temptation" (Pl. X), shows the garden in full bloom. A large tree laden with apples is growing on a verdant lawn; back of this are many more trees seen in the distance. Eve, an arm upraised, is about to pick an apple and offer it to Adam standing near her. Above them the snake is coiled in the tree. The scene suggests quiet and contentment. The second picture represents the Angel of God sending the two out of Eden —"Expulsion from Paradise" (Pl. XI). Here the trees are bare, the branches menacing. Adam and Eve are seen from the back, leaving the garden, as the heavens threaten. It was amazing to see so young a child select and project the meaning of the two different states of consciousness. This demonstrates magnificently the strength and power of spiritual inspiration. Robert's work illustrating the Bible is more profound, both aesthetically and morally, than his other work.

Another picture from the Bible, the concept of Creation by a boy of fourteen, conveyed the vastness and majesty of the earth, the water, the heaven, and man coming from the hand of God.

A girl of fifteen painted a picture called "The Origin of Life" (Ill. 33). In it the dark part represented the unformed life in its beginning, the light parts were emanations arising from it. The unformed life was a deep mysterious purple, and the emanations were painted in pearly shades of light grey with rose and violet light.

Barbara, a girl of ten, was deeply interested in Greek history and mythology. One of her subjects was Prometheus giving the fire to earth; another was Pygmalion and Galatea. A third, reproduced here, was "Fight on a Wall in Ancient Greece" (Ill. 34). The whole concept is free and daring. Though Barbara executed the drawing with only a simple white line on black, she still gives a plastic quality to the design. How vivid her invention was, is shown in the way she draws the warriors climbing up on each other's shoulders and the way she represents the gods overhead directing the battle.

When Linda was ten, she painted in bright colours a picture entitled "The Pied Piper of Hamelin I" (Ill. 35). It is a happy fantasy of this tale and entirely fitting for the age of the young artist. The theme must have intrigued her because five years later she drew the same subject a second time (Ill. 36). Notice how the characters of the story are treated and how the interest has shifted. In the first picture, the emphasis is on the gay, happy children; in the second, the emphasis is on the eerie quality of the Piper. Both drawings show originality.

S.J., a young woman of twenty, came to me to study painting. When we discussed her problems, and she tried to formulate what she wanted to do, I found her confused in her aims and in conflict over various interests. She was interested in science, landscape gardening, languages, and painting. She had already attended two different universities, remaining only a year in each. She left both schools because of disappointment in their methods of teaching. She thought the courses were dry and boring with no sustenance or nourishment for her soul.

We set to work, painting from many different approaches: first, going through the liberating exercises I have described; next, working from imagination as this approach eliminated her fears of not being able to express herself according to naturalistic standards. When we did approach the study of objects, we began with very simple forms, thus building up her self-confidence. The elements of design, colour relation, and texture were gradually acquired and she made great progress in her work.

I helped to clarify her desires by having her make a list of the "pros" and "cons" of each subject. By the time she was through giving thought to the issues, she was able to convince herself that her greatest desire was to express herself in her chosen field of creative work, painting. Through this analysis we discovered that the thing which prevented her from making the decision previously was fear of her own inadequacy and subsequent failure.

X. GARDEN OF EDEN—TEMPTATION. Drawn after hearing the story.

XI. EXPULSION FROM PARADISE. Drawn after hearing the story. Both pictures by
Robert R. at seven years of age.

XII. A Sound Picture. Drawn after chanting "AH"

XIII. Dancing in the Wind. Suggested by the sound picture above.
Both pictures by Miriam at fifteen years of age.

She was, however, subject to spells of discouragement and depression, often saying she could not paint. At such times I would try various ways of inducing quiet, trying by this means to allow the unconscious to bring forth images of her inner state and her deep problems and unblock her.

She had had a very unhappy childhood and its memories of resentment and hatred were still with her, chaining her to the past and preventing her from putting her energies fully into the present. In this present there were beneficent influences of which she was not always able to make use.

One day, when she came, she was in a very discouraged mood. "I can't paint at all," she said. "For several days I've tried and I'm

35. Pied Piper of Hamelin I. By Linda at ten years of age.

36. PIED PIPER OF HAMELIN II
Same artist, at fifteen years of age.

completely blocked." So I suggested that instead of making a direct active effort we should try the quiet receptive way. She agreed, and sat for half an hour with her hands over her eyes, resting and introverting. When she took her hands down she said, "I saw myself standing in a swamp, my feet held by vines growing around them. Above them was a great white light. My hands tried to reach it, but my feet were held in the swamp and I could not."

I suggested drawing the image with coloured chalk. When she tried, another image came, even stronger. Ill. 37 is the first of the series: the

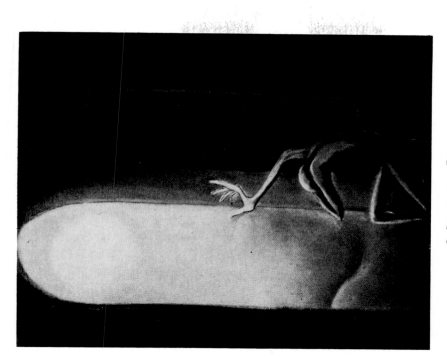

38. STRIVING TO RISE
By S.J. at twenty years of age.

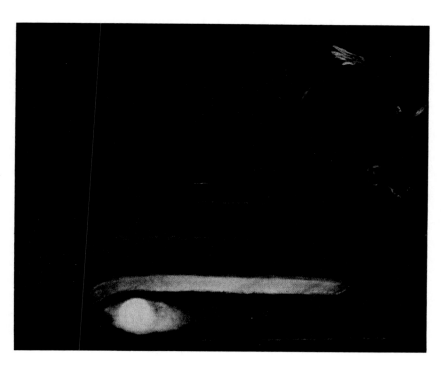

37. IN CHAINS
By S.J. at twenty years of age.

light is there seen through an archway. The girl is crouched on the ground, held by chains. Her position indicates her agony.

In the second picture (Ill. 38) the setting is the same, but the light is greater and transfigures the landscape. The girl has shed her chains and is trying to rise.

In the third (Ill. 39) she has drawn an embryo. She said she felt she had to go back to be reborn. In the fourth (Ill. 40) the light is golden and the figure kneeling faces it. She has lost some of her chains, but her hands are still bound. The drawing of her shoulders and hands is again very expressive of the suffering she is experiencing—but she is on the way to liberation.

These drawings are illustrative of the way in which the unconscious mind brings forth pictures of the inner struggle and conflict, and by showing them to the student enables her to see herself, face her problems and gradually liberate herself.

In this case, the girl's problem dealt with the need of freeing herself from her past, which contained very unhappy experiences in childhood. The resentments and hatred she felt kept her chained to the past and interfered with her growth and development, but as she realized it through this catharsis in her art, she gradually lost the chains which held her, and she concentrated on her painting which developed rapidly and amazingly well.

Her life became fuller and more satisfying during the course of this winter's experience in this work. New avenues for widening her religious and social contacts opened up. She found a simple church in her neighbourhood. The minister was a young man of humane philosophy and broad religious views. In them she found answers to her searching and doubting mind. One day, after services, she approached the minister, telling him how much she had enjoyed his sermon and that she would like to discuss her problems with him. She found him sympathetic and helpful and subsequently joined this church. She now felt that she belonged to a group with which she was spiritually harmonious.

A secondary interest followed. She found that an art teacher was needed for the children of her community. She gladly undertook the work with a twofold effect on herself. The teaching helped to formulate and clarify the ideas she was receiving from me so that she painted with more direction and she also felt she had won a place in the world where she was useful and was really needed. All her life she had been a receiver from others. Now the situation was reversed and she found strength in imparting wisdom to others.

On the social side, her relation with men had been negative. She feared any contact with them and what little she had had, ended in failure. Now for the first time she was able to make a warm, friendly relation with a boy of similar interests. He was writing and studying music. They soon attended concerts and exhibitions together, stimulating each other in a new, emotional and intellectual life. When the relationship progressed she was exuberant and happy; when it became tangled she became correspondingly depressed.

However, through the release in painting and the beginnings of finding herself as an individual, she found channels for her religious and emotional life.

39. EMBRYO. By S.J. at twenty years of age.

40. PRAYER. By S J. at twenty years of age.

Before this first winter of work was finished, she became completely convinced that she wished to make painting her career. As Paris still holds out its great lure for young painters, she planned to go there for an indefinite period. She has been there seven or eight months. The first few months were taken up with seeing this new world and absorbing its beauties and richness. She went through a period of discouragement, not finding any teachers who gave her what she needed. She has now made a good routine for herself. She works from the figure every morning at La Grande Chaumière and nearly every afternoon she works in her own room, painting and learning by herself.

The last two pictures of this group, illustrating the place of imagination in the development of the individual through art, are made by a very sensitive girl of fifteen years.

The first is the notation made after chanting the sound of "AH" (Pl. XII). It is like a bundle of wheat. The colours are soft yellow and blue against black. The second picture, called "Dancing in the Wind" (Pl. XIII), grew out of contemplating the first and in developing the images which followed. It was done by Miriam whose work is described in Chapter XVII. The girl wrote about this picture as follows:

"The Four Daughters of the Wind are frolicking with their Mother. They are merry because soon Autumn will come and then, together with their Mother, they will roam the earth to battle the snowflakes."

The chanting has harmonized Miriam and made possible the expression of latent ideas and fantasies on a level higher than she was capable of before.

This picture embodies just that magical quality a fine imagination infuses into a work. Imagination is both the tool of the mind and its animation; it stirs in us the voice of the bird, the lilt of the song, the beat of the heart, the wind in the trees; above all, it is the voice of the universe calling us to look through the world of sense to the eternal.

CHAPTER XIII

The Training of Observation, Recollection, and Perception

If the doors of perception were cleansed, everything would appear to man as it is, infinite. For man has closed himself up till he sees all things thro' narrow chinks of his cavern.

—WILLIAM BLAKE

THE three faculties of the mind—observation, recollection, and perception—are closely related. The exercise of one has a reciprocal effect on the others, thus forming a spiral development. Observation is the power to absorb appearances of objects through gazing at them. If we observe accurately and intently while looking at something, our impression of the object will inevitably be truer and more enduring than if we have given merely an absent-minded glance. Our recollection will be keen in proportion to the quality of our observation. Measured in terms of time, when we see with our total attention, we are using the present moment to fullest advantage for the future.

Memory is the power of recalling things seen, but I prefer to use the word recollection—it has a wider meaning. Dean Inge says: "Recollection is the power of active search and recall. It demands a higher kind of volitional and rational activity than memory. Memory in a sense constitutes the empirical eye. It is of images only—spirit needs it not; we do not remember recollections, we possess them—or they us." Thus, in "recollecting" we bring out images of deeper significance than by merely remembering.

Perception is sometimes used in its limited sense as similar to observation, but I adopt its broader definition—the seeing within and through the object. Perception in this sense connotes the addition of feeling and thought applied to the object so that the observer comes to conclusions about it—in other words, sees its meaning, its quality, its purpose, and its design for him, the painter. "In the Far East sketching from actual objects does not mean working from a model so much as training an artist in the observation of that which is real. According to the Chinese idea, the spirit of all phenomena originated in heaven and was formed into shape on earth; every phenomenon is endowed with spirit and is a worthy subject for a picture; each is an inspiration for a painter who, by searching inquiry into its peculiar nature may succeed in grasping its very spirit. Thus an artist is urged to examine every significant feature of his subject and to imagine himself to be it to express its spirit."[1]

In reviewing these three faculties, we find that there is a time-sense in each of them—observation entails full exploitation of the present; recollection, an exploitation of the past; and perception holds what is yet to be created. The interrelation of these three and their effect on one another will be demonstrated in the following lessons or exercises used for the development of these faculties.

First, the conception of their use and value must be simply stated to the pupils, discussion being adapted to the age of the students. I do not explain in detail to very young children. I merely put an object before them to draw, take it away, and say, "Now see whether you can draw it again." The process takes care of itself. In older children capable of a longer span of interest and understanding I tell as much as I think they will grasp.

In selecting an object or scene for the first study in observation, it is easier, of course, to find something in the studio, such as a still life, a corner of the room, or one of the pupils posing. The students look at the subject attentively and draw it to the best of their ability while it remains before their eyes. Allow about twenty minutes or a half-hour for this first step, which is observation. Then take the model away. Now ask the students to draw the same thing from recollection. Give them a fresh sheet of paper and allow the same amount of time in which to draw. You will hear groans and complaints of such difficulties as these: "I can't recall how she sat," and "I can't remember how her arm went." But the students must do the best they can. They will be discovering their inattentiveness, how much they have missed seeing.

This effort to recall will stimulate the children to greater consciousness

---

[1] *Encyclopædia Britannica* on "Far Eastern Method"

41. First Sketch in the Zoo
By B.B. at sixteen years of age.

42. Second Sketch in the Zoo
By B.B. at sixteen years of age.

in their next attempt at observation. The model will pose again, and they will have a second opportunity to observe. You may hear exclamations such as, "Oh, *that*'s the way her arm was placed!" or "*That*'s the way her head was turned!" Remarks like these indicate how much more quickly and aptly the children could have taken in what they saw. The effort of recalling and the negative result woke them up to the wasted opportunity. The second time they will absorb more completely; the faculty of observation has been made keener. As they work, the students show delight over their increased power of sight.

The fourth step will be made from recollection again, but that, too, will be more active. The power of search will be more fruitful. The young creators have had time to think and feel about the object or scene, to come to some inner conclusion about it, to exercise the artist's prerogative of selection and choice of what is important. In other words, perception will enter in and the drawing will develop design, originality, invention, and even abstraction. For this fourth part of the lesson I do

44. CLOWNS AND JUGGLERS. By Armand at nine years of age.

not limit the students in time. In fact, that study may develop into a painting which takes three or four studio periods to complete, according to the student's plan, interest, and ability to carry on a more mature piece of work. Below is a detailed demonstration of the steps of this exercise, with animal drawings made at the zoo and developed in the studio.

THE TIGER

B.B., a sixteen-year-old boy, selected as his subject the tiger. From the drawings which follow we notice how working from recollection has given his imagination an opportunity to function and has increased his capacity to draw with distinction.

His first drawing of the tiger (Ill. 41) is fairly crude. After working from observation on the menagerie, he returned to the studio and tried to draw from recollection. He discovered he had not observed keenly and couldn't get the movement of the animal, couldn't remember how the stripes went, and felt generally discouraged. So he returned to the zoo and made a second sketch. His first remark indicated how his power of perception had increased. He said, "Oh, that's how the stripes go— and I see he moves in a slinking motion, just like a big cat."

That day he made the second sketch (Ill. 42) of the tiger. He now felt that he understood the animal well enough to incorporate it in a picture. He planned a circus moving through the streets of the city. The whole composition is well conceived, both as to design and colour. And in it we see what he has learned about the tiger—its character and integrity are preserved; he is a big beast, partly tamed, but still himself as he ambles through the streets of the town.

45. HORSES RUNNING. From memory. By a boy at fifteen years of age.

He called this painting "Tiger in Circus Parade" (Ill. 43).

From this experience we see how swiftly development can take place. The experiment deals with both concrete and intangible aspects of art. We intensify the power of observation and recollection and "cleanse the doors of perception". Thus the artist really begins to develop.

The last illustrations in this chapter are not the result of the foregoing series of exercises, but were done from only one observation and one recall. They do demonstrate, however, that previous training has prepared the children to use these powers of observation, recollection, and perception as any real artist must.

The illustration, "Greenwich Village" (Pl. XIV), was done by Robert F., a boy of sixteen years. It was painted on a beautiful June day. He came to the studio in a rather happy frame of mind, saying how much he enjoyed coming to paint. He said he would like to go up on the roof and look at the city. So up he went, and stayed a while enjoying the sights and sounds of Greenwich Village. When he came down he painted the picture as he remembered the scene. It is a well-constructed painting, both as to form and colour, and indicates the strength of his power of recollection and composition.

"Clowns and Jugglers" (Ill. 44), was painted by Armand shortly after he had seen a circus. Notice how much he must have observed in order to recall the character of each clown, the concerted movement of the trapeze artist, and the dexterity of the juggler. The arrangement and construction are, of course, of his own design.

"Horses Running" (Ill. 45), by a boy of fifteen, shows an unusual ability to recall movement and animal structure.

The procedure of observation and recall is the common method of all artists. I have merely analysed the process and put it into the form of a simple exercise. The results obtained are illustrated by the efforts of these children.

XIV. Greenwich Village. By Robert F. at sixteen years of age.

XV. The Sun. Free expression regained. By Jody at four years of age.

CHAPTER XIV

The Growth of Form and Design

THE SENSE OF FORM AND DESIGN IS INBORN

THE birth of form in art has its parallel in nature. In the scientific accounts of creation there was first a condition of vapour and dark chaos. Form came slowly through many stages before it crystallized. Form followed the same pattern in the growth of art. I have been observing the drawings and paintings of very young children, from three years of age on, to try to discover the nucleus of form, how it reaches out to express itself, what first breaks its normal expression, and how to recapture its initial impulses.

Form exists in every realm of creation, from the tiniest snowflake to great solar systems. It is integral to the whole nature of men—physically, psychically, and spiritually. Each drop of man's blood contains infinite patterns; his whole physical structure of bones, muscles, and nervous system is the most complex and beautiful design.

Since man himself is in the form of a complex organic design and exists in a world built on corresponding patterns, it is inevitable that his art should originate in design. The arts of primitive people reveal this clearly. Their design is much more powerful and integrated than that of much of the art of so-called civilized people. The same is true of children's art work—a truth which has only recently been recognized. Young children exhibit a strong innate sense of form which often fades as they grow older and which is lost to most adults. This blight may be traced to our educational system, to the atrophy of the instinct of form through stupid teaching, imitative drawing, mechanical filling-in of spaces, or dry copying of objects, all of which crush the normal, vital sense of form and ignore the real beauty and dignity inherent in the child's own expression.

In the very first paintings of a child, we can trace the process by which form emerges from chaos through its own drive. We can also observe how it may either be lost by mistaken teaching or maintained if encouraged freely, the type of form native to each child being preserved. Following the growth of the children's art through adolescence, we can study the progressive evolution of form through design, first in one dimension, just a moving line, and later through two- and three-dimensional expression. We can also note how the power of observation increases with the acquisition of truer knowledge of natural laws. When the early instinctive sense of form lessens and the influence of the conscious mind begins, the beauty of form increases in ratio to the artist's knowledge of the laws of nature.

Leonardo's work provides the highest example of how natural laws may be used intelligently. His profound knowledge of the laws of nature in the mineral, vegetable, animal, human, and planetary worlds revealed itself magnificently, triumphantly, in his art.

The work discussed below has been selected from many children's drawings and paintings to show the development of organization in their art and the crystallization of form into a unified design.

The first series of pictures, done by Larry, a boy of three and a half, was selected because it illustrates so well the chaotic state and the first appearance of form.

The child had been attending a play school where the children were given paints. The teacher, however, had no realization of the importance of free movement. Her pupils, through their eagerness to paint, had developed tight muscular habits and very poor co-ordination. It was much harder for the boy from this school to find his own form than for a child who had never been conditioned badly.

The painting I call " Chaos" (Ill. 46) typifies the work the boy had been doing for a year. It is natural for a child to begin this way, but, with a little help on co-ordination of the body, the chaos should pass quickly into form. This child was in a rut; he was "daubing" and was quite self-satisfied with his dripping puddles. His imagination probably covered the deficiencies; it will at that age.

He said to his mother, "I like painting in the studio, but I don't need a teacher; I know how to draw."

46. CHAOS. By Larry at three years of age.

47. EMERGENCE OF FORM FROM MOVEMENT. By Larry at three years of age.

Having found him resistant to suggestion and hearing that quotation from his mother, I tried to reach him indirectly.

"Do you remember how your Daddy showed you how to play tennis last summer?" I asked.

He nodded, "Yes."

"Well," I said, "when you lift your brush to come down on the paper you should do it with a big sweep just the way you raised the racket to hit the ball." I lifted his arm once and let it come down; he liked the movement and smiled.

On his next paper, which I have called "The Emergence of Form from Movement" (Ill. 47), he made a circle, and then continued to make outlines of half-circles, each resting against the other. The tennis ball may have suggested the beginning, but the circular design arose from the movement in his arm.

As he found his arm and hand making form, his mind must have jumped to other possibilities. Soon afterwards he began with straight lines, then built squares on top of each other, and called the result a house. Next he tried a grasshopper which had a slight suggestion in it of the great bent legs of the insect.

The last of his pictures is "Giraffe" (Ill. 48). He had admired a giraffe which an older pupil was doing and said, "Show me how to draw a giraffe." I countered, "First go to the zoo and look at the giraffes." He went, and the next time he came to the studio he produced his giraffe which, for a child of his age, shows great powers of observation and recollection. The body is well drawn; the way he put in the back legs is quaint, but the head is much too big. He commented, "I know the head is too big, but I saw it that way." It is possible that the child confused the head with the neck. "Trees" (Ill. 49) was painted at five years, showing a continued development of form.

This series of a beginner's drawings is valuable to show how form first appears and how the boy's painting changed from fluid gropings to two-dimensional form.

Another group was done by a boy of three on the day he began painting. The child came into the room where the tables were arranged, each with a paper, brush, and pan of paint, and went straight to a table. He dipped a brush in some paint and proceeded to smear the paint up

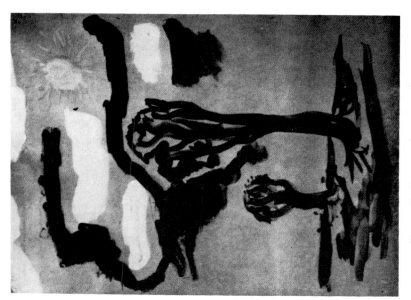

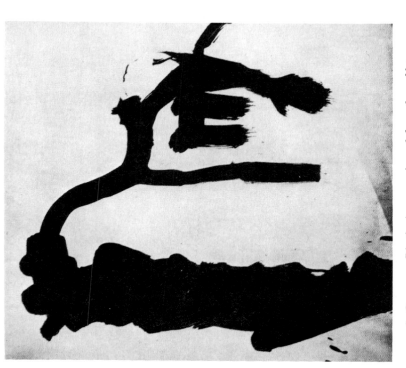

49. TREES. By Larry at five years of age.

48. GIRAFFE. Rhythmic expression of form from Nature.
By Larry at three years of age.

and down and all round, covering his lines with others as fast as he made them. His first effort was a mass entirely without form.

After he had made quite a few paintings of this type, I took his arm and swung it to and fro to give him a sense of rhythm. I had not expected any definite response, but, to my surprise, the boy then made a series of lines. This was a direct reaction to having his arm swung. The movement had given him so much control that he was able to make lines and leave them uncovered. Next he tried to make a window, but kept filling in the form and thus losing it. The boy was greatly disappointed not to see the window each time. Eventually he realized that if he left the outline he could still see the window. Following this experience, he became more ambitious and did a painting he called "Our Sedan Roadster". This sequence shows the beginnings of form as another little child discovered it.

The next painting reproduced is the expression of a four-year-old who discovered the centre as nucleus and the use of diagonals in design. She expresses the diagonal by means of dots as well as lines. I've titled it "The Centre as Nucleus for Design" (Ill. 50).

A boy of eight discovered form through the use of a basic recurring movement which goes forward, stops, and returns in a manner very similar to the Greek motif named "Running Dog Pattern" (Ill. 51). The dual movement in the child's drawing resembles waves as they curl and pile up over each other. This is the same kind of duality found constantly in Chinese art in which pairs of opposites are called by such various names as wind and water and mountain and water. It is interesting to observe that the child discovered this dynamic way of creating form by himself.

"My Stars" represents a purely expressionist type of art. It was drawn by a girl who had been taken outdoors at night and who had seen the stars for the first time. As soon as she arrived in school the next morning, she said, "I want to paint the stars!" She took a big brush and dipped it first in scarlet paint, making a quick, big flourish up and down across the page; then she repeated this gesture in blue, green, and bright yellow, one colour below the other. The girl was expressing the excitement she felt on seeing the stars. There was no attempt to represent them as such, but how much more effective was this form of expression

50. THE CENTRE AS NUCLEUS FOR DESIGN. By a girl at four years of age.

51. THE RUNNING DOG PATTERN
An eight-year-old discovers forward and return movement.

than the conventional conception of yellow dots on a dark blue background. Her form expressed her personal sense of wonder.

HOW A NATURAL TALENT WAS DEFLECTED BY MISTAKEN TEACHING

The following group of pictures was painted by Jody, a very happy,
lively little girl of four years. The vigour of her stroke makes one feel
these pictures just had to be painted. She was so full of energy and
desire that she painted eleven pictures in her first lesson. Before I knew
it, I would hear her little voice say, "But I want another one" (meaning
another piece of paper). The reach of her arm was wide and flowing;
her mixture of colour made the richest and subtlest of harmonies, and
her innate sense of design and form was startling. "Here," I thought,
"is the embodiment of creative power still unharmed!"

She began the first of the drawings reproduced, with a small dark
circle, filled it in, swept a larger circle around the first one, spattered
a series of dots around that, and then surrounded this design with a
larger enclosing circular sweep of lighter colour. A short perpendicular
stroke connected this whole form with a wide black square which framed
the inner part of the picture. The whole is a beautiful abstraction, but
one can sense in it the laws of nature existing in growth. In this picture,
called "Discovers Square, Circle, and Centre" (Ill. 52), Jody has combined forms having their symbolism in historic art. The Chinese, in
particular, have used the circle to symbolize heaven and the square to
symbolize earth. Without being aware of it, a child may unconsciously
repeat the race symbols.

Jody's second picture is another abstraction, "Forms Within Forms"
(Ill. 53). The design suggests fruit, or seeds in a pit, or two people in
a house. It could be anything because it possesses a quality of universal
form. These selections are but a few from a great outpouring which kept
up all through the spring until the studio closed.

Jody returned in the autumn. A change took place in her work. The
glory diminished; the paintings became scanty and few in number; the
great ebullience ceased. What came now was, by comparison, a mere
dribble. The form and colour became commonplace. I wondered what
could be the matter and made a few suggestions such as using a larger

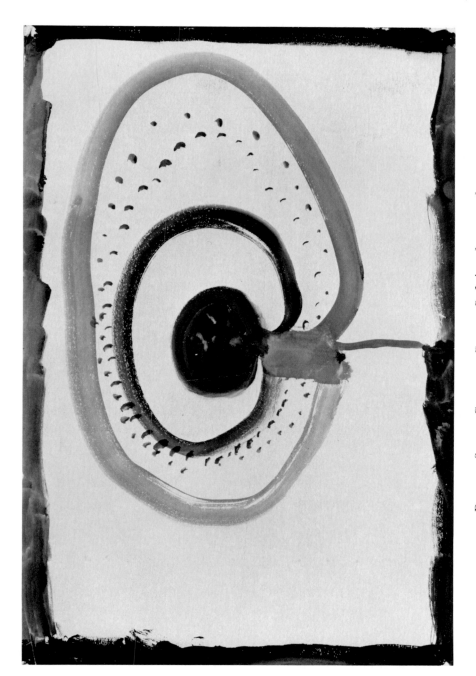

52. DISCOVERS SQUARE, CIRCLE AND CENTRE. By Jody at four years of age.

brush and freer movements. Jody was unresponsive, however, and I did not want to press her.

One day I spoke to her mother, showing her a picture Jody had just done—"Retrogression" (Ill. 54). "Do you notice any difference between this and her former work?" I asked.

"It's not so good, is it?" the mother responded.

"Her work has definitely changed and lost its original power," I replied. "Can you think of anything that may be causing it?"

"She has gone to a kindergarten the last five months and they gave them stencils to fill in," the mother said. "Could that have had anything to do with it?"

"Why, certainly," I said, "that must be exactly what has changed her course. This apparently innocent occupation set up and guided by her kindergarten teacher has become a new artistic ideal for her. Jody now thinks filling in a square carefully is the test of a successful drawing. Adults don't realize how utterly malleable a young child is; and when the adult in charge is completely ignorant of the creative process, she has not the dimmest idea of the damage she is doing. This is a remarkably clear explanation of exactly what is happening all the time to the native ability in children to find form themselves. It is crushed out so easily because children are defenceless. They are not yet conscious of their own expression. Through their simple trustfulness that 'teacher knows best' they are misled; they learn to abandon their real form for a broken substitute."

I then began trying in various ways to recapture the "first, fine careless rapture". I tried free movements without any success. Jody would make them willingly in the air, but as soon as she turned towards the paper, she constricted again, making separate little shapes and filling them in meticulously. I brought some large brightly coloured vegetables and fruit to the studio—an egg plant, an orange, a red apple. We played ball with them. I hoped that seeing and feeling these bright objects might do something. Jody enjoyed the game, but it had no effect. These devitalized drawings continued for weeks. I wondered whether her gift was lost for good.

Then I remembered something I had seen the child do quite often in the early days. This was first painting a frame around the edge of the

53. Forms Within Forms. By Jody at four years of age.

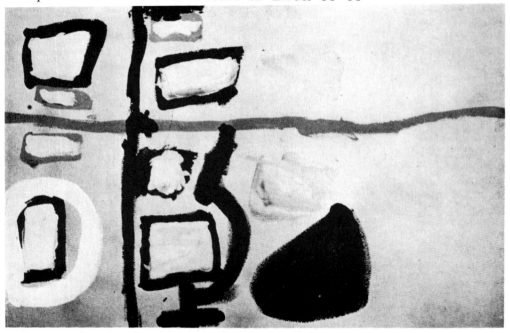

54. RETROGRESSION. Caused by use of a stencil in school. By Jody at four years of age.

paper and then making other squares within that and other forms within that. It had been the way in which Jody seemed to organize her pictures.

At the next lesson I said very casually, without any pressure, "How would you like to begin this picture with a frame around it?" Jody did so quite naturally as she had done before. Next she divided the picture vertically, then horizontally, then diagonally, so that she made a completely unified design. But she followed this by filling in each partition with a different colour, then putting spots and patterns of other colours on top of the first. The painting was not as free-flowing as her early designs, but it showed a return to a whole idea which seemed like the beginning of recovery from the injury she had received.

As the weeks went by Jody gradually recovered her self-confidence though it was months before she regained it completely. The last picture of the series, which she called "The Sun" (Pl. XV, facing p. 153), has her original spontaneity and daring. It is a great whorl with rotating rays giving off light, colour, and energy.

This little girl's experience clearly pointed out these truths to me: natural gifts can be obliterated by careless or ignorant teaching; our responsibility to nurture the latent possibilities in the children is very great; we as teachers must observe and learn from the children's progress or regression what is happening to them and then we must find what means we can to avert the retrogression and cultivate the latent abilities.

In all the pictures reproduced so far, the children have found their form directly. One discovered the straight line; another, the circle; another, the square; the next, the diagonal; the last, the spiral and the combination of the square and the circles to make a two-dimensional representation and finally reach objective form, demonstrating that its origin is innate in human kind.

The uniqueness of each child's own expression of form was graphically demonstrated by a little boy of eight when I was teaching at Walden School. He drew a wall-eyed horse with a little boy on its back mischievously pouring a pitcher of water over another small boy who was running away. The whole picture, drawn in an angular fashion and with delightful swiftness of movement, is quite humorous. The horse's body and head are each oblong. The ears are triangular and the tail straight; the legs are sharply jointed. I had been teaching only a short time and was not yet fully aware of the need of preserving the child's own style. My first impulse was to show the boy how a horse's back had a double curve in it. The boy would have none of this advice and actually pushed me away, saying very firmly, "*My* horse is square!" (Ill. 55). How could a teacher be taught a better lesson? The child had evidently looked at horses, seen the essential form as oblong, and had thereafter drawn it that way. Fortunately he had sufficient faith in himself and enough strength of character to assert his will against mine.

The basic pattern of this horse picture is made from the straight line and the square. Their forms are characteristically masculine and, although not confined to boys, they are very frequently employed by them.

The next picture, "A Beach Scene" (Ill. 56), was done by a girl of twelve. Her design is based on the curve and rounded forms which are characteristic of feminine expression. She has achieved a fine plastic quality and a well-balanced design.

55. "MY HORSE IS SQUARE." By a boy at eight years of age.

DISCOVERING DESIGN

Although the process of finding form and design is largely creative
and spontaneous, at times one needs to guide and stimulate these natural
powers, keeping on guard, however, against teaching a too formalized
scheme of design.

Many people ask me, "When do you teach technique?"

My reply is a question to them. "What do you mean by technique?
Isn't it another name for skill? And doesn't skill come from effort and
practice? And doesn't the great desire to create form the emotional drive
which makes a willingness to labour until skill is attained?"

The principles are revealed instead of being given as rules, and from
there each child discovers his own form, his own style. With our new

concept of education, we realize now how much damage has been done by false teaching. The illustration I gave earlier in this chapter of the almost irreparable injury done to a free child by teaching her to fill in stencils is a perfect example of the false approach. This does not mean that we cannot help a child acquire skills; it does mean we must wait for the right moment and then work constructively. Art must be born before it is clothed. I believe that in painting, above all things, it is essential to think of technique last. The moment we are taught art, we cease to be artists, and anything real that comes through comes in spite of what we have been taught, rather than because of it. What we need to be taught is not art, but to believe in ourselves, our imagination, our senses, and our hands, to free our bodies and our spirits that we may work and live according to our visions. From failures and

56. BEACH SCENE. Curved forms. Plastic quality. By a girl at twelve years of age.

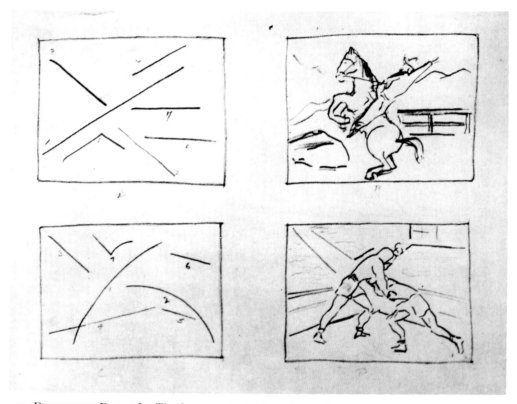

57. DISCOVERING DESIGN I. The figure on the left is made one line at a time as the empty spaces suggest the need. The figure on the right is always a picture suggested from looking at the balanced line on the left.

victories come skill, and skill itself is technique. Spirit creates its own forms.

However, there are times when stimulation is valuable. Recognizing that the sense of design is an organic part of each human being and knowing that a child stirred to awareness of that aspect will respond eagerly, I have invented a little game that seems to work well in most instances. It is an intuitional rather than an intellectual approach, another example of direct use of the native ability of the child.

The exercise or game which I use to teach design is demonstrated in the drawings above; the procedure is described in this report of an actual lesson.

The pupil and I sat down together at a table with pad and pencil.

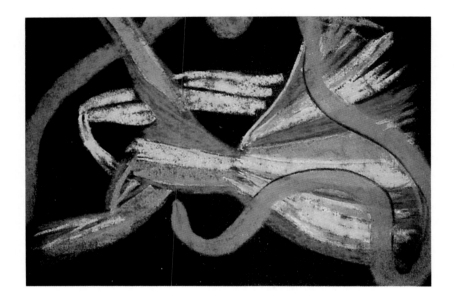

XVII. Woman Dancing with Serpent
Suggested by sound picture XVI.
By Linda at fourteen years of age.

XVI. Sound Picture
Abstraction drawn after chanting "LL".
By Linda at fourteen years of age.

XVIII. The Stars. By Miriam at seventeen years of age.

I asked him to sketch a few oblongs, saying, "We are going to play a game together, just with a few lines and spaces. Look at these four lines you have drawn (Ill. 57A); they are the first lines of our design; they frame a pure white empty space. We'll take turns, each drawing a line. Each time a line is drawn the appearance of the design will change. Each new line must be put where it is needed in relation to what is already there. Now we shall see what will happen. I am going to begin by putting a line anywhere I want to in the whole space."

I drew a line, diagonal no. 1. (The reason for my drawing the first line is that, when the pupil makes his first contribution, he *must* immediately face the problem of where his line should go in relation to a space already broken.)

Then I said, "See, the oblong is changed. It is no longer a simple unit; it is partly divided. If you could make only one line in this design, where do you think you'd put it? Where is the *space asking for a line*, and what kind of line will you make?"

The boy took up the pencil and considered. He sensed the largest empty space and put his line in that part. (The line is usually made either parallel to or in opposition to the first line, showing the instinctive sense of balance present in all children.) In this case it was opposite to the first line, line number 2.

After this we played the game alternately; I made line 3, he made 4, I made 5, he made 6, and I made 7. At this point he remarked, "I think that is enough."

"Well," I said to this boy, "how would you like to make a drawing of any subject you choose and base it on the balance we have worked out in our game?" He agreed to try. Illustration B is the result—a sketch of a rider and a horse.

Illustrations C and D are a repetition of the exercise. In this instance I dropped out of the game and let the boy play with lines and spaces by himself. It is interesting to note the invention the game has awakened. The play with lines and spaces has increased the pupil's awareness of design. Now when he plans a picture he will unconsciously feel for the fundamental relationship of all parts to each other. His basic line will form the axis for the forms he adopts. Ill. 58 consists of four similar sketches illustrating the same idea.

58. DISCOVERING DESIGN II. See note under 57.

This exercise can be carried further in the use of tones and value relationship and also in the building up of colour as design.

A little incident occurred recently which demonstrates how an older boy understood this exercise and developed his own ideas about it. I was teaching a new boy this way of developing organization in his picture.

He was a bit sceptical. As the pattern grew and he saw it, he said, "Oh, you mean this is a way to make a modern picture!"

I started to explain that design is an important part of modern art, but that he did not have to make abstract pictures just because he constructed the design abstractly. At this point David, a pupil who had overheard our discussion, interrupted: "The lines are the bones of the picture, like a skeleton. You can build forms around them just as you can put the flesh on a skeleton." The new boy listened attentively and grasped the idea from this simple explanation and made use of it in his next work.

SUMMARY

In my many years' work with children of all ages, I have become firmly convinced that sense of design as well as sense of form are innate. I believe that these elements lie in each individual's nature and can be called forth in the various ways that have been elucidated. The process has been traced from the first manifestations of a three-year-old through to the work of the more mature student.

PART III

Practice

THE CHILD

Foreword to Case Histories

THE children selected as exemplifying the practice of the principles explained in this book came to me through my present position as consultant to the Counseling Centre for Gifted Children at New York University. They represent the most recent developments in my teaching. I began this phase of my work in 1936, while still director of my own School of Art in Rockefeller Centre, New York.

Professor Harvey Zorbaugh founded the clinic for the gifted child at New York University. As a result of his excellent work as director of Lower North Child Guidance Clinic in Chicago, an institution for juvenile delinquents, he was invited to come to New York University and open a clinic in their School of Education. He contended that much was being done for the deficient, but very little for the brilliant and talented; his aim was to establish a place where highly gifted children might develop. Perhaps it is among these, he contended, that we shall find the leaders of the race. The staff of this clinic is made up of experts in the fields of psychology, psychiatry, pediatrics, social case work, education, and vocational guidance. In the vocational work Professor Zorbaugh required the advice of specialists in music, science, and art. He invited me to become Consultant in Art and, in that capacity, to judge the art submitted to the clinic, to select the gifted, and to advise the parents.

I soon found myself formulating a method based on my principles of teaching. It was in the form of questions to myself. This interested Professor Zorbaugh and he asked me to write an article for the *Journal of Educational Psychology* about my method of judging art. Following are quotations:

"A METHOD OF JUDGING THE ART OF A CHILD

"We discern the gifted child in art by various signs. But it is not sufficient to judge his ability by intuitive judgment. There are definite qualities in art deriving from the human functions and the individual's use of his powers that may be classified and used as a guide in deciding whether or not the child is gifted.

"For years I only judged intuitively when people brought me their children and asked, 'Is he talented?' but now I am forced to reason and weigh and discover what were the elements involved in my decisions.

"Looking over the art of a child in order to judge his ability, I have in mind four essential factors and the degree of their development by which to measure his talent. The factors are:

Factors	Mode of Expression	Varieties of Forms
1. Body	Movement (Quantity)	1. Quality of Line 2. Rhythm 3. Balance 4. Observation
2. Psyche	Contrasts (Quality)	1. Quality of Feeling 2. Sense of Life 3. Dynamics of light and dark 4. Richness of Colour
3. Mind	Organization (Intensity)	1. Imagination 2. Design 3. Form 4. Space 5. Relativity
4. Spirit	Emanation	Essential Quality

"I can judge whether he is using his body well by the strength of the rhythmic movement, the kind of line he uses, the kind of balance achieved, and the quality of sensation exhibited.

"The second factor to be noted is the quality of the feeling of life, great intensity, awareness of quality, a high degree of sensitivity. All these belong to the emotional or psychic content of the work. The use of colour and the values of dark and light are expressive of this aspect.

"The third factor involved is the power of the mind, which is indicated chiefly through the degree of design and organization in the work. Other elements which come under this heading, that I would observe, are the sense of form and space and balance; in other words, the relativity of everything in the picture.

"The fourth and most vital factor in the judgment of the child's work is the spirit or emanation of the whole. If he is functioning well and simultaneously on the first three factors, it is very likely that the fourth will follow, because when the whole child functions, the spirit awakens."

The purpose of the Counseling Centre is purely advisory; it offers no instruction. But when the art of some of these children interested me, I offered to take them into my school. That is how I began teaching them.

I joined the staff of the Counseling Centre for Gifted Children in 1936. This work is continuing.

I am giving the history of five of these children, showing in each case the problems encountered and the method of dealing with them, and using the method of scientific report, so that my readers may follow the work of each child from the beginning of his study through many years.[1]

[1] "At its highest development the language of reports is known as science. . . . By highest development we mean greatest general usefulness."—Hayakawa, *Language in Action*.

CHAPTER XV

Pedro and Robert—The Parents' Contribution

PARENTS' MORAL SUPPORT ESSENTIAL

PARENTS believe that their children are either talented or not, that they can draw and paint by virtue of a gift they were born with, or that they were born without this gift and, therefore, will never draw or paint. This belief is not true. The average child's power of expression in art can be developed simply and naturally. Art is a normal expression of the human soul, and each individual should have some form of expression as a means of developing that inner life. Not all children need to draw and paint, but for the very young it is one of the simplest and most easily used forms of art expression.

The development of the child's art may depend largely on the attitude and understanding of those around him towards his first efforts. Parents may be much more helpful than they dream possible. By using their intelligence and intuition in co-operating with the teacher and by keeping suitable materials easily available, they can contribute their share towards their children's growth.[1]

The average parent who is not an artist believes that he or she has no capacity to influence or advance the art expression of his child. If, however, parents would keep in touch with the teacher and understand her aims and method, they could be of inestimable value. Each child has his own difficulties to overcome and needs the support and understanding of the home in his efforts to overcome these. Often, through lack of this understanding, children lose faith in their own expression and subsequently lose all interest in art.

The imaginative, artistic child sees things differently from concrete, conventionally-minded people, whether parents or classmates or regular

---

[1] Chapter II described conditions favourable to creative work. These can be adapted to the home as well as to the school.

teachers. The conventional world impinges, and the child is not strong enough alone to fight for his integrity. At this point the moral support of the parent is important.

Here, as examples, are two boys, both gifted. Six-year-old Pedro was originally a free child who became deflected by conventional social patterns. His work had an Oriental quality, great richness in colour, and intense upspringing life, expressed in fine, two-dimensional design. He produced prolifically, needing very little help during the first year. His extremely unconventional pictures were, to some eyes, difficult to understand.

After about a year and a half a gradual change could be noticed. Pedro, influenced by concrete-minded schoolmates and teachers who found fault with his lack of correctness, was losing his richness and spontaneity; his work was becoming more conventional.

This always presents a difficult problem because it means that the child is losing faith in his own vision and is taking on an imposed outer standard—not the standard of the artist and creator, but the minute and photographic-representative standard of a classroom teacher —and without design as a base. The young child has an innate sense of design. These outside influences disregard that sense and substitute likeness of an object as of first importance. In reality, it is design that is basic.

Pedro's imagination was still active and fruitful, but the tendency to make small, cramped drawings increased. No sooner had I helped to free him one week than he would drop back the next and lose all he had gained.

These interferences might have been overcome if his parents had been more understanding. They not only did not help him at home, but they did not care enough to get him to class regularly. If it was not convenient for his father to bring him, Pedro missed his class. His interest gradually waned until he finally stopped coming altogether. It was a pity, because the boy had a very real and original talent.

Robert R., the youngest student New York University ever had, won a scholarship to the Counseling Centre for Gifted Children when he was four years old. His story shows how a child may benefit from intelligent parental support (see Ill. 59).

When his mother brought Robert to class, she referred occasionally to remarks Robert had made about his drawings and even his comments on life. The boy's remarks and his mother's anecdotes interested us so much that the mother was asked to write down what she could recall of her child's beginnings and how she had dealt with these efforts. These notes form a background for Robert's story and at the same time supply important data for other parents to read, for they show how fragile beginnings can be fostered.

Mrs. R. wrote as follows:

"I definitely remember Robert's making a Humpty Dumpty and a cup and saucer at the age of three. He knew what he was doing. He never fumbled; he always handled a pencil correctly. When he was four he was ill for about two months with an infected gland, and I had to read to him while he was in bed. Worn out with reading, I started to draw pictures and tell him stories about them. I'd have children in a playground in swings, and then I'd skip to a country house and a tree. That became a little boring, so I said, 'Suppose you do something, Robert. You put in the children—your own little friends, Susan and Lewis and the others.' He liked this very much, and I was surprised how well he could do it.

"Once I drew a country house and told him a story of the farmer, but Robert didn't even bother to listen. He was bored and started to work by himself. When he called me in, I could tell by the tone of his voice that he was terribly pleased and satisfied. He had drawn a row of wooden soldiers. From that time on he went all over the country in his drawings—porters with valises, boats, baseball games, cowboys, Indians—he never stopped. He used a complete pad. The pictures told a story, and he would talk to himself. If you went through the mass of pictures you could see the story.

"When he was four and a half he went to the clinic. The day I brought him in he did a boat. When we got in the class, I think he was a little bit lost. That big, big paper—he just couldn't keep his thoughts concentrated to a point where he would finish the subject. I think he would forget what he wanted to say.

"One day Robert made a black door in a red house in one picture. I said, 'Why, Robert, people don't have black doors in a red house.'

59. ROBERT R.'s PORTRAIT. Shows his deep concentration and at same time his relaxation and ease of movement. Taken at six years of age.

He answered, 'But the door is open, and don't you know that when a door is open and you look in the house, you can't see anything, and the opening looks black?'

"I brought home a stick of grey chalk one day and said, 'Look, what lovely chalk you have. That would be awfully nice to make an elephant.' So he made it and was very much surprised that it looked like an elephant. He concentrated so hard on making the drawing that he didn't make another elephant for almost a year. He wouldn't even attempt it. He is so afraid of doing anything that he thinks won't come out right.

"He represents the various countries which he draws by the different kinds of trees he makes. His Mexican pictures all show cactus. He uses palm trees for the warm climates, fir trees for the north, and oaks around New York—so he associates trees with parts of the country. He wanted to make penguins and he knows they are up in the north. He made a cabin and then put in fir trees, and I said, 'I'm sure that there are no fir trees where the penguins are.' But he said he didn't care, he wanted the trees.

"One of the little sketches which I did not save was a picture of angels flying in the sky. I said, 'Robert, you left the wings off this angel.'

"He answered, 'Well, that angel doesn't need wings because he is God and can fly without wings.'

"He has a love for the spiritual and unknown. He can name all the planets and loves to study the heavens. He asked me today, 'Why is it that you know words and yet you don't know how to read them unless you study them?'

"He makes many remarks which show he is thoughtful. 'At the age of two you start talking and all of a sudden you have to study reading. How is it that I know so much when once I knew nothing?' When he started school he said, 'I won't go to school until I'm a man. I don't want to spend all my life in a schoolroom. I'll go until I learn to read, that's all.'

"He does not like to waste a picture, so he will often go back and finish one he has left, although not with the same enthusiasm as if it were fresh. He won't even give a picture away unless he himself is satisfied with it. One of his little friends was in the hospital and he said he wanted one of Robert's pictures to look at when he came home.

60. THE SKIER. Submitted from home. By Robert R. at four years of age.

61. BASEBALL GAME. Submitted from home. By Robert R. at four years of age.

62. THE SHIP. First drawing in class. By Robert R. at four years of age.

Robert put himself out to do a picture with everything in it to amuse a child—a circus with all the animals, elephants, a man charming snakes, monkeys sliding down poles, and on top he had trapeze performers. There wasn't any space without something in it—it was a picture that a child would love. The boy was delighted and gave Robert a baseball bat in return. Now Robert is doing another picture for him, of war, fire, waves, and all sorts of fighting themes because Robert thinks this will please him.

"He wants to know all about art, and says, 'Does everything I put down on paper actually exist?' "

When his mother applied for a scholarship at the clinic for Robert, she submitted many small sketches. Some of these have been reproduced.

For so young a child they show a remarkable ability to organize a scene, characterize life, and convey the intended idea. They show movement and swift humour. All parts are related. One finds a sense of space and movement.

In "The Skier" (Ill. 60), notice the character of the jump, the motion, and the suggestion of the place—mountains, the sudden drop, and the snow below.

"Baseball Game" (Ill. 61) is a humorous presentation of the game.

Because of the high quality of the sketches submitted, Robert was awarded a scholarship to study at the clinic. At the time he received unfortunate publicity: the newspaper reporters focused on him because he was so young. This, of course, was not good for him. The reporters

63. THE CIRCUS. Made after Robert R.'s return to class at four years of age.

64. SERIES OF MEN WORKING. By Robert R. at four years of age.

65. By Robert R. at five years of age.

66. By Robert R. at six years of age.

kept coming to his home wanting to photograph him, and his playmates all twitted him about it.

When he came to school, he did not do well. It may have been the reporters' effect on him, it may have been that the group frightened him, or it may have been that he did not like the larger sheet of paper. At any rate, after a month or two, his mother said, "I think you made a mistake about Robert. He isn't doing well at all. Wouldn't you like me to take him out of the class?"

I replied, "No, I am sure that I did not make a mistake, but Robert may be too young for the group. Let me give you materials—paper and chalks—and you let him work at home. I can see that you two have a close, sympathetic relation. You know how I handle the class and what he needs. Why not try it for a while? Then when you think he is adjusted to using the materials, bring him back."

This plan worked very well. Mrs. R. kept Robert home for a month and encouraged him to draw a little nearly every day. She showed him how to move his arm freely and employed other methods I have described for easing tension. Slowly Robert became accustomed to working with the larger paper. The rather awkward drawing, "The Ship" (Ill. 62), is an example of the kind of work he first did in class. On his return to the studio after the period at home, he showed a new orientation to his drawing. An example of the work he did then is "The Circus" (Ill. 63). It has his former assurance in the line, and he has added tone which gives the drawing more life.

During the next year Robert's work became much more mature, richer in colour, more complex in conception, and very expressive of what he felt and thought.

His mother has realized that in spite of his love of his work, Robert has a tendency to stop in the middle and leave things unfinished. By her own sympathetic guidance she has helped him to overcome this tendency to a large extent and to produce a great deal of good work at home. He is a shy child who tires quickly. He is also easily distracted by others from his work but is stimulated by coming to the clinic and seeing the work of the older children. The combination of the two influences, school and home, has been most fortunate in advancing his development.

As time has passed, Robert has gained constantly in his ability to express himself. Many subjects have interested him, and, during the subsequent years, these subjects have each reappeared. I have grouped each series over a period of several years to show clearly how his concept and execution of the subject developed during that time. From the study of these pictures we can see Robert's innate humour and delightful imagination and can trace his growing power of observation and ability to find his own form and to express it.

The first group is called "Men Working" because Robert himself uses that expression frequently. The boy is unusually keen in his way of observing human beings. What he has seen has touched his sympathies deeply and has brought out a humane understanding of people's burdens. Take, for example, his first drawing of this subject (Ill. 64) when he was only four years old. Here are workmen pushing their loads. He could not have expressed the weight and difficulty of the labour so well if he

67. SERIES OF PRIZEFIGHTING. By Robert R. at four years of age.

68. By Robert R. at five years of age.

69. By Robert R. at six years of age.

70. Parade of the Elephants. By Robert R. at six years of age.

71. CIRCUS RIDER ON A WHITE HORSE. By Robert R. at seven years of age.

72. LAMBS IN SPRING. By Robert R. at eight years of age.

had not been conscious, to some degree, of its arduousness. A drawing done one year later shows a gang of men hammering at a construction (Ill. 65). The third is an interpretation of men excavating (Ill. 66). The treatment of the tone values brings out grimness. Note the keenness with which he has portrayed the men—some running a steam shovel, some hammering, others filling a wheelbarrow; over all, there is the definite sense of labour.

Prizefighting has also interested Robert. In the first sketch done at the age of four (Ill. 67), his chief interest was in the two boxers. In the second sketch, drawn a year later (Ill. 68), his interest extended to the ropes and posts around the ring, with some slight suggestion of the audience. The last sketch (Ill. 69), done when he was six, embraced the whole. We have the ring with prizefighters and referee, the great spotlight overhead, the reporters and radio men at the ringside, and massed galleries of spectators. Through it all he used rich darks, medium greys, and lights to great advantage. His characterization is acute, as, for instance, in the referee.

Robert's interest in the circus has been intense, and he has done many pictures of it over the years. He has depicted the familiar trapeze artists and tight-rope walkers, each performing his stunt. He has portrayed the pompousness of the elephant, the antics of clowns, and the strutting of the trumpeter. When he was six, he drew "Parade of the Elephants" (Ill. 70). The spatial comprehension in this picture seems to me an outstanding achievement for a child of that age. He created this effect by means of the dark curtains separated to show the light between, the trapeze artist suspended in just the right spot to make

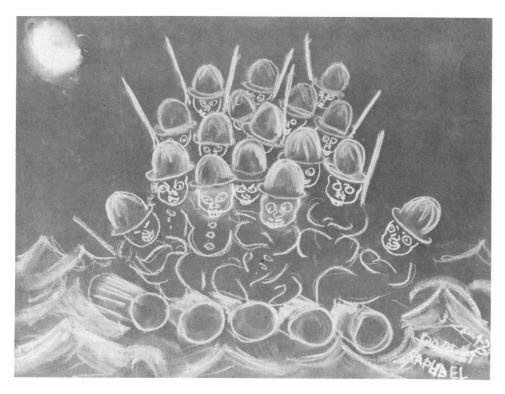

73. The Japs are Coming. By Robert R. at eight years of age.

balance in the picture, the heavy elephants parading and performing across the whole arena with the trainers, whips in hand, controlling them, and the straw scattered in the foreground. His interest in the circus continued. At seven he drew "Circus Rider on a White Horse" (Ill. 71). He has caught the weird motion and light of this particular act intensely and poetically.

During his eighth year, a new mood and interest appeared—something gentle and poetic. He drew a tender and delightful picture of lambs in spring (Ill. 72); the colour was as delicate as the drawing. He then did a few landscapes and tree studies. One had a hillside of many shades of green; in the foreground were delicate dark branches, and on the ground some huge, beautifully drawn scarlet mushrooms.

Another influence was World War II. Robert did parachute pictures and soldiers fighting. He drew one picture in black, green, and yellow chalks called "The Japs are Coming" (Ill. 73). In it he invested the Japs with a menacing quality quite uncanny for one of his years. "Sailor on Leave" (Ill. 74) was another aspect of the war, showing his humorous observation.

Robert is very fond of horses and has drawn them in many moods. In one drawing called "Running over the Hills", they were free; in "Ploughing" they were harnessed and at work. These were drawn when Robert was eleven. "Horses Communing" (Ill. 75) expresses the boy's fine understanding of the sympathy between the horses.

A new interest—Negro dancers—developed at this time. "Hot Jazz" (Ill. 76) is a very daring interpretation of it. The rhythm and colour suggest the music and the mood.

The next picture Robert did was "Moses' Farewell to His People" (Ill. 77). The boy had shown an interest in the Bible before—his picture of the Garden of Eden appears in Chapter XII. But in this portrayal of Moses, Robert has reached a higher level of spiritual expression than in any of his previous pictures. Here the form and content are in equal balance; the drawing is fine, and the conception profound. The figure of Moses is heroic—he expresses great sorrow, dignity, and resignation. The procession conveys the spirit of the occasion, and the promised land is well suggested. Robert made this drawing when he was twelve years old.

His work has taken a new direction in the past few months. Now

74. SAILOR ON LEAVE. Drawn from scribble.
By Robert R. at nine years of age.

thirteen, Robert is developing new interests and ideas as is common at that age. Not only is the subject matter different, but the treatment is more serious and more mature. The child is looking with new eyes at his world of art.

Serious and honest, he will never leave a drawing or painting that does not satisfy him. An indication of the quality of his work can be found in the delight which other children take in it. Evidence of the true artist's temperament is his willingness to paint only when he really feels and understands what he is trying to do.

These evidences of an unusual talent make one pause and realize

75. HORSES COMMUNING. By Robert R. at eleven years of age.

76. Hot Jazz. By Robert R. at eleven years of age.

clearly that the teaching needed is not in showing such a boy how to draw, but in helping him to keep a balance within himself as a human being in order that he remain productive. When he becomes discouraged, tone him up; if he becomes inflated, cool him down; but at all times keep his interest going so that he produces continuously.

When a boy is as gifted as Robert, there is danger that he will receive more praise than is good for his equilibrium. It is important that all his other normal activities should be kept up for his general development. Robert's mother is well aware of this need and therefore continues to encourage his other studies and sports.

It is through this co-operation between parent and teacher that we hope his work will continue to grow.

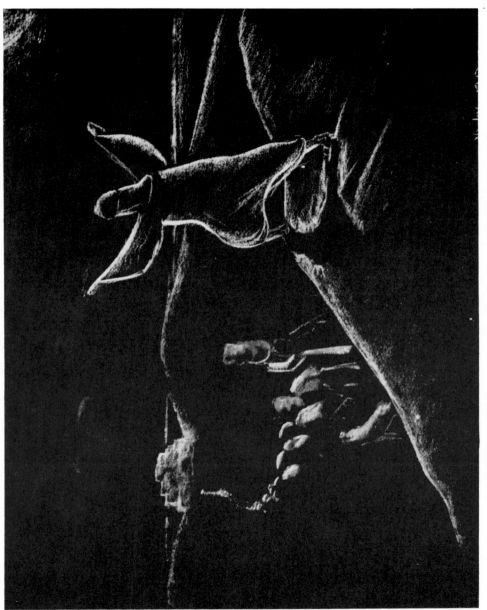

77. MOSES' FAREWELL TO HIS PEOPLE. By Robert R. at twelve years of age.

CHAPTER XVI

Linda—The Continuity of Art from Childhood through Adolescence

LINDA's older sister was a member of my class. One Saturday morning Linda came with her mother and sister and stood watching the others with a very wistful expression on her face. I said to her, "Would you like to draw, too?"

"Would I?" she countered, and hopped on to a stool like lightning. She stayed that morning and has kept right on ever since. She was eight years old when she began in my school at Rockefeller Centre. She continued her work at my studio in Washington Square with the group of children from the Counseling Centre of N.Y.U. until she was eighteen.

All through these ten years she has been a most prolific artist. She is independent, decisive, and clear in her own mind about most problems. Her work has always been full of life and interest. During the first four years she was entirely occupied with the child world, gaily painting in bright, pure colours. When she was thirteen, however, this interest waned, and she began painting subjects of adult life, people in a restaurant, the market place, religious scenes. Her power of expression showed a lapse from the old courage and assurance. She must have felt her difficulties because there was also a loss of enthusiasm. I noted, along with lack of confidence, less enjoyment in her work.

It is generally accepted that the child-artist's talent evaporates at adolescence, but no valid explanation accompanies this theory, and not everyone agrees that it is true. Linda's case is a normal one and a consideration of her loss of interest and its renewal may contribute the opposing point of view.

The changes at adolescence are common knowledge, but I review them to suggest what teachers may contribute as the problems are revealed. With the organic changes, the emotional and spiritual asserts

78. TWO WILD DONKEYS FIGHTING. By Linda at eight years of age.

itself. A higher potential for art expression asserts itself. This must be fully recognized, or the creative activity will cease because it falls below the dream and the need. The surge of feeling and aspiration disturbs the established flow and needs new strength and fresh forms of expression.

At the same time there also occurs a quickening of the mind; new standards develop, and, with them, increased self-criticism. Many students stop work because they develop a sense of inadequacy. Definite help is needed in bridging the gap between feeling and expression and in lifting the work up to the new level.

In Linda's case this difficult period was bridged, and her work continues. Her history therefore is presented in its sequence as the others are, but with emphasis on this transition because her pictures reveal the release of this new material and her progressive strength.

13

79. FAMILY AT THE ZOO. By Linda at nine years of age.

The pictures she drew when she was eight showed her humour and playful side. One she called "Two Wild Donkeys Fighting" (Ill. 78), and said, "The wild donkeys are in the woods fighting over the grass. The other animals are all amused." It is truly childlike—a fantasy of wild animals.

Her pictures were frequently concerned with family life and happy children at play. One called "Family at the Zoo" (Ill. 79) is a scene in front of the elephant cage. It is painted in a child's naïve way of presenting the important elements clearly and succinctly. The children's upraised arms express their enthusiasm in greeting the elephants; the father's downward gesture says clearly, "I've had enough." There is an indication of a design sense emerging. This was painted when Linda was nine.

The following year she developed her fantasies of happy children in every sort of occupation and always wrote about them on slips of paper. She painted "The Maypole", "A Rainy Day", "A Spring Day", "The Policeman", "Shopping", "The Balloon-Woman", "Children Home from School", "Bedtime", "Children Wading", "The Snowman", and "The Circus". These pictures were an unusual chronicle of child life expressed with real understanding.

They showed acute observation, good design, and the human touch in which she excels. She herself was very alive and joyful while working; she knelt, she sat, walked away, and came back many times during the morning. In this way she constantly judged and changed her work. During that winter she made great progress as is shown in "Airing the Dogs" (Ill. 80) and "Flying Kites" (Ill. 81).

80. Airing the Dogs. By Linda at eleven years of age.

81. FLYING KITES. By Linda at twelve years of age.

82. A Girl Weeping. By Linda at thirteen years of age.

When Linda was thirteen, a change began to show in her work. She stopped painting children and began addressing herself to the activities of the adult world. These pictures were all executed in a thin, insecure manner. The abundant output diminished to a desultory trickle. She seemed to have lost interest; certainly her eager enjoyment changed to indifference. It looked very much as if her talent might drift away as her interest waned. She did not even preserve these pictures, with the exception of one which we both thought was a little better than the others. A painting of her family, "Hanukkah Festival", is revealing of her state. She presents the mother as very big and strong and the father, who is conducting the ceremony, as very dignified. She herself is still very small and unimportant. "A Girl Weeping" (Ill. 82) was also painted at this time; it is a poignant expression of one mood characteristic of adolescence.

As I have said, definite help is needed during adolescence in bridging the gap between feeling and expression and in lifting the work up to the new level. To meet these needs there are three important contributions we can make.

First, on the physical side, there is a special need to invigorate the body with the exercises in movement and breathing gymnastics; they release the unconscious content of the moment and bring out a new rhythmic expression.

Second, let the child feel that you sympathize with and understand his new interests, new forms, new search. Counsel him to be patient and willing to have his pictures unsatisfactory; explain that he is now working on a deeper level, and will necessarily have new problems. Help the pupil see his journey in art as a whole, and place this present phase in relation to the rest. Thereby he will release and dispel doubts and fears of inadequacy.

Third, encourage the pupil to study the masters, both old and new, to examine their methods and processes and so to work and develop his own.

Such advice will help develop power consciously—what had been done unconsciously and carelessly in the early stages may now be done with thought, care, and effort. Such is the definite transition from play to work. If children see these matters clearly they will find renewed inspiration and enthusiasm to create.

When I tried the sound and breath experiment with Linda, the effect was immediate, apparently lifting and penetrating the veil which covered feelings and interests waiting to be brought to life.

Her first colour-sound picture, "Triangles and Circles" (Ill. 83), came from the sound *A-U-M-M-M*. She made a squeaky sound, said it was very pointed, and made holes in the air. She drew three or four yellow triangles. This was for the sharpness the sound had suggested. She said she chose yellow because a circus had very squeaky noises, and yellow reminded her of a circus. She drew straight black lines at the bases of the triangles because everything else was sharp. Black was used because a "cat makes squeaky noises, and all *real* cats are black". A grey background was used because it represented air that was thick—a cloudy day. Black circles were drawn in the upper part of the picture to designate

83. TRIANGLES AND CIRCLES. First picture made after chanting. By Linda at thirteen years of age.

the holes which she said the sound cut in the thick air. She seemed happy after drawing the picture and talking about it.

The next picture was done spontaneously with no sound or breath preparation, but it followed naturally after the release her sound picture gave her. She called it "Going Home on the Bus" (Pl. I, Frontispiece). It is a mother with her two children seated in a bus; the children are asleep beside her and the conductor is standing in the aisle. Linda explained: "It is night and they are all tired out. The woman has rheumatism. She did not want to go to the circus in the first place, because she said, 'No lady goes to the circus.'"

This last remark was a rebuke to her mother. Linda evidently regards

84. SOUND PICTURE AFTER CHANTING "EE". By Linda at fourteen years of age.

85. GIRL THINKING. Suggested by preceding sound picture. By Linda at fourteen years of age.

86. Cosmic Laundresses: a Fantasy. By Linda at
fifteen years of age.

the circus as an outlet, a kind of abandon, and the mother's attitude acts
as a barrier. This was her last picture of children. The fact that they
are sleeping suggests that she was unconsciously saying good-bye to her
childhood. The presence of the conductor shows the male interest coming
through. This picture was the preface to her real adolescence.

At the next lesson we practised chanting sounds again. Linda used
the sound "EE". Although it was done spontaneously, reproducing
what she saw when she chanted, it looked like a picture of sound-waves
(Ill. 84). The colours were very harmonious and almost mathematical
in relationship. In the upper half the wave line was purple against a
background of yellow and red. In the lower half it was reversed. A
yellow wave line was drawn against a red and purple background.

Immediately following this sound picture Linda conceived another

87. Children Buying Chestnuts. By Linda at sixteen
years of age.

picture called "Girl Thinking" (Ill. 85). It was evoked by the notation
just described and the same colours are employed.

She wrote this about her painting: "A young girl sitting under the
weeping willow tree on the edge of a lake with her feet in the water.
She is just sitting and thinking. The sun is shining, and her flesh is yellow
because she is nice and warm."

This picture opens a new phase in Linda's work. The colour is more
subtle—quite different from the brilliant primary harmonies she used
for her earlier pictures. From the psychological point of view, the
unconscious symbolism is apparent. It is the beginning of her young
womanhood. She sits in thought under a tree with her feet in the water.
The tree is life, a masculine symbol; the water is the unconscious, a
mother symbol. The girl is alone and feels herself apart from others.

Another abstraction, reproduced in colour, was drawn after Linda had chanted "LL". The colours are red, green, and light yellow (Pl. XVI, facing p. 168).

"A Woman Dancing with Serpent" (Pl. XVII) was suggested by the vigorous rhythmic form of the abstraction. Linda has expressed the young woman meeting life with outstretched arms. A serpent, the ancient symbol of wisdom, dances around her. The painting is so fresh and genuine, so obviously inspired from within, that I find it extremely moving. In the first sound pictures she retreats from life to be alone; in this one she goes forth to meet life.

Linda's period of insecurity had now been bridged; she was well on

bigger than I am they will be able to draw a picture of you.
But there was the same sad answer,
Thank you but I have tried. I have tried big people and little people I have tried everybody and everything. Nobody can see me. Goodnight little girl.

The little girl walked home. She thought about the dragon but she didn't tell anyone because she knew they would ask;
how big is he?
what color is he?
what does he look like?
and not even the dragon knew the answers.

88. ILLUSTRATION FOR HER OWN BOOK. By Linda at seventeen years of age.

the way to orienting herself to the world of young womanhood. The work of that last month seemed to show a new vigour and a new direction.

In the following autumn she began with a strange fantasy about "Cosmic Laundresses: a Fantasy" (Ill. 86). It has the old freedom of conception, but more form and better drawing.

This is what she said about it: "Every night when it's dark and windy, if there are no stars and no moon, the phantom washerwomen come out. They are laundresses who have been doomed to fly the sky for seven years looking for a golden line to hang their scarves upon. They are guarded by four great phantom trees that have hundreds of eyes which follow the laundresses all night as they haunt the skies."

Along with these changes in Linda's painting, there was a change in her demeanour. Quiet, shy, and retiring for a while, she began to laugh and talk with the boys in a happy, natural companionship.

One of her most recent pictures is "The Wailing Wall". The women of Jerusalem are coming to the wailing wall to weep and moan over their sorrows. This drawing originated from Linda's chanting the sound of "OU", which suggested sorrow and lamentation. It is a mature conception, strong in design, plastic quality, and essential feeling.

When she was eighteen, Linda entered Black Mountain College, where she is majoring in liberal arts. If her interest in art continues, she wants to illustrate children's books, preferably of her own writing. The last two pictures, "Children Buying Chestnuts" (Ill. 87) and "Illustration for Her Own Book" (Ill. 88), show a return to her original interest— child life—but are now done in a more mature manner preparatory to professional illustration work.

CHAPTER XVII

Miriam—Art Leading to Contemplation

ELEVEN-YEAR-OLD Miriam was one of the many children who competed for a scholarship at the clinic without success. Both Miriam and her mother were extremely disappointed. The mother offered to pay the small tuition fee if we would permit the girl to enroll in the school for a short time in the hope that she might show more ability. I agreed to take her on trial.

Although her first few months' work was not very encouraging, the girl showed such unwavering interest and eagerness that she was asked to stay on. New potentialities showed themselves. Her latent ability soon began to take form, gradually grew into a real talent, and later revealed an artist and thinker of unusual maturity for a growing girl.

Her record begins with a drawing made the third week after her entry, "A Girl Offering Flowers" (Ill. 89). We can read at once her fear of failure in this picture. The cramped lines indicate a tense, confused use of the arm muscles. The expression of terror in the girl's eyes tells the same story. However, the rich deep black of the background and the unconscious use of light behind the figure presage the rapid development which came later. The picture is very much like the artist herself at that time—sensitive, timid, aspiring.

Later that year Miriam used water-colours and found them liberating. The swish of the big brush and the flow of water encouraged her to overcome her fears. As she continued to work with water-colours, she gained in assurance. In the latter part of the year, she was given charcoal to work with and was taught more about construction and design. This training brought definite growth in organization, with finer quality of feeling.

The next autumn, the older members of the class were given an opportunity to sketch out of doors. They spent an hour in the morning

89. GIRL OFFERING FLOWERS. First drawing by
Miriam at eleven years of age.

in Washington Square under the supervision of my assistant. Her report
of the experiment and its effect on Miriam for two successive Saturdays
is quoted below.

October 14. We went into the park and sat down for an introductory talk.
I gave the children a little of the background of Washington Square, its
significance to New York City, and its reputation as an artistic centre. We
noticed the contrast between the old red brick houses and the modern sky-
scrapers; the colourful variety of people—those who might have slept on the
benches all night, crisply shaven men on their way to business, the strolling
artist comfortably attired in slacks and moccasins, the well-dressed little
children with their nurses, and the urchins running wild. We saw the traffic
and the general excitement of the Square.

I told the children to look not only at the face and clothes of a man when they were sketching him but to notice also how his clothes were creased and wrinkled in certain ways because they had been worn in different ways on each person.

Miriam approached this work with great enthusiasm and serious interest. Though she is a very reticent girl, she exclaimed, "This is wonderful! I like this!" Her park sketches were done with great conviction and a new maturity. In "Park Bench" (Ill. 90), she seemed to catch the character of the people.

October 21. Miriam continued doing some very good sketches, some of them showing a definite sense of humour. I also discovered that she seemed to assert herself in this phase of the work. For example, I have never seen her write her name so positively. With only a blank piece of paper in front of her, she nevertheless had written her name in bold letters across it. The release she experienced in this expression gave her a sense of achievement and self-confidence which may be very important in her development.

During these weeks of outdoor sketching Miriam acquired a new ability to compose her material and became aware of the importance of balance through opposition in line, masses, and form. In this phase of her work, the subject matter was used to develop the power of the mind in organization. The next period deals with release through imagination.

I have already told of reading from the Bible with the object of giving the group a fresh stimulus. To this practice Miriam responded fervently. Evidently of a deeply religious nature, she was happy to be able to put her conception into form. The Christ story particularly appealed to her. She drew a dramatic picture of Christ in prison, a fine black-and-white of the Annunciation, and a powerful painting, "Christ Walking upon the Water" (Ill. 91). This was done very simply in blue, white, and yellow. The sea was dark, with huge mountainous waves; the fishermen in the boat pointed at Christ with tense excitement, and Christ Himself was painted with sweet benignity and tenderness as He stretched out His hands to them. The whole possessed powerful movement, permeated with light.

This last picture is the first to reveal the depth and quality of her feeling. It also illustrates the stimulating effect of occasional reading from truly elevated literature.

I noticed that Miriam was timid about producing her own subject matter. In one of the projects just recounted, she was brought into contact with the visible world through visiting the park, and in the other

90. PARK BENCH. By Miriam at twelve years of age.

she was brought into contact with the invisible world of the spirit through the Bible. Now she seemed floundering by herself, unable to bring out her own ideas. I thought this was the right time to talk to her about herself as the source of unlimited material and to suggest ways of tapping this source.

At the beginning of the lesson I sat down with Miriam and said, "In looking over your work for the last month or so, I notice that you have made several starts, but have finished very few paintings—all of them more or less trivial in character. This means to me that you have not connected your outward expression with your inner capacities. You have within you memories of a great variety of experiences—scenes of crowds with exciting events; fires; storms; accidents; scenes of quiet— perhaps country meadows at evening; scenes of intimate human life,

91. CHRIST WALKING UPON THE WATER. By Miriam at thirteen years of age.

92. FAMILY QUARREL. By Miriam at fourteen years of age.

simple things with your friends or family—sometimes jolly, sometimes angry, or even sad. Do any of these suggestions appeal to you? If not, be quiet a while and let your memory bring you its own picture."

After a pause, Miriam said, "I wouldn't want anything to happen to my mother."

I said, "What picture does that bring to your mind?"

She replied, "I would rather work it out."

I left her alone to make some sketches. By the time I returned, she had made a very interesting drawing. "This is a family quarrel. There is a picture of the mother," she explained, "the two children, the mother-in-law, and the husband. The mother-in-law is jealous of the wife, so she tells stories to the husband, and the husband scolds the wife. Here the two children are with the wife, and the mother-in-law is with the husband."

The subject matter for this drawing, "Family Quarrel" (Ill. 92), was brought up through the technique of turning the child's thought to her own life-experiences. This approach nearly always produces authentic work, provided, of course, that the teacher is sensitive to the child's unspoken reaction as the talk goes on. The teacher's suggestions must be put forth tentatively and delicately, almost impersonally, for, even though she is helping the pupil to self-revelation, she must make him feel the subject is a universal problem.

Miriam had planned to make a painting from this sketch, but her interest was diverted. I had just decided that some of the older boys and girls were ready for the experience of drawing from life and had engaged a model to pose for them. Miriam joined this group. For the time, her interest and development was devoted to a study of the figure.

A second year concluded with a record of more definite progress than I had dared hope for.

One of Miriam's greatest interests is the dance. In the following autumn she made a charming colour sketch of a group of girls: one at the piano, one playing an accordion, and two dancing—in the foreground were the heads of the spectators. The whole was bright and gay and full of action. The faces were omitted, but were not missed because the young artist achieved a plastic quality which expressed her concept well without detail. The sketch was important, because it was her first expression of the dance, and, as we shall see, this theme led her on and brought out her hidden love of grace and beauty.

At times she wished to draw landscapes from memory. Next came a richly coloured autumn scene in ochres, bronze, and green. It was fairly well composed and created the mood she desired, but the colours were used carelessly and did not create plastic form.

Whenever I think a student is in need of refreshing some aspect of his work, I suggest a return to one of the exercises described in previous chapters. At this time, I thought Miriam was getting a little confused in her use of colour, and I asked her to return to its simplified use. By this I meant selecting one colour carefully, adding a second choice after deliberation, and then proceeding to make a picture with these two. Later a third colour was to be chosen and a second picture made, using the three colours. Miriam did as directed.

Her first choice was dark green; her second, bright red; her third, lemon-yellow. With these colours she made a swift, strong sketch called "The Ballet Dancers". One dancer is standing in the light, about to pirouette; the second is seated, watching her. The whole picture is done very simply, and the girl has achieved the plastic quality which her landscape lacked. It also has a suggestion of underlying meaning to give us insight into her human problems. The two figures could be aspects of herself—the one ready to dance, the other contemplating herself and wondering, "Dare I choose the art of the dance for my career, or must I be practical?" That was the problem she herself was facing.

When she returned to the studio after Christmas, Miriam began a picture which held her interest for several weeks. During this time its form changed, but underneath the desire was to construct her dreams of wealth and beauty. At first, it was an elaborate house with balconies and archways and a cobblestone roadway leading up to it. When I asked her what she was doing, she said, "It's a wealthy house, or it could be a castle in Spain."

As she continued, Miriam added iron grills on doors, windows, and balcony. Then she told me the picture had changed into "an old courtyard in medieval France, the scene of closely guarded life. Here lords and ladies laughed, and children played."

Later on, she said it was the courtyard where Marie Antoinette was taken prisoner. With this story in mind, she elaborated the picture and worked on it so long that it lost all form. She became dissatisfied. It was not good enough to go on with, and yet she could not get interested in another subject.

I remembered how the year before the mention of her family had stimulated her to work; I also knew that childhood recollections frequently break a block and start something new, so I asked, "Can you recollect any scenes of your childhood? Wouldn't that interest you?"

She made several abortive attempts. In each, she left herself out of the scene. I could tell by this omission that her interest did not lie there. Up to this point I had failed to help. It seemed wise to take her into my study and try to draw her out alone. Perhaps she could not get started on a new subject because she had not really finished with Marie Antoinette: perhaps the queen was a symbol of something important to her which held her bound. I asked her what the story meant to her.

The question pierced her silence. Her attitude changed, and she spoke freely. "I've read of Marie in my history class, and liked very much the way my teacher talked about her. Marie represents royalty to me, and aristocracy, and all the fine things of life. I remember her letters; they are human and reveal a tender character which I admire greatly. I wept when I read the story of her death."

It was evident from Miriam's words and manner that the queen did symbolize this dream which began as a castle in Spain and ended in the courtyard in France. Perhaps because the picture was unsuccessful, Miriam needed to talk in order to clear her mind of preoccupation with this idea. Talking about it apparently did loosen its hold on her, for now she was quite ready to leave the subject and start on something else.

Her next picture turned out to be an ocean scene with a lighthouse on brown rock. The sky was blue-grey and white; the ocean, dark blue with white caps. In the symbolism of this picture, we see what the release did for Miriam.

The girl had come to a point where she was held by a devotion to Marie Antoinette and what she stood for. She might have remained at this point indefinitely. But this cleansing took Miriam out of a situation which has tied up so many artists in the past—possession by the symbol. If a child sticks to one idea too long, try to find out what the idea means to him. You will release him and help him constructively to widen his horizon.

A little later Miriam was shown the exercises for sound and deep breathing with the purpose of recharging her energy and stimulating her use of colour. The training was of extraordinary value to her, since it made possible the lifting of the weight of conventional form and led her swiftly into a rare expression of her own imagery and philosophy.

She described this period of work in a letter, from which I quote:

During my third year in the class I started to use sounds as a source of inspiration. This was done by letting out all the breath possible, then on the "in" breath, to chant a syllable or vowel, such as "ah". The reason for first removing all the air in the lungs was to increase the intake and improve the co-ordination of brain and muscle. This expiration of air left a waiting, eager

93. A Woman Before Her Mirror. By Miriam at fifteen years of age.

attitude. A deep, prolonged intake with the vowel being chanted at the same time was accompanied with swinging movements of the arms and body. This gave a feeling of freedom, and, through that, forms arose. The breath was exhaled with another vowel and resulted in a vision of colour and the beginning of creation. This deep breathing is continued until the colours and forms associate themselves and are grouped to form a composition. It is while using the colours suggested that the real feeling comes. As I translate my visions and thought on to paper or canvas, the body merely obeys the brain. I mentally associate the forms with things in my life or just remember things I have felt or seen and what they mean to me. These thoughts are responsible for the strokes on paper or canvas.

If I am satisfied or interested in my thoughts, the brain and the hand co-operate and the results are better than if I am emotionally disturbed or failed to really appreciate ideas given by breathing deeply. I have found that by forgetting all emotional strain I possibly can, and obeying ideas created

94. THE SPIRIT OF GIVING, RECEIVING, and GIVING.
Sound picture made after chanting "UMMM". By Miriam at sixteen years of age.

by breathing, I can, as a rule, achieve satisfactory results. But this doesn't always work. Little things I have seen or heard or felt keep interrupting my thoughts and destroy the co-ordination between my brain and my hand, and my work shows lack of concentration. It is when life means most and seems dearest that best efforts are found.

The path Miriam followed in the new world which opened up to her was very direct and apparently easy. She seemed to enjoy the breathing and chanting, showing much less self-consciousness than most pupils. Evidently, colour and forms appeared readily to her inner eye, because after a very short time she began to put down several colour abstractions expressing the various vowel sounds. The following examples show the type of work she did after singing these vowel sounds.

1. *Title:* "A Woman Before Her Mirror" (Ill. 93).
    Sound: UMM.
    Colours: Soft blue-green, shades of pink to orange, and white against black.
    Description: The design is rich, flowing, and oriental in quality. The woman is gazing at herself in admiration. Perhaps the woman's interest in her own appearance expresses Miriam's growing self.
    Her Comment: "A hand came down from space and let out a dancer. The dancer may dance and be gay until she has broken a law or ceased to dance well, then the hand will take her back."
    My Comment: The concept is a little ahead of the execution—as if she sensed a moral law of the universe and simultaneously realized the inevitability of man's breaking the law and the meting out of justice which rests within the law itself. It seems strangely wise and knowing for so young a girl. As she progresses, her pictures and statements become more and more expressive of vision and beauty.

2. *Title:* "The Spirit of Giving, Receiving, and Giving" (Ill. 94).
    Sound: UMMMM.
    Colours: Yellow, brown, green.

Her Comment: "Some people ask without thought, seeking gain only for themselves. Some ask for others, hoping to gain favour for themselves, but some there are that ask for others alone. These people are given an inner glow which causes them to rise above the others."

My Comment: The grouping of the figures is well done, the reaching hands are the "grasping ones", the kneeling figures are the partially unselfish, and the central standing figure receiving and surrounded by light is "the highest one". The rays below her are also significant, and at the same time strengthen the composition.

3. *Title:* "The Master of All Forces" (Ill. 95).

   Sound: H-I-I-I.

   Colours: Blue, flesh, gold light in the background behind Deity.

   Her Comment: "He controls all forces, and plans how they can best be used to aid humanity. He is a supernatural being and can feel no pain. Because of this He has difficulty in knowing how to keep His forces from becoming harmful to mankind."

   My Comment: This last picture of Deity marked the climax of a series, beginning with the dancers, going through the dreaming boy, the idea of law, the ideal of giving, and finally reaching God. Then she rests and contemplates the problem of good and evil.

In the following autumn the flow of her work continued. She chanted each time, and found her inspiration from it. Her subjects always dealt with human aspiration or failure, frustration or achievement, and each time she wrote her thoughts after drawing the picture.

The last one she drew, called "Stars" (Pl. XVIII, facing p. 171), shows how she has developed through her art. Compare it to her first drawing, "Girl Offering Flowers" (Ill. 89). They have something in common, an imaginative concept expressed with conviction.

Of the picture "Stars", she wrote:

The girl as she looks from her window does not see the stars as the scientist or the businessman or as the housewife—but she sees them as tiny figures

95. THE MASTER OF ALL FORCES. Sound picture made after chanting "HI".
By Miriam at sixteen years of age.

holding the light to strange and beautiful dream worlds in the palm of their hands. The world around her fades away and she becomes one with them enjoying the freedom of the air and the frolics with the wind.

My comment was:

Through the breath, the dual movement of deep exhaling and inhaling, she has touched her soul and brought it to life. The chanting of sound has harmonized the whole self and made possible expression of latent ideas and images on a much higher level than she was capable of before.

In the same spring Miriam applied for and won a scholarship to the Parsons School of Design. When she was accepted, the director wrote her a letter welcoming her to the school and complimenting her for her "unusually fine and extremely original" portfolio of work.

CHAPTER XVIII

Steven—An Expression of Dynamic Force

THE dynamic force in the personality of the artist is what makes his picture live. Colour, form, design, each contribute, but the magic which fires and welds a painting into a fine work of art is the expression of this dynamic force. Whether the artist paints bread, apples, machinery, or churches, the picture lives only as intensely as he lives; his force transferred to the inanimate makes it animate. A person endowed with such fire is apt to be headstrong and aggressive and, in consequence, will arouse battle in those around him. Emotional tensions and explosions inevitably occur and inflict wounds. These wounds may be forgotten by the conscious mind, but remain buried and act as interference to the full expression of the artist's dynamic power. A situation of this kind does not appear in very young children, but is more likely to be a problem of adolescence.

This chapter relates the experiences of a boy with this kind of dynamic nature and its attendant emotional difficulties. Steven was a friend of one of my pupils. His curiosity had been aroused by this boy's enthusiastic report of the individual quality of the work in the group. One Saturday morning Steven came in to see for himself. He was a strong, fine-looking, well-built boy, mature for his fifteen years. He immediately recognized the atmosphere of independence among the students who were relieved of restrictions such as he had met in school, and was impressed by the new and stimulating approach. He told me he wanted to work here and thought that perhaps he could express himself as he truly desired, but had not been permitted to do elsewhere. He submitted drawings which were extremely fine and showed great talent. He was accepted at once and began to work.

Frequently sullen and closed to criticism or suggestion, Steven was undoubtedly richly gifted but very difficult to help. At times I became troubled and discouraged about him; yet I always found some way to meet each new impasse. And although the changes were slow, he did begin to overcome his difficulties during the two years he was my student.

One unfortunate tendency of Steven's was to destroy most of his drawings before he had finished them. Beneath this apparently harsh self-criticism, he was, I thought, really manifesting an attitude of self-destruction. His selection of subject matter, frequently dealing with violent death, tended to confirm this thought. But as time went on the great strength in his work began to emerge.

Drawing in black and white appealed to Steven most. He liked using a soft stick of lead so he could produce rich, black tones. At this time he was inclined to get his work too black and smudgy. He was not interested in the middle greys needed to join the black and whites and make the whole more plastic. He was full of extremes and still is, though to a lesser degree. When he used colour, it was lurid and over-lush, showing little awareness of colour relation and no balance in the handling of it. Here follow selections from the notes I made of his record. They deal with situations which reveal his problems, his boggings down, and the beginning of his emergence.

October: The painting, "Horse and Buggy in a Storm" (Ill. 96), shows a bleak, harsh mood. The horse is thin and worn, struggling to make headway against the beating rain. Pictures of this nature may have a subjective meaning, expressing the artist's own mood.

November: Steven made a very good drawing of a derrick on a wharf. We discussed the colours to be used—which ones would be expressive of the subject matter in the drawing. He said, "Red, steel blue, and black." For the first time he used his colours organically in the structure. I noticed that although he had earlier resisted my talk about such use of colour, he was now beginning to incorporate it.

December: Steven has a tendency to use harsh black strokes and tones in all his work. The model posing today was a delicate old lady. Steven used his usual strength and made a drawing quite out of character. I explained to him how each situation and type of human being or animal could have a quality of line and tone expressive of its own nature. For examples I selected subjects which would particularly interest a boy: a boy playing with his puppy might be expressed with delicate lines

96. HORSE AND BUGGY IN A STORM. By Steven, at fifteen years of age.

associated with gentleness and affection; a football game could be drawn with strong lines; and a war scene could be interpreted with brutal and smashing strokes. I asked him to try this and to notice at the time how muscular tension in his arm changed from gentleness to power, according to the feeling which he wished to express, just as in music the change from *pianissimo* to *forte* requires different pressure on the keys of the piano. He made some experiments and found how to make a more delicate drawing, but he evidently was not ready to put the ideas into practice because he continued to make the same over-strong black lines. Steven seems to need for the present to go his own way using the "smashing" technique.

January: Steven has been painting a scene of an excavation. When I last saw it, it was strong and full of possibilities. While I was occupied with someone else, he became discouraged and destroyed his picture. I was disappointed to see what he had done and explained to him the necessity of asking for help when he is discouraged and cannot help himself. "It is at the low point in work that a teacher is most useful because at that time when you cannot find the solution yourself, you may be ready to listen to what someone else has to offer. If you destroy your work without showing it, then you cut off your opportunity to receive help and to learn."

February: This month we held an exhibition of the religious pictures which the children had done from Bible readings. Steven worked on his picture long and earnestly. It was a painting of the Crucifixion (Ill. 97), showing with great intensity the suffering of Christ. Here, for the first time, colour was understood.

March: For some time I have felt that Steven has been undergoing some kind of inner struggle. It is particularly obvious in his resistance to any teaching. I have concluded that the best solution is to give him materials and let him work alone for a while. Perhaps he can find his way in solitude.

April: Steven has drawn several war pictures, chiefly of soldiers wounded or killed. One called "Death" (Ill. 98) is especially gruesome; it depicts a soldier caught in a wire fence. He is decapitated, and his head has rolled off his body. Steven evidently relishes doing scenes of suffering and horror.

97. The Crucifixion. By Steven at fifteen years of age.

The idea of leaving him alone is working out well so far. He must have been constantly hectored elsewhere to have become so hypersensitive to any suggestion. Even though I see his need of criticism, I do not say a word for the time being. It is more important for him to enjoy his freedom and heal himself through it.

May: The year is ending. Steven has completed a fine painting, a man returning to his cabin with his horse. The two are attacked by wolves. The scene is bleak, the horizon is brightly lighted, but there are dark clouds and foreboding rocks and trees. The whole mood is one of terror.

October: Since returning to the studio this fall, Steven has shown a great interest in making careful drawings of interiors of industrial plants. His technique in the use of lead has improved. These pictures have some interweaving tones of grey and are more plastic in character. The one reproduced is called "Machinery" (Ill. 99).

98. DEATH. By Steven at fifteen years of age.

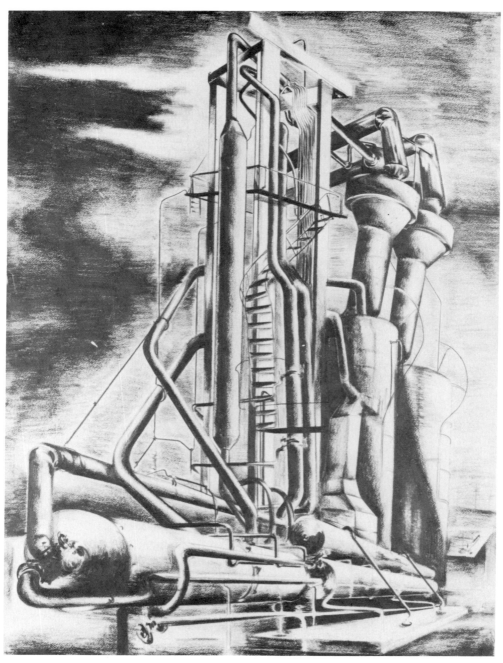

99. MACHINERY. By Steven at sixteen years of age.

February: Steven and I had lunch together today. The talk, friendly and quiet, brought forth at least one past difficulty and a statement of the problem which confronts him now. I told him that many of his pictures showed disturbance or shock—the storm, the decapitation, the automobile crashes, all revealed it. I asked him whether he knew of anything which had upset him.

He immediately spoke of his music. He said he knew he had been good at it, that his teachers had given him great encouragement, but that he had been neglectful of practising. This angered his mother intensely. After many scoldings and reproaches for not valuing the sacrifices she had made, his mother discontinued the lessons. Now, Steven said, he regrets it very much, for he really loves his music—he "just could not practise then".

I told him that his failure to practise could have been due to changes going on in his whole structure and that it was a pity he and his mother did not realize that it was natural for a boy to be restless and unorganized during adolescence. "However," I said, "if you realize what you lost in not being able to direct yourself at that time, perhaps you will be able to concentrate better on your present situation. Do you want to tell me what is troubling you at the moment?"

He replied, "I unexpectedly graduated from high school at mid-term. I had been told that my marks were not good enough and that I could not graduate until June. Apparently those in charge changed their minds, because I'm through with school now and faced with decisions to make. I don't know what to choose or how to go about it."

"What are the choices you have in mind?" I asked.

"There are three things I want to do, and I don't see how I can do them all. One, I must get a job of some kind and earn money. Two, I want to continue my art. I want to make it my profession, but I don't want to do commercial art. And, three, I want to continue my general education with some evening study if I can—my teacher at school urged me to do this."

That was the situation, and we talked until we came to the following conclusion. A job was essential; he had one or two possibilities offered him and would definitely take one. As to continuing his art, I convinced him it would be possible to use his own style and quality in some form

100. LIFE STUDIES. By Steven at sixteen years of age.

of commercial art without destroying his integrity. Since he needed
further training, I told him I would send him to an evening class in a
good art school if he would let me. These two choices were agreed upon.
The third—his desire to continue his general education—would have to
be put aside for the present until the other two were further achieved.

After this talk, Steven seemed relieved and ready to face his problems.

February (three weeks later): Steven is now attending an evening
school. He wanted to draw from life first, said he was sure he needed
that. He seems very happy at being in this more professional class; he
is proud of being the youngest in it—most of the men are over thirty.
"Life Studies" (Ill. 100) is one of his sketches made at this time. It is
included to show his ability to use delicacy without sacrificing strength.

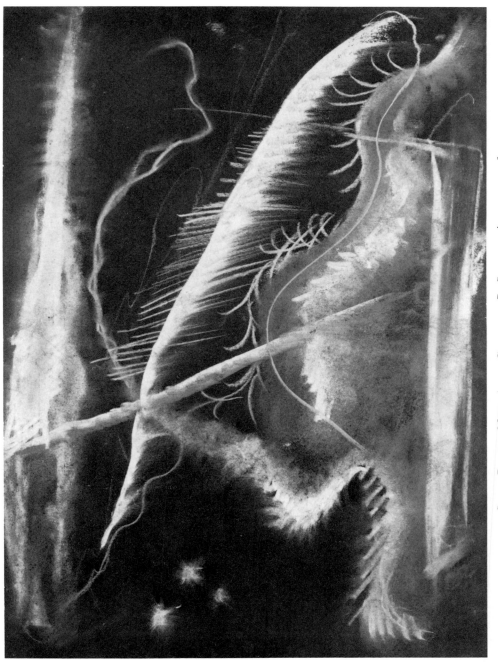

101. Sound Picture Made After Chanting. By Steven at sixteen years of age.

102. THE STEEPLE. By Steven a few years later.

April: Steven has again become interested in the Crucifixion theme.

May: I persuaded Steven to experiment with sound today. It was quite a victory for me, considering his resistance to any suggestion. The sound picture (Ill. 101) which he created after chanting is done in black, pale yellow, and green. It is extremely beautiful in design. Unfortunately it is the only one he did. It must have had some good effect on him, however, for immediately afterwards he took a large canvas and painted a very powerful picture of a cathedral with crowds of people in the plaza. "The Cathedral" (Pl. XIX, facing p. 256) is painted behind in heavy strokes of black, blue, and red. The sky is very light and clear in yellow and light green. The people massed below are in black and scarlet. This is a great step ahead, both in painting and the revelation of his own growth. It is a fine example of dynamic force freed, beginning to fulfil itself. A few years later he called to see me, and brought his portfolio of recent work. The water-colour titled "Steeple" (Ill. 102) shows his progress. There is delicacy, yet strength, feeling, and organization. He continues to paint.

CHAPTER XIX

Harold—Mercurial Temperament Brought to Stability

AN unusual portfolio of work was sent me by the Counseling Centre in March 1936. It was the work of Harold, a boy of twelve. I was favourably impressed and wrote this report:

"I think this boy is distinctly gifted, with good possibilities of future development. He should have opportunity to study. The qualities I find to recommend are: movement, a rhythmic line, and balanced arrangement. His imagination is rich. Most of his pictures are permeated with a real sense of life. His design is fairly good; the pictures are well organized for a boy of his years. He has an individual point of view and a keen power of observation. His recordings of people's lives—in the streets, selling at pushcarts, going to work, sitting in parks—are quite mature. On the debit side, his work is often inclined to be overshadowed by conventional techniques. Sometimes the drawing is cold and hard, showing a lack of emotional development. This is also evidenced in a poor colour sense and a lack of richness and warmth in his pictures. He needs to have his senses and feelings brought out; his approach is too intellectual. I feel sure that, if his feeling is awakened and brought into expression, he will find a new depth and originality in his art."

"Moses on Mount Sinai" (Ill. 103) was one of the pictures he submitted to the Counseling Centre. My specific comments on it were:

1. *Movement:* He has expressed the strength and vision of Moses. There is a fine, strong power in the concept, and some of the lines are good: in the head and cloak, in the birds, and particularly in the clouds. The drawing of the arm, hand, and staff is rather weak.

103. MOSES ON MOUNT SINAI. Submitted for entrance.
By Harold at twelve years of age.

2. *Dynamics:* A grand feeling of life and intensity and high quality
   of imagination.
3. *Organization:* Good feeling of space and distance and design. Form
   could be stronger.
4. *Spirit:* Very remarkable. Has a rare quality of depth and understanding that might develop into great art.

After receiving this report, the Centre accepted him as one of the
children whose cases were to be recorded. I subsequently admitted him
to my school in Rockefeller Centre on a scholarship.

Harold's personality was gentle, but evidenced strength of purpose.
He was sensitive, kindly, and thoughtful of others, eager to learn, and

very intelligent. As he worked, his chief limitation was a tendency to accept superficial success. That continued to be his major difficulty in the five years he was with me. But patience and friendly talk over the problem always kindled new effort, followed by more sincere work. It is fair to state that Harold, now twenty-three, has outgrown this weakness completely. His outlook is thoughtful and searching; he is ambitious, industrious, and modest.

When Harold first came to my school, I gave him materials and told him to draw anything he wanted. He did "Greek Warrior" (Ill. 104), with a temple in the background. It was fairly well drawn, but the colour was quite insipid and sentimental—a queer mixture! The composition was fair, but it was weakened by imitation of history book illustrations and the lack of understanding of colour.

The best way to make students sensitive to colour is, I find, to reduce the number of colours used to two. Through the very limitations imposed on them, they become inventive and extremely conscious of when they are using first one and then the other. I invited Harold to work in two colours. He chose black and yellow and made a landscape. Through its richer tonality and handling of the design, this drawing revealed deeper sensitivity and feeling than any other of his paintings up to that time. In addition to the work in colour, he participated in the exercises for freedom and co-ordination. These exercises began to release him, and he even attempted to express such abstract ideas as conscience.

At about this time he began to express interest in Judaism. His picture, "The Rabbi" (Ill. 105), done during his first year, was a youthful interpretation of a theme which became his central interest when he was about twenty-one. He used the Rabbis as a symbol of the spiritual man.

The last picture he made in the spring of his first year with me was of some cattle being driven home in the evening. I considered it an important step forward for him, because it definitely dealt with a deeply buried "feeling-side". This was the first time that he had successfully expressed it.

From time to time I wrote down our conversations and steps in the boy's development. The following pages are excerpts from the records I have kept of Harold's work. If the conversations quoted dealt with a specific problem, I have illustrated it with a picture.

104. Greek Warrior. First-year work.
By Harold at twelve years of age.

SECOND YEAR (AGE THIRTEEN)

October: A definite step forward over the summer. Harold has digested
his experiences from last spring, and his work now has a new richness
and warmth, combined with an added power of organization remarkable
for a boy of his age. His subjects are frequently historical—for example,
a scene in an Egyptian street. I said to him: "These pictures have certain
fine qualities, but they all deal with foreign countries. How would you
like to find material from your own experience—things you know about,
that have impressed you or interested you?"

בית אל   בית זין

105. THE RABBI. By Harold at twelve years of age.

He replied, "I get you. How about football practice? I love to watch that, even when I'm not in it, and that would be swell stuff to draw!"

"Try it," I recommended.

He made a strong drawing, "Football" (Ill. 106), showing the action and spirit of the game.

(From that day on, his interest in what he has seen and felt in the life around him in the street, park, or market has increased constantly. "Pushcarts" (Ill. 107) illustrates this period. It embodies his acquaintance with the materialistic outlook, an attitude which he has had to combat constantly. He has drawn and painted market scenes frequently and always reveals something grasping, cruel, or tragic.)

From time to time Harold has made remarks like the following:

"I like the lower East Side, particularly Orchard Street. The people are very interesting to paint, and they have so many interesting characters. For instance, you see every sort—the poor, foreigners, coloured people, old hoboes—all buying. I like best the places where there are pushcarts and market streets. I only see it once in a while, but when I do, I keep it in my mind and draw it all from memory.

"I can remember that part of the city very well, but when I walk on Park Avenue, I don't remember it after I've gotten home. The poor children haven't many playgrounds, and, when there are any, they are so crowded the children have to play in the streets. Little Italy and all the other neighbourhoods like it make very exciting scenes. You sort of want to help those people if you can by showing the ones who haven't been there what it's like."

November: Harold's drawing and composition have improved so much that he has been admitted to the class with older students to study lithography with Emilio Amero.

December: His lithography work is coming along well.

January: Harold is now working in tempera with Amero.

February: Harold wishes to earn his living by some form of commercial art. We have an excellent evening class in modern fashion and advertising, and, eager to try this new work, Harold has entered. The teacher is an artist in the best sense. I think it will be interesting to see what he can do in this class. Although very young, Harold is developing great assurance in his drawing.

April: I find his progress encouraging. What he has built up in creative ability and assurance is not destroyed but applied to a concrete problem. This combination of pure and applied art is what I am trying to work out for these young people. In this way their art training can contribute to a well-rounded life, helping them become healthy, happy individuals finding satisfaction in work, artistically and practically.

THIRD YEAR (AGE FOURTEEN)

January: Harold is in his third year with me. Some of his large chalk drawings are quite remarkable in their characterization of life, composition, and colour. During these last few months, however, he has had a setback. His work has become more pinched and conventional, and he has lost a great deal of his power. He must be watched or else he may throw away, unconsciously, all that he has gained.

March: He has taken a big step forward again. This is how it took place. Harold had been drawing fairly well from a Negro model for

106. FOOTBALL. By Harold at thirteen years of age.

several weeks. I planned that the group which had worked from the model should leave that objective approach for the moment and return to purely creative effort. Harold made a small sketch and brought it to me. It was a picture of three men around a fire in various stooping and standing positions. One of them was forging a blade. The picture struck me as rather meaningless and ordinary without much conviction in the drawing. I asked Harold, "What are you trying to draw? Does this picture mean much to you?"

He answered, "No, it doesn't mean much of anything to me. I was trying to make a group of men in the positions I had seen the model take; I thought I could make use of the studies of the past few weeks."

107. PUSHCARTS. By Harold at thirteen years of age.

108. FLEEING REFUGEES. By Harold at fourteen years of age.

I realized then that he was working in a most external fashion, not using his own reactions to life. I continued: "Well, you say it doesn't mean anything to you, and it really couldn't because you have merely taken human attitudes which you have studied and deliberately forced them into a composition. That is not the way to create. The only possible result of such an experiment would be a little added facility in drawing. Stop a minute and think whether there is anything in the world that you are deeply interested in—something which you feel strongly about, either in your own personal experience or in the world about you."

In a flash he replied, "I know. I've been thinking a great deal about the Civil War in Spain and how sad and how terrible it is. I'd like to make a picture of that."

"Go ahead," I told him.

In a short time he had made a sketch, "Fleeing Refugees" (Ill. 108), which wonderfully expressed the tragedy and pathos of the persons represented. Not only is it fine in feeling; it is remarkably well drawn and composed. This is no facile sketching of a scene, but a deeply felt agony, an identification with each sufferer here depicted. It is just one more confirmation of my firm belief as a teacher that the creative ability of each pupil is stirred when deep feeling is touched.

Harold followed this sketch with a large drawing which he finished in coloured chalks. The final picture contained all the vitality and meaning of the little sketch.

When he had finished that, we had a discussion over what he should do next. The very natural thought came to him that he would like to do something from life. We looked out of the window to see whether anything there appealed to him. He responded to the outlook with enthusiasm. It was a scene of the city's roofs, water-tanks, and human beings in the streets below. He said, "I feel just like doing that."

He set to work and made a strong, well-composed picture expressing an angle of New York quite his own. He is now in his stride again.

June: Next year I want to watch Harold to see that he does not run off into triviality, but builds his work from a deeper level of expression.

FOURTH YEAR (AGE FIFTEEN)

October: Harold's chief difficulty is in not seeing his picture as a whole. His tendency always is to get interested in one figure or, at the most, two, and to work them out in detail, regardless of the design as a whole. He sometimes uses only one-half of the sheet. I made a special effort to make him understand the relationship of the parts to the whole. I asked him to make many very small oblongs or squares and design in them the ideas he was considering in order to define what the figures were doing and where they were located. The idea finally penetrated, and the result was that he made a very good drawing. I intend to urge him to begin each time with these small sketches.

November: Following our plan, Harold made some small sketches for a big drawing of a funeral. The lower part was well organized with the mourners walking to the tomb, but the sky and whole upper part were empty. I told him to turn the paper upside down to judge what the sketch still needed. Then I pointed out that the upper part of the paper was very empty, and that he must do something to the sky to make it contribute to the design. The sketch had great feeling in its representation

16

of a funeral cortège at the cemetery—the atmosphere was bleak, the mourners bowed. Only the improper relation of the forms disturbed it. After more work Harold finally overcame this fault and completed the picture well.

January: Harold has been having difficulty in getting into a new piece of work, so I sat down with him and asked him whether anything was troubling him. He admitted that his teacher in school had been condemning him for doing drawings with tragic themes. She had particularly disliked one he called "Mine Disaster". He said, "She looked at my drawings and started to discourage me by saying that everything I did was false and untrue, that I hadn't experienced anything. She said all my pictures seemed so sad, that this is a happy world, and there was a false note in my things. In one of the pictures, a scene which I couldn't have seen, I said I knew how I would feel if I did see it, but she said I wasn't there. She has me entirely discouraged."

I reminded him that he had to stand up for what he was doing. I told him that if, at this stage of his life, things seemed tragic, he should paint them that way if he wanted to, but that he would pass out of this phase and paint later from other states of feeling. I told him of Picasso, who in a period of ill health and great sorrow painted all his pictures of the blue period and who later, when he was in love with a beautiful young woman, had painted his pictures of the rose period. This talk relieved Harold's mind of the disturbance from his teacher's remarks. He now seems at peace with himself and has settled down to good work once more.

February: About the beginning of this month I became aware of a drop in the quality of the work of all the students in Harold's group, of a general state of repetition and monotony. I considered how to rouse the pupils. Now, I decided, was the time to use thought as a stimulant and to read to them from some great literature something which would move them to think in more impersonal, universal terms. Choosing the Bible, I read the passages dealing with the Creation, Adam and Eve, Moses, and Noah. I finished with selections from the New Testament.

Realizing that most of the children were sensitive and receptive, I thought it likely that hearing the familiar Bible stories under these sympathetic and unorthodox conditions would awaken a fresh reaction.

Some responded eagerly, some held back. On the whole, I should say that the experience was fruitful.

Harold at first was reluctant to participate. Then he got the idea of doing "Adam and Eve in Modern Dress" (Ill. 109). The result was a very strong drawing, original in conception and passionate in its expression.

I asked, "How did you happen to think of doing Adam and Eve in modern clothes and surroundings?"

"The people seem so remote in the Bible," he replied, "that I wanted to bring the story closer to us to show that the people in the Bible are real today, not mythical. I don't know why I put them in a bedroom; it just worked out that way in the composition."

FIFTH YEAR (AGE SIXTEEN)

October: Harold has come back, as usual with a setback. He started off with a market scene again. It was a repetition of what he had done many times, only not so good. It lacked life and design.

We discussed the picture. At first Harold rather defended the painting, saying that the people had character and that he had seen them driving hard bargains. As we continued talking, he spoke of his confusions and conflicts. He told me that he really wanted to paint the working man and the injustice and cruelty he saw around him constantly. When he was much younger, he expressed the same thought which now is evidently growing stronger. I suggested that he change his symbol from the commercial to the human and see what that might bring out. His somewhat close, sullen look gave way to a smile. His swift response was, "What I would really like to do is a self-portrait." That, of course, was excellent. He wanted to objectify himself, to see what he really was.

January: All through the winter, on and off, these self-portraits have appeared. Harold painted a profile of a young man seated with a thoughtful, somewhat wistful expression. The young man wore a blue shirt and was painted against a dark background. He did a series of studies of young men—farmers, woodsmen, and others—always out of doors, always alone, and in rather low tones and cool colours. He told me he felt unhappy, that his friends did not care about art and laughed at him when he was serious. "Sometimes I go out with the boys, expecting to have fun, but I never enjoy it because I'm really alone," he declared.

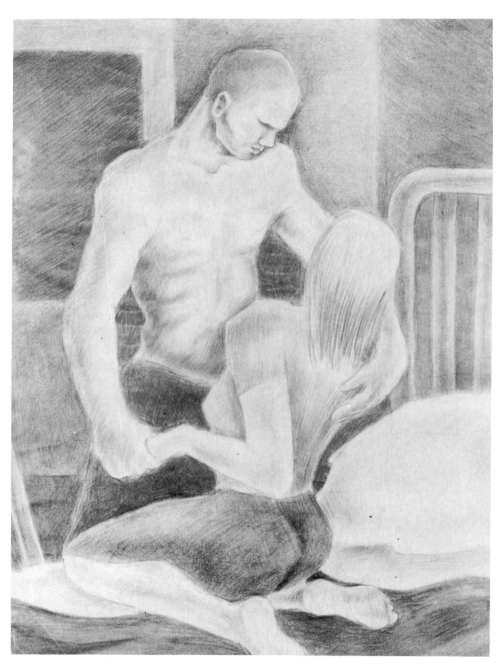

109. ADAM AND EVE IN MODERN DRESS. By Harold at fifteen years of age.

One of his pictures was of a man outdoors standing in the foreground; in the middle distance was a barn, and in the background were the sky and earth. He called it "Alone". The man wears a blue shirt, his hair is black, and his expression is troubled. The barn and earth are brown; the sky is a dull bluish green. He said, in speaking of the figure, "He is not in a happy mood."

"Is something troubling him?" I asked.

"He is reflecting on his life."

"What are his reflections?"

"The bad things, not the good things. He is evaluating himself, thinking about what he has done, and he realizes he hasn't done anything at all."

"What were the good and bad things?"

"I haven't gotten that far," Harold replied. "He is just evaluating himself."

This conversation obviously reveals that Harold has again identified himself with the subject of his picture. He is going through a severe but healthy process of self-discovery.

February: Harold has just graduated from high school. He received several awards in connection with his art: the St. Gaudens Medal (given to the most gifted student from all the high schools in Greater New York); a year's scholarship at the Art Students League of New York City; and four prizes in the "Scholastic" competition at Macy's. He is still continuing with his Saturday morning class at the Counseling Centre.

When Harold went to the Art Students League to select his courses, he decided to study anatomy with George Bridgeman (now deceased), who was famous all through the United States for his excellence in teaching this subject. It interested me intensely that this boy with his long experience in freedom in art should be so anxious to learn the construction of the body and ready to do dry, hard work to get this knowledge.

Harold's first response to the League was one of great pleasure and excitement over his new life. Being among older students in a recognized art school thrilled him. But this thrill has been followed by great boredom and irritation over the work. He told me he had to go out into the hall and pace up and down to be able to endure it. He has been put to work on casts which he finds dull and difficult.

March: Harold has changed his opinion about the League again. When I recently asked him about his work, he replied, "It's swell." He has been learning much and is now getting used to the grind.

He mentioned another problem.

"Sometimes I like to distort things, but the others say, 'It's rotten,' and 'It stinks.' "

I reassured him, "Don't let them influence you in this matter. Distortion has its meaning for you. It is an emphasis; through this emphasis we work towards expressing a meaning. Such exaggeration may almost appear to be caricature, but it is more than that. If you give it its expression when the need is there, you will return to normal in due time. As you study from life, your power of observation will become more acute so that you will be able to draw the norm well and will distort only when you really wish to. This knowledge about distortion will permit you to judge your friends' criticism in a new way. I want you to learn to hear and endure their criticism, to judge its value, and, if you think they are wrong, to develop enough strength and self-confidence to be true to your own conception always. That should be your guide."

I told Harold I felt that, in his great desire to attain technical development, he was over-estimating it to the detriment of his original creative power.

April: Harold frequently comes to the studio after his work at school is over for the day. Sometimes he experiments in new ways of painting, sometimes he wants to talk, and we have had long and heated arguments about many of my principles of teaching art. He is weighing his new experiences in the school against his early training in the studio, and evaluating both. One of his major problems still concerns distortion. He has a strong inclination towards distortion in his design, and I think it is a genuine characteristic of his art. He has found his fellow students and many of his instructors antagonistic to his ideas. He can't accept their criticism and yet he can't quite go on in the face of it. I have tried to build up his self-confidence and readiness to withstand the assaults of his comrades and teachers.

XIX. THE CATHEDRAL. By Steven at sixteen years of age.

XX. The Strikers. Drawn after chanting "EE".
By Harold at sixteen years of age.

"The artist is a nonconformist," I told him. "He must cut his own way, create his own style, and believe in himself. That is the most important thing to learn."

May: Harold came into the studio intending to paint for a few hours. He found himself empty of any ideas or images. I suggested that he try the technique of chanting something he had never done before. "I have been having such wonderful results with some of the other pupils, and, so far, none with you. If you have any confidence in my guidance, you will do this breathing and make these sounds. You will find that a new understanding of colour will come, and you will contact deeper expression from your unconscious, which is, after all, the artist's deepest source of inspiration."

Harold gave himself up to the experiment and went out into the hall to be alone. He used the vowel "E" to breathe and chant on. He returned quite aglow and said, "I have a whole picture that came between the "EEE" and "OH" sounds. The word that came to me was 'strike'. I saw a picture of strikers, for whom you know I have great sympathy."

He made a huge painting on a black canvas, a finely balanced, daring composition—"The Strikers" (Pl. XX). The hands of the man holding the placard are intensely powerful, revealing Harold's feeling about the importance of hands, which he always distorts. It is his way of saying something about the power in man's hands. I think this is by far the best piece of work he has done, and it came directly after his first real use of deep breathing and intoning to harmonize himself.

After finishing the oil painting, he was convinced, for the time at least, of the value of this technique of breathing with sounds and wanted to try it again. Of his own accord he selected a piece of black paper to try a small chalk drawing. He went out into the hall to breathe and move and chant, made the sound of "OU", and said it suggested cold and loneliness. A snow scene in which there was a great expanse of cold, quiet snow expressed that mood. He called this drawing "Winter Cold".

May (two weeks later): Harold is very uneven in his work. One day he paints something big and broad and strong and then the next day he drops back into a small, petty way of expressing himself. I came into the studio today and found him painting in a very cramped and small way a picture called "The Berry Pickers" (Ill. 110). It was conventional

110. THE BERRY PICKERS. An example of niggling tendency.
By Harold at sixteen years of age.

and timid. I felt discouraged that this should happen after his recent progress, and told him so.

He said, "I know there is a difference between this painting and 'The Strikers', but I think this kind of work is suitable for illustration, which I may want to go into for a living."

An argument ensued in which I tried to show Harold that a man like Daumier did his cartoons for newspapers without debasing his art, and that among his contemporaries Don Freeman and Albert Hirschfield have done magnificent drawings in their cartoons and illustrations. I said, "They have refused work many times when they felt they would not have complete freedom to do as they wished. They have not sacrificed

111. The Futility of War. By Harold at sixteen years of age.

artistic integrity in order to earn a living. They are both successful and both fine artists."

Harold was greatly surprised by my statement and said, "I thought commercial artists had to do work they hated, that they had no scruples and would pick up every job that came their way." He seemed relieved to find he didn't have to do dull factual drawing if he wanted to earn a living by his art.

Of his own accord he now wished to try chanting and painting from inward vision again. He went out of the room to be alone. I could hear him chanting through the wall. The sounds were beautiful and clear and intoned like the singing of choirboys. He caught an idea immediately, came back, took a large sheet of black paper, and began to draw. With a few coloured chalks, he made a sketch of a crippled soldier selling poppies. With a few strokes all the suffering of war was in that picture. It is a poignant expression of Harold's strong anti-war conviction, revealing at the same time his sympathy for the blind. He called it "The Futility of War" (Ill. 111). I asked him to write down just what took place, and bring it to me next time.

This is what he wrote: "Before I began to breathe, I was determined just to breathe and sing out sounds and forget everything else. After the breathing, I felt so refreshed and full of vigour that I wanted to work despite the low feeling that I had before. I wanted to draw a head that had some feeling to it, so I started to do a soldier selling poppies. The result has given me more courage to listen to you and really to open my shell and emerge."

He felt great satisfaction with this picture, admitted it had both meaning and plastic quality, and that it made "The Berry Pickers" look slick and cheap.

He said, "I begin to see the possibility of using real work in commercial art."

June: Harold drew a series of black and white sketches of life in Harlem. One called "Harlem Doorstep" (Ill. 112) shows a development in his technique and less exaggerated distortion than some of his younger work. He seems to have assimilated the idea of working towards illustration honestly without resorting to over-naturalistic and petty drawing.

During the summer of his seventeenth year, Harold passed his

112. HARLEM DOORSTEP. By Harold at seventeen years of age.

examination for Cooper Union. He entered in autumn and enjoyed his work tremendously. He made friends with boys of similar tastes and interests and won the respect of his teachers and his fellow students by the high quality of his work. By this time he had apparently learned how to work steadily.

Harold's compassion for the suffering he saw daily in the streets moved him to paint these Negroes gathering remnants of coal. The gauntness of their bodies, the cold barrenness of the street, and the gloomy colours used, all made this a strong expression. The painting is entitled "Coal" (Ill. 113).

113. COAL. By Harold at seventeen years of age.

114. SILENCE. By Harold at eighteen years of age.

The following year he entered the army and remained away three years. While Harold was in training in the south, he saw many Negroes and was again touched by the burdens they are forced to bear. "Silence" (Ill. 114) was drawn on a postcard which he mailed to me.

When he returned from the heavy fighting in Germany and France, Harold was naturally restless and unable to settle down to painting at once. Because he had the returned soldier's problems of adjustment and found he could not begin to paint again as he had hoped to, I tried this experiment with him to help him reorientate himself.

I asked him to close his eyes, put his hands over them, let his memories

115. My First Spanking
By Harold at twenty-one years of age.

go back to early childhood, and then to recall his very first experiences. Harold was quiet for a time. Then he jumped up and said, "I remember my first spanking and how bitterly offended and angry I was with my mother for striking me. I'll make a picture (Ill. 115) of that scene."

Later, he explained his drawing to me. "At the time I was three years old. Whenever I urinated, my mother held the chamber-pot for me. On this day, an interfering friend of my mother's came in. She remonstrated with my mother, saying, 'The boy is being spoiled. You should teach him to urinate alone.'

"So, on the next occasion, she insisted that I proceed alone. I remember that I felt hurt and angry. If I couldn't have her help, I refused the pot and wet the floor. In her anger, my mother gave me my first spanking. Although I knew the punishment was justified, I felt wounded and crushed.

"This was my first rebellion against the world and I was defeated. In the picture I made the figure of myself very small and insignificant in contrast to my mother, who towered over me. The presence of my mother's friend and my father added to my humiliation. She looked on sneeringly, and he watched helplessly. No one came to my rescue."

He evinced great satisfaction in the drawing, and soon closed his eyes again to repeat the experiment of using his memory. This time he recalled a visit to his grandfather. He said about a drawing which he

116. MARKET SCENE. Derived from scribble.
By Harold at twenty-one years of age.

named "Grandfather", "My grandfather is standing in the sunlight; he is stooping over me, giving me a coin. His white beard shines in the sun; his head is large and strong in contrast with the small face of the child. We are so different, yet we are of the same blood. One day I will be like him; once he was like me. There is a quiet, pleasant feeling. The child does not realize how much of life's heartaches will visit him before he is like the old man."

A third memory came to him when he was quiet again. This time he recalled being home alone in the apartment. He was expecting the return of his parents. The bell rang, he went to the door eagerly. But instead of his parents there stood two bearded old men—tall, dark, and foreboding. He called this "The Strangers". He was again frightened and made the same gesture with his arms that he had made in the picture of his first whipping.

In thus re-living his early life Harold brought out various emotions —terror, tenderness, and panic fear—which were parallel to the emotions he had experienced in the war. In so doing, he released the present tensions which troubled him. A second effort to loosen Harold and to get him painting again was through the use of the scribble, a device he had not employed for many years. A theme which he had formerly used often—selling—now reappeared.

"Market Scene" (Ill. 116) is an echo of his earlier drawing of the same subject. In it he depicts the hard bargaining merchant and the brusque housewife whose secrets he knows so well. But now the work is more mature in every way. The line is fine, the design is alive and well co-ordinated, and the characterization of the people acute.

These two experiments succeeded in liberating Harold so that he was ready to begin to paint again without hesitancy and confusion. He returned to Cooper Union and continued his studies there.

He was then in his third and last year at Cooper Union. Meanwhile he had become my assistant teacher in the art classes of the Counseling Centre for Gifted Children, and in teaching found expression for his out-going nature. He shared his art-experiences with the children in such a way that they found him an understanding teacher.

His painting developed; he began to find his own style. His deep interest was in interpreting the religious mystic. "The Rabbis in

117. THE RABBIS IN DISCOURSE. By Harold at twenty-one years of age.

Discourse" (Ill. 117) and "The Angel" were done at this time. "The Rabbis in Discourse" is one of a long series of paintings which he painted for a whole year. "The Angel" is a second theme that held his interest. Sometimes the Angels lead him on, sometimes they are destructive and lead to death.

Harold planned eagerly to start work by himself immediately after his graduation. He was greatly encouraged in this ambition by his instructors at Black Mountain College, where he spent the previous summer.

He has written this about his plans for next year, when he will really paint alone:

> I feel as if I were standing on the threshold of art, or as if starting out on a grand adventure. I realize I have scarcely begun to paint, that so little lies behind me, and so much lies before me. Formerly I had the misguided conception that art was my own personal thing, but now I see it everywhere. I know that I am but one of many who live, breathe, and make art.

As I study Harold's pictures of the last ten years, I see clearly a thread, an underlying motivation, running through them all. It is the drama of his unfolding human sympathies reaching towards and penetrating more deeply into the mystic perception of human beings. Starting with his evaluation of Moses, in which he expressed the strength and wisdom of the great leader, his sympathy goes to the downtrodden—first to the underpaid worker, then to the oppressed Negro, and later to the suffering and purified Jew. In reaching and expressing the complex of his own people, Harold is facing himself squarely. This is the first step towards self-realization.

THE ADULT

CHAPTER XX

An Artist, Blocked, Breaks Through

T.G. was an artist who had already established herself. Having illustrated books, painted murals, exhibited and sold her own work, she was in no sense a beginner. I met her in Mexico. A mutual friend introduced us, thinking I might be able to help T., as she was in an extremely depressed state over her work. She was still very young, but felt she had come to a place in her work where she was just repeating herself. "Can I be finished at twenty-eight?" she asked.

She invited me to her studio. From the pictures she showed me, I saw at once that she was gifted. But her work was too hard and polished to satisfy a woman of her warmth and vitality. The people were well drawn but static; the buildings were architectural and too intellectually composed. I could see she was still under the influence of teachers with an outlook different from her own. As I looked over her work, she exclaimed, "Here I am in Mexico where I have been longing to come and paint, but I can't find the form to express the country and the people. All the drawings which I have done here look similar to work I have done in the past, and in other countries. Mexico has a colour and character of its own, but I am not able to convey it!"

I realized that there was a wall between the strong emotions Mexico had aroused in her and her ability to express them. The fantastically beautiful world of grim mountains, tropical flowers, wild clouds, and gentle Indians had touched her deeply, but her cold drawings showed that there was no link between her feelings and her art. One of these drawings she spoke of is "Two Boys and a Rooster" (Ill. 118). I told her what I felt caused her problem and outlined roughly the way (through the scribble) that I thought could help her find the link between emotion and drawing. She listened with quick understanding, became excited at the prospect of finding a way out of her dilemma, and wanted to begin

118. Two Boys and a Rooster

at once. As we were in her studio with materials at hand, we set to work. I took her away from her drawing-table and asked her to stand up to begin her work. In spite of the formalism in her art, she was quite untrammelled underneath and able to react with swift imagination to my suggestions of free movement and rapid scribbles.

Fortunately, she kept these first pictures because they form a clear record of what took place within her psyche. In the first scribble, "Sleeping Woman" (Ill. 119), she perceived a figure asleep as if still unborn; the cord is about her, and the head is shrouded in darkness. In the second scribble, "Awakening" (Ill. 120), she saw the figure of a woman about to rise. In scrutinizing the lines, she saw in them a figure still tangled in the cord, trying to get up. This symbolizes her effort to throw off her habitual way of drawing which kept her soul down and

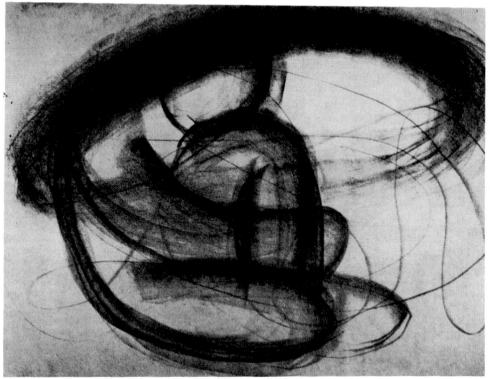

119. SLEEPING WOMAN. First scribble.

bound. This drawing pictures her awakened soul. She saw in the third scribble the head of a woman with eyes open in a startled expression. It is a portrait of herself looking out with wide eyes on a new world. The mouth is not yet drawn—it is as if she were still inarticulate. She called this scribble "Vision" (Ill. 121).

T. told me she felt as if she had gone through something of great importance to her, as if a shell had been broken. This release from sleep to a state of new sight all took place within two hours at our first lesson.

I left the girl in a changed frame of mind, ready for work. She continued using the scribble as a means of stirring her imagination. In the next scribble she pictured a group—"Mexican Women Praying in the Churches" (Ill. 122). These sombre little figures kneeling in devoted groups in the churches had made a deep impression on her, and now,

120. Awakening. Second scribble.   121. Vision. Third scribble.

in her new approach, she was able to envisage them in a beautiful and simple design.

Later she developed this idea into a painting, "Mexican Women Praying in the Churches" (Ill. 123). She remarked. "This is the first time I have captured the spirit of Mexico."

122. MEXICAN WOMEN PRAYING IN THE CHURCHES. Fourth scribble.

123. MEXICAN WOMEN PRAYING IN THE CHURCHES
Painting developed from the fourth scribble.

CHAPTER XXI

A Strong Wish to Draw Brings Results

THIS is a story about the releasing of a talent dormant since childhood. The whole occurrence is very recent, and no one can predict whether it will bear fruit; but the dam has been broken, the stream is prolific, and the promise of further development shines out in the display of a rich imagination and the rare ability to express plastic form through a pure, beautiful line.

One day a woman, who looked about fifty, walked into my studio. I asked her why she came. She said, "I've always wanted to draw, but nothing came of it, though people kept saying I had talent and tried to teach me."

"Do you know why nothing came of it?" I asked her.

She answered, "I think I do, but maybe it's a mistake. My mother said one day, 'You're always drawing, but where does it get you? Why don't you draw me something proper, copy a real picture?' So I set to work and copied a picture with great care. I thought I had done quite well and showed it to my mother with pride, hoping that now she would praise me. She just glanced at it and said with complete finality, 'That's no good at all, a very childish drawing.' I was so humiliated that I have never forgotten it. But, of course, I don't know whether that's the reason I never went on."

I told her I thought the fact that she remembered this incident so vividly showed the depth of the wound and that most likely she had put her finger on what it was that had thwarted her aspirations. Unfortunately this kind of thing often happens when parents don't know anything about creative expression and don't realize the importance of encouragement.

"Now let's go back to where you left off," I told her, "and see whether we can't begin again."

124. Two Figures Talking
Found release in scribble with white pencil on black.
Shows immense power of imagination and expressive line.

We went to the easel, and I explained to her how she could begin
to dispel her dread of difficulty by beginning again. I have written fully
of the release through rhythm, movement, and line, and will not repeat
our conversation covering these points.

She enjoyed doing the scribble and always saw something in it
immediately. In the beginning she showed a strong preference for using
a white pencil on black paper; playing with this delicate pure white line
fascinated her. Two examples of this type of drawing are reproduced:
one (Ill. 124) she called "Two Figures Talking"; another, "Woman"

(Ill. 125). The woman made dozens of these, nearly all being of people looking, as she said, "through veils at life".

One day I told her about contour drawing, a method by which one does not look at the paper while drawing, but instead one keeps one's eyes on the model almost constantly. This lady found contour drawing a great delight and proceeded to draw by the hour anyone who would sit for her. "Former Ambassador Litvinoff" (Ill. 126) is one of her contour drawings done in pencil. The artist is Madame Litvinoff, wife of the former Russian ambassador.

The next step was an unexpected one, showing how strong was the confidence re-established in her. She had just written a story for *Vogue*. The editor wanted illustrations and suggested that the author make them. Madame Litvinoff asked me whether I thought she could do it. "I've

125. WOMAN. Continued freedom through use of white
pencil on black.

126. FORMER AMBASSADOR LITVINOFF. By his wife, Ivy Litvinoff.
By Courtesy of former PM.

never yet made a planned drawing," she said. "They've all been scribbles."

"Well, try," I answered.

She brought me some first attempts she had made at home—two women facing each other diagonally, both sewing on one garment. There was some indication of good drawing in it, but almost complete lack of understanding of the human form. There was, for example, little understanding of how the head showed from behind the shoulder or of how the hands looked holding the material. I posed for her. She improved, but still didn't quite grasp the idea. After all, it was a big step to take with no preparatory practice. Then I drew her in the same position to show her more definitely what I was talking about. She caught on very quickly and spent the morning drawing hands and shoulders and all the other parts which troubled her.

127. THE TEA PARTY. Illustration from story in *Vogue*. Done after six lessons.
By Courtesy of Condé Nast Publications.

128. SELF-PORTRAIT, MADAME LITVINOFF

In a few days she had made three drawings to illustrate her story. I think they are very charming and full of fine human characterization. *Vogue* accepted them and has given me permission to reproduce one: "The Tea Party" (Ill. 127).

I must confess that Madame Litvinoff's progress has been unusually rapid, but behind this progress are several evident reasons. The talent was always there, but not used. Expression of the talent was brought about through re-establishing self-confidence and leading her to a direct method of drawing where her interest took her. Added to that is a great dynamic energy, an intense love of drawing, and a determined will.

The last thing she drew was a "Self-Portrait" (Ill. 128) in ink, which revealed an extraordinary power to express character in line. She has since returned to Russia.

CHAPTER XXII

A Woman of Fifty Makes a New Life

B.H., a woman of fifty, had been married twenty-five years to a college professor. Her three children were grown up and independent. Now, with fewer family duties, she had begun to study art for her own pleasure. She also did a little teaching, but did not take either pursuit very seriously or derive much satisfaction from them. However, she did believe that a woman should have some interest outside her family. Strongly imbued with sympathy for the Negro, she thought she might like to teach Negro children—but even that idea was not very clear or strong in her mind. B.H. was also interested in civic work and belonged to various organizations. Relations between her husband and herself had been unsatisfactory; the breach had grown wider through the years. She still cared for him, but, realizing that he had lost interest in her, permitted him to get a divorce. She disposed of her belongings, packed her clothes in three suitcases, and left home to find a new life for herself.

She came to see me very shortly after the divorce. She had heard me lecture at her college on the therapeutic value of art. In the confusion of her own unhappiness, she recalled the help I had given others and now sought it for herself.

I noticed at once an outer mask of cheerfulness and triviality. This came between us, making it difficult for me to make a serious contact with her. She could not quite bring herself to tell me what she really hoped to get from me. To my questioning she merely answered, "Oh, I want it for my own pleasure in painting and possibly to do some work some day with children."

In response to this general statement, I said, "Perhaps it will be best, then, if I start with my usual method of releasing people physically to do freer work and then go on to imaginative work."

B.H. responded only superficially. I did not seem to touch her unconscious at all. Another indication of her lack of seriousness was the fact that she immediately threw away her drawings. This really hurt me because it showed the low value she placed on her own efforts. I was about to mention this, but checked myself because it seemed a waste of time to tell her. By the end of the first lesson I felt I had not given her anything and doubted whether I could do much for her. Her approach was so superficial; she seemed to prefer chatting to working. After revealing herself more honestly and deeply, B.H. proved to be a truly serious and extremely intuitive person. She had, I discovered, actually read my thoughts that day and knew that I had felt she was not worth bothering with.

Before her second lesson, B.H. and I had lunch together. Conversation broke the ice. When she told me of her personal problems, I answered that I could see a connection between her attitude during our first lesson and her home life. This attitude, I added, was perhaps largely responsible for her sense of inadequacy as a woman. In the way in which she threw away her work and belittled it, she was also belittling herself; her work was a projection of herself, and if she showed no respect for the one, she could show no respect for the other.

I said, "Perhaps you have not given a real place to yourself in your life, but have lived entirely by that morality which places duty to others ahead of duty to yourself. If you really want to make a new life for yourself, you must regard yourself as something of great value. Perhaps your husband lost his affection and respect for you just because you lacked sufficient respect for yourself. This is your second chance. You have done your duty as you saw it in the first chapter of your life; you have won certain real values from it, and you still have your children and their love. But now you have a whole new world before you, in which to find the meaning of life through your own development."

Tears came to her eyes as she said, "I know you are right."

After lunch we went to work and she made a series of drawings, all coming out of the scribble. She commented on each one as follows:

"A Woman Carrying Burdens." On this day I had a remarkable experience. It was shown to me that I had not properly regarded and respected my real feelings about my art. I discovered that I had not really nurtured

18

the spark that was within me. My first scribble showed me with a heavy burden on my back. My eyes were turned away from the wings in the back of the picture which were there to carry me high where I really want to go, where I must go to be fulfilled.

"A Woman Praying Before A Shrine." On this same day I am repentant and ask forgiveness of the Goddess of Art, or the divine within me, for my stupidity, and I make a vow to reverence my feelings about art and never to speak lightly again of any power or force that makes me want to paint.

"Reaching Out." In this one I feel humble. For the time being I am turning my back on outside things. I have given so much of my life to my children and friends that I have never taken time enough to do the things I wanted to do. I hope it is not selfish. In my scribble I see many mountains. I call them beauty, truth, hope, love, helpfulness. The figure is reaching out to them.

"The Rest of the People." On this day I had a door opened to me. I saw a vision of life as it might be lived. When I shed my burden, I felt right away that I wanted to help other people shed theirs. So this scribble is a picture of me taking the rest of the people up to those mountains with me. They start overburdened and heavy with *things*. As they climb, the burdens are cast off and they will reach the top, light and free.

This series of drawings was extremely significant, like a series of dreams. Her symbolism is easy to read. It is universal in character and has been used in art through the ages. Through her talk with me, her unconscious was stimulated, and the material in the pictures makes a pattern of her present and future states.

When she had finished these pictures, B.H. said, "I've done enough for today; I'm tired."

She lay down on the sofa and slept for two hours while the rest of the class kept on working. She slept so soundly that one little boy actually sat on her head without awakening her. When she finally awoke, it was dinner-time, and she felt greatly refreshed. As she said good-bye, she thanked me for the experience and told me that I had given her hope and a new outlook.

She left New York shortly after this meeting. Subsequently she wrote me of her wanderings during the next year and of how she finally settled in a western city whose quality and flavour appealed to her. There she began to make friends on a new basis in which she received as well as gave; then she began to look for work. After a long search for a suitable opening in teaching, she finally found what she wanted in a Negro settlement. She wrote me happily of her work there and of that of the individual children, and even sent me some of their pictures.

She said that in the slums in the Negro section she found a place where she was needed. She mentioned taking the children to an exhibition of great master-works of art given in that city. Some of the children found there a picture full of scribbles similar to the ones they had made, and were delighted to find that artists also found their way by scribbling.

A few years later she wrote again and told me she had settled in Florida, where she had bought a little place of her own. She said she had finally reached the point where her own painting came first. This was the real goal she had in mind, and she is finding great satisfaction in her work.

CHAPTER XXIII

H.F.—Creative Energy Channelled to the Practical

THE case described here shows how, after the self has been awakened by original creative work, the power developed may be turned to practical use in some form of craft in industrial or in commercial art.

H.F. was a young Polish immigrant. He had been a student for five years. He was talented, very ambitious, and hard-working. An example of his work, "The Fight", was drawn when he was thirteen. One spring day he came to me and said, "My father says I must help support the family; he has taken me out of high school and wants me to become a baker like himself. I don't want to; I won't do it. If I once become a baker's apprentice, I can never get out of it. It means working all night and sleeping all day. My father never sees my mother; that's no life. And, besides, I want to be an artist!"

I said, "Well, if your father won't support you while you study, I don't see how you can do it. I think you'll have to go to work."

He became excited and shouted at me, "What! You say that to me, after *you* put art in my blood!" Those were his very words. They both frightened and amused me—and placed a very heavy responsibility on me. He was so serious; the words were so heroic! But I did feel: "If I have influenced him and he really wants to make a fight for it, I ought to help him." So I said, "Well, you could get a daytime job in some business other than baking, and I could send you to an evening commercial school."

At first his pride rejected the idea. I persisted: "You have to look at life this way: we have to learn to receive as well as to give. For your development now you need parental backing. Your parents cannot give it to you or will not give it to you through lack of sympathy for your needs. If I have 'put art in your blood', as you say, I am a kind of contributing parent, and I am ready to accept my responsibility if you assume yours, which is to make something of yourself."

"If I let you do that for me, what can I do for you in return?" he asked.

"The return does not have to be in the same measure. You will give help to others when the time comes—and that is the way things work out in this life. A child seldom gives back anything like the devotion and love he receives from his parents; he gives it to his own children, and seeing that, the parent is fulfilled," I replied.

He seemed immensely relieved. It was a new code for him, and he accepted my offer with grace and real happiness.

He began searching for work and found many small jobs, as usher, package wrapper, and clerk, which enabled him to contribute to his household. Meanwhile he studied at a free W.P.A. school until he could be admitted to Pratt Institute's evening school. He was extremely faithful and industrious. Very soon he had learned enough to get small jobs in commercial studios and shops and, within two years, he had a good, steady position as layout man on the newspaper *PM*.

Throughout those two difficult years he was aware that the foundation he had gained in free creative work gave him what he saw lacking in most of his fellow students. He has since reported that adaptability to any situation or any new medium came easier to him because of the self-confidence gained from his diversified studies.

We have been in close touch with each other ever since he left my class. At that time he wrote me that he wanted to start a class in commercial art for my older students so that, while they were still in high school, they could get the fundamentals of their "profession" and be spared some of the struggles he went through. We corresponded—and planned his class.

Soon his class became a reality. Five of the older students, boys and girls between thirteen and fifteen years, were in it. They brought their lunch Saturdays and at 1.30 H.F. came in from his work and became the professor. It really was delightful to observe him. He was a much more exacting teacher than I; he expected perfection from the class and home work to boot. I remember the first day he gave them a little talk on commercial art. It began this way: "Here you have a good time.

You just paint what you want, but in commercial art you have the customer. You must learn to satisfy him, too." They listened attentively. I don't know what they thought. Then he continued:

"Come here, all of you, gather round me, and I'll show you how to fasten your paper, use the T-square and triangle and the drawing paper."

His pupils worked steadily and loved it. He found great pleasure and satisfaction in this work. He would not take a cent of pay, saying, "I want to give them what was given to me."

This sounds a bit like a morality play—perhaps it is and perhaps that is why I tell it. Efforts to help young people do not always turn out so well. Even if they are talented and ambitious, opportunity is dissipated if there is a lack of sense of responsibility or stamina.

One aspect of H.F.'s story which gives special satisfaction to me is his return to the group with his contribution. It means that a pupil has matured and discovered that the principles upon which he was reared have worked; they have given him those qualities of initiative, self-confidence, and active imagination which have helped him to meet life. To these have been added a technical education which makes possible a practical commercial art career.

This situation, in which an older student teaches the younger ones, contains important values for both sides. It establishes the double rhythm of giving as well as taking. The one in the role of teacher is required to formulate his ideas and finds great satisfaction and clarification from the effort. The younger ones look up with great curiosity and respect at seeing a one-time fellow student in this role of responsibility. I think it brings them to a realization that the serious part of life is not far removed from them. I can imagine that, as the other students grow up and disperse into different fields of activity, they may return as H.F. did and teach the younger students their special pursuits, based on the principles with which they began. This would build a sound basis for art training.

Another aspect of H.F.'s development which gives the story a poignant value is the devotion, steadiness, and persistency with which he fights for his goals. All through his job and his army training he has made use of every opportunity to the full to do his best work and to gain from the experience. His strong sense of responsibility, his faithfulness to his ideals, and his actual achievements are very touching.

During the last nine years H.F. has written me continually and kept notes about his life. They tell of his hopes and despairs, his disillusionment when exploited, and his indomitable courage. The sweetness of his nature comes out in these touching letters.

Born in Poland twenty-five years ago, he recounts how he arrived in this country at the age of ten and even at that age found that life for him was, vaguely speaking, a continual struggle between financial and domestic troubles and a growing interest in art. The impressions of the years in Europe still persisted quite vividly in his memory—a small home, comfortable in spite of the lack of modern improvements, and situated in the midst of a dull village where life was quite uninteresting. His education, he observes simply, was not much to speak about, for it was confined to a Hebrew school. Even at that time his greatest enjoyment was in drawing.

"It was night when we entered New York harbour, and the bright lights of the city sort of left us breathless for a while, and soon after we shouted with the rest, with joy. That scene will always remain in my memories."

"Electricity, running water, and a genuine bathtub were thrilling discoveries when we entered our new home."

The surroundings were of no significance, for his father was earning very small wages, and a better neighbourhood to live in was quite impossible. But this certainly offered a new change.

It was not until he entered school that he began to realize what this new world offered. At last he had a chance to learn to speak English well enough so that the neighbourhood boys whom he envied were able to understand him. With this triumph he could enjoy school more deeply. Teaching was different from that on the other side. His interest in art continued, and it was then, at such an early stage, that he decided on his future. His sole ambition was to become an artist. Fortunately he received much encouragement from teachers and students.

His teacher in public school, who had been a student in my class in Creative Art for Teachers at New York University, brought him to my attention; he received a scholarship in my school. Of this he wrote:

I was very much impressed and delighted with the manner in which I was taught. Freedom of expression was the dominant note, and as years went by, I realized more and more how valuable the training was. Many students in other schools, I noticed, were finding difficulty in obtaining the spontaneous feeling often necessary for a good piece of work. I can remember very clearly my first impressions at the Cane School. Before me was a scene beyond my wildest previous dreams. Many students were working, each absorbed in his own work; many were standing or walking about examining their work from a distance, looking at it from different angles, then coming back again. It was all very exciting to me.

One exercise I can't forget was that of holding a piece of coloured chalk firmly in the hand and swinging the arm completely with the body relaxed following the movement of the arm on a large piece of paper for a minute or less, then standing back and trying to find some interesting dominant forms that would be developed more completely in the next step.

As I progressed, I was introduced to different mediums and methods and studied the various phases of lithographic reproduction under Charlot and Amero. Here I had the opportunity of watching topnotch men at work, and had great pleasure in seeing my work reproduced. I carried my knowledge to the public school, where my work was outstanding. I was soon given a scholarship in the Music and Art High School.

He continued working in our Saturday morning class; his work showed imagination, but lack of anatomical structure. Largely because of his great need, I decided to have a model for the class. He wrote of his experience in drawing from the coloured model who posed as a lion hunter:

I believe I was never so inspired during my whole art course as when I drew from Wollen, one of the world's greatest living models. By that I refer to his posing, the way he swings gracefully into an interesting position, and swings out just as gracefully. I also refer to his costumes, which were really a part of him. As some art students know, he is African-born. Wollen has many charm bracelets and weapons which he wears when posing to help create his lion hunts and other such scenes. I feel as if I am witnessing the hunt; you can nearly tremble with excitement; you can picture the scenery behind the exciting poses.

From this experience of drawing from life he painted the picture called "The Lion Hunt" (Ill. 129), in which he used his studies of Wollen,

129. THE LION HUNT

the model, but composed his idea of the jungle and the hunter in the picture. It was a definite step forward for him.

That spring of this same year his father took him out of high school, in his first year, saying that he would no longer support H.F. as he was old enough to work and bring in some money. I did not see the boy for six months. He recounts his experiences during that time:

My father insisted upon my looking for a job, hoping to discourage me in my art and compel me to become a baker as he is. I realized that my artistic training was not of a commercial standing and that I was unfitted to look for art work just yet. But I began to comb the city for any sort of employment so that I would be able to ease the situation at home, financially and with my father. Day after day I spent roaming the city streets up and down and going to employment agencies in an effort to get a job. I was discouraged and thought of seeing Mrs. Cane. She had no way of helping me get a job but suggested that I needed training in commercial art if I wanted to make that my work and offered to send me to Pratt in the evening. She scolded me for not coming sooner because it was now after the autumn term had started and I could not get in until February. Meanwhile, she said, I could go to some W.P.A. school, have practice, and do drawings to show at Pratt. Her encouragement made me feel better and ready to go on. I had been so anxious to get a job that I had put aside all thought of getting help towards school.

Then one day I landed a job as a shipping clerk. At first the very idea of getting some sort of job made me feel comfortable at my employment, but after a while I felt that I was getting nowhere fast and looked about for some chance to get further art training. A W.P.A. school offered an opportunity to learn something of commercial art. Here I found that my recent training gave me an advantage over other students who were less able to work freely. I soon gained a little recognition for my efforts and had several posters hung at an exhibit. Before long I began to feel that further advancement at this school was limited and began to think of a more substantial training.

I thought of Pratt Institute, but since my small earnings were needed at home, I didn't see how it was possible to go there. I kept thinking of Mrs. Cane's offer to help me at Pratt. I felt a little bit funny at getting such help for nothing. I thought of such benefits only in connection with stories I've seen in the movies.

He wrote me two letters during this period:

October 18. . . . I wrote and told you that I wasn't very satisfied with the school I'm attending. On the contrary, I'm beginning to enjoy it a great deal. I was so enthusiastic when I left your home after that scolding, or rather encouragement, that I began to work hard immediately. I received a job as an usher a couple of days later. The day before you wrote the letter, I was called for a job as a shipping clerk. Immediately I took it because it paid more. I have to pay the agency my first salary which is ten dollars. The expenses are great, because I can't eat at home for four days in which I study in the evenings. But that doesn't bother me because now I can bring in the house five dollars a week for my board.

I have set a plan in three different steps. 1. Study at this school until I enter Pratt for the interview. I can show the work that I'm doing here and others. 2. Study as hard as I can at Pratt. 3. While attending Pratt, I will look high and low for a job as an apprentice.

This evening when I came home, my mother told me that a sign painter had been here and wants to see me for a job at his place. He had seen signs that I had made for various stores around my neighbourhood. I will see him this Saturday afternoon.

December 1. Dear Mrs. Cane: I have been wanting to write to you, but I haven't had any important news. Today I have received the interview appointment card. I am to be interviewed this month at Pratt on December 14th.

I have been waiting for a copy of cartoons that I've made for calendar reproductions for an egg company that I wanted to send to you, but they haven't come yet. I received ten dollars for it. The man claims that since he has distributed the calendars in the vicinity of his egg farm, he has had his business increased.

My work at the Brooklyn Art Centre has been very successful. I produced two outstanding posters which I imagine will be very useful for the interview at Pratt.

Never before have I reached such high confidence in myself. Wanting art to be my livelihood was quite a dark passage. Now I can see that not only have I received a good course in fine art, but I built a great foundation for commercial art. I've seen how students in my present commercial class struggle for composition, balance, freedom, combination of colour, because they didn't obtain a foundation in fine art. I feel so lucky at having obtained the qualifications they lack that it makes me feel quite different than I did in the past. My work that I have produced at school is not merely sign painting or a poster. I apply my fine art as well.

He was admitted to Pratt and wrote me of his plans for the term:

January 7. . . . I chose the layout work which consists of rough drawing to finished work, a combination of what we learned in the past year. Other subjects, such as rendering of merchandise, are quite important, but I feel that I know my mediums, for I have practised various techniques at your school, and also at the Music and Art High School. That's why I chose layout.

About my job situation. Well, I'm still working, and I expect to be laid off soon. If I am, I'll apply for home relief. I'll let time take its course because I'm trying my hardest to attract their attention to my capability to do what they demand.

Mrs. N.'s husband is trying to obtain a position for me, and through my own effort I'm still plugging by telephone and answering ads. in the paper. I may obtain a position sooner than I think. I certainly do hope so.

From his journal we have these comments on his early days at Pratt:

Pratt Institute afforded me a chance to learn the fundamentals of commercial art, and the teachers there inspired me to such an extent that I often remained out of bed until very late working on my assignments.

After my job as shipping clerk had lasted about six months I received an offer from a friend to use his cellar as a studio. He was a florist and had seen me do some sign painting in my spare time and thought I should go in for sign work as a profession. I was ambitious to earn money through art work, so was quick to get going on the idea. I proceeded to clear out the florist's cellar, with the aid of my brother and some friends. Then I realized how bad the cellar was, the leaking floor, the stench of the flowers stored there, and the need for artificial light all combined to make me abandon the idea of a studio. I felt a little ashamed to back out after all my enthusiasm and felt a great relief when Mrs. Cane expressed her understanding of the entire situation.

Several letters informed me of other activities of his.

May 2. . . . I made signs for a man's store here in New York. He is going to open a place in Binghamton and has asked me to go up with him and get it ready. He asked me whether I was able to decorate his store by making signs, posters, murals, etc., and I said "Yes", even though I knew I had no experience in this respect. The idea of making a complete display for a store excited me, and I felt that the experience would be useful, so I accepted.

I've been to a sign painter I know and asked him how to go ahead. He has given me lots of information. My employer is going to pay $15.00 a week. I'm going soon, will write you all about it.

May 25. . . . Dear Mrs. Cane: This is the third week of my work here. The store looks beautiful, better than we expected. My work isn't through yet. I have completed a sign six by twenty feet, various displays, and advertisements for circulars and newspapers.

The people are very nice to me. I like the town. It seems that I have at least two or three more weeks of work. So far my work is satisfactory, and I find it very enjoyable. I'm praying that I will receive this job I told you about at the factory.

On his return to New York after completing his job at Binghamton, he was quickly able to get a summer camp job. His letters from camp follow:

July 10. . . . I got a chance to go to a summer boys' camp. They asked me to supervise in the production of a stage set of Gilbert and Sullivan's *Mikado*. Here's a new job, something I've never tackled. Before leaving New York I went to the Public Library and studied the opera and made blueprints to work from. Now here at work. The stage set is two stories high. I'm surprised it's going so well. I had plenty of nightmares and hard work, but am happy it is going well. I like it here, and it's quite a change from my last job.

After the camp job he came back to New York. Through his former public-school teacher he received a job in an advertising agency.

From a letter of February 8:

> The job is swell. I'm learning new tricks every day, things that I couldn't possibly learn in school, and I find it terribly interesting and enjoyable. Here are some of the things I do: illustrating, lettering, layouts, pasting copy, illustrations and photographs for reproduction. I see actual work being done here, from setting up machinery to finished reproduction. You see it is a process house that I'm working in. I watch them carefully at work in my spare time.

On March 8 he wrote:

> At school I'm doing better than ever, and there's a reason for that. You see, Mrs. Cane, I do my preliminary work for a problem in class and receive an O.K. At work there is spare time where I develop the idea and have it criticized again by the art director. He shows me some professional touches and the fast ways of executing the finished step. I then do some of it at work in the lunch hours before going to school (I have about fifty minutes); on Saturday we work a half day, and I remain for the rest of the day and work. I then finish up at home. My average this term may be 95 per cent. The teacher likes my work.

A little later H.F. wrote me of his idea of teaching commercial art to my pupils. I encouraged the suggestion and, turning formal, he wrote back:

> I wish to take this opportunity to express my thanks for your consideration of my recently submitted plan. My enthusiasm in regard to the suggestions I made and your consideration permit me to exert a great deal of effort in making a very complete plan. The hardships I've had until obtaining a commercial art job make me feel that perhaps I may be able to present my experience and knowledge in a new light, with emphasis on the more practical way of adapting oneself directly to a position as a commercial artist.
>
> I certainly will do everything in my power to make this undertaking a success. I hope that I can help these students in almost the same way that you have aided me.

A few months later he said:

Several things have happened since I last saw you. First, I received an interview with *PM*. The odds were against me because the paper is unionized, but the man was impressed by my work and did everything he could to get me the job which paid thirty dollars a week as an apprentice. I had to make many calls before I received their decision. You can imagine how I felt during those few days. I couldn't eat, sleep, or work. My mother thought I would collapse. Unfortunately I was turned down with the explanation that union pressure forced him to accept someone else.

I heard the underlying reason. They had a coloured boy capable of holding the job, who was a guild member and had preference for that position. They felt that since I was presently employed and he wasn't, he would have a more difficult time getting a job. I feel pleased at their decision and think their policy is very liberal. I went so far as writing a letter of appreciation and asked them to keep me in mind.

Six months later *PM* sent for him; he received the much-desired opening. They took him on as layout man; later he became staff artist. While there, he had opportunity for a variety of experiences and new responsibilities. For instance, in an emergency he was assigned the job of bringing out a week-end edition alone, doing all the layout and art editing himself. He remained with *PM* two years. During that time the war broke out. He made his first contribution to the war with a poster called "On the Job" (Ill. 130)—on opposite page. The Museum of Modern Art had a competition for war posters. H.F.'s poster won honourable mention and was exhibited all over the country with the show. Soon after he volunteered his services and entered the army. He stated his capacities and asked for some work in which he could use them. Right after his basic training, while stationed at San Francisco at Western Defence Headquarters, he was given poster work for training. Later he was selected as art director of the *Fourth Air Force Clipper*, one of A.A.F.'s outstanding magazines. On the side he designed stage sets for army theatricals. Then he became a member of the art staff of *Air Force* magazine in New York City. He received a personal letter of commendation from Lt.-Gen. J. L. DeWitt for outstanding individual work. He was given the Army Commendation Ribbon for this work. Next he was sent to Orlando, Florida, to be art editor of a secret paper for officers. While working on this assignment he made two posters which

130. ON THE JOB. Made for poster competition at
Museum of Modern Art.   Won honourable mention.
By H.F. at twenty-one years of age.

received recognition.   One was used for the play, *The Philadelphia Story*,
the other as an Ordnance poster.

When the time came to separate from the army he found work for
himself at Paramount Pictures in New York, doing art work for their
publicity.   But he was not content to remain in a job of this kind.   Ever
since he had been out West with the army, he had dreamed of going back
to Los Angeles and starting an advertising business of his own.   Now he
decided that the time to take his chances had come.   He went in June.
He has been in Los Angeles six months, first working for various agencies,
then starting out for himself.

The last picture of his reproduced here, "Publicity for Paramount"
(Ill. 131), is used because it shows that he has achieved a synthesis of
art adapted to commercial use.

Though he achieved all this without even a high-school education, H.F. feels that his education was not thorough enough, and has therefore decided to take advantage of the Government's education provision for veterans and has entered the Art Centre in Los Angeles for a three-year course in fine arts and commercial arts. The last year is termed "The Masters Course", and he is determined to graduate from that in order to be among the first in his field.

131. PUBLICITY FOR PARAMOUNT. Professional work done in advertising job for Paramount at $75 per week. By H.F. at twenty-five years of age.

PART IV

The Healing Quality of Art

CHAPTER XXIV

A Modern Psychotherapy

As soon as it is light in man, it is no longer night without.

—SCHILLER

IN a primitive society every man uses all his powers in order to survive. Within him is an unconscious desire to achieve perfection. All his occupations, such as housework, hunting, and fighting, give him opportunity to fulfil those healthy desires, and in so doing he serves both society and himself. In our industrial civilization, however, society profits most if man functions continuously in a limited, repetitious field. The assembly line is an extreme development of this tendency. But there is no satisfaction for man in this method of earning his living because his unconscious need to grow is denied; he has no chance to exercise his creative faculty.

This kind of productive organization throws modern man into great conflict—the conflict between his individual need and the good of society. As individuals we need a varied existence, with an opportunity for play as well as work, for the irrational as well as the rational. Primitive man used his creative ability naturally in making his clothes, utensils, and habitation. We should learn from him and use art freely in our lives to bring back the balancing and health-giving qualities of creating.

The words of Schiller quoted above express very simply how art, which may illumine man, can be a healing agent. Many suffering individuals, frightened and insecure, feel lost; for them it is "night without". If that darkness persists unbearably long, the result may be a breakdown followed by mental illness. Painting may be one way these persons can lift themselves to a healthier condition. However fragile the effort and unformed the art, the persons creating it experience a new breath of life; they share in the creative pattern of the universe; they know its pulse and, for a flash, feel godlike in their new power. A candle is lit; the dark is dispelled. This is only the beginning. Afterwards the journey consists of steps forward, retreats, and steps forward again.

The process of recovery in clinical cases is similar to the development in normal ones. We should realize that a great number of our normal problems are attributable to some inhibition which needs release through the arts. The difference between "normal" and "abnormal" is more in degree than in kind of cure. The method is simple. First, a *rapport* of confidence and friendliness must be established between the pupil and the teacher, so that the pupil will feel that what he is going to do is easy and pleasurable. And, second, a play approach must be developed towards the work—even for adults. Play with line gives rhythm. Play with colour and light gives contact with nature's health-giving forces. Play with fantasy touches the irrational, which frequently uses symbols as a means of expression. The symbols are of importance because inherent in them is the dual character of the real and the unreal. In this way the symbol becomes the intermediary between the conflicting instincts in the pupil, which are often the cause of his difficulty. Fixations and fears buried in the unconscious are also brought up through fantasies, and when they are expressed in a person's art, they act as a cathartic, they are a cleanser. From the working through of many experiences, both negative and positive, comes the gradual emergence to clarity and peace.

Art has therapeutic value for the normal as well as the abnormal. A great many problems with merely "slow" or "difficult normal" cases arise from emotional tangles causing repressions or destructive trends which can be cleared up through simple art experiences. Out of the genesis and development of his drawings we can trace the whole development of the individual. The different stages seen in his drawings afford an opportunity to recognize his disturbances. The fact that nearly all disorders of the mind and soul shake self-confidence is one of the most important axioms of the modern psychotherapy. The normalization of the creative power would mean not only the adjustment of self-confidence but also the rehabilitation of the whole mental habit.

There are naturally many cases of "type-problems" to meet. These cases range from the tiny child too shy to mix with other children, through the school-aged child who is only "slow normal" in his studies, or one who could be classed as "difficult normal" in his emotional state, or one who is backward and subnormal mentally, through the adult with his more complex personal and social problems, and on to clinical cases involving real illness. Many of the psychiatrists and analysts who are treating such patients have found it desirable and effective to use art expression as a supplementary treatment.

I have described in the following pages several cases which exemplify these type-problems.

CHILDREN

1. Jimmy was a boy of three who had come to school for the first time. An only child accustomed to playing alone or with adults, he was so shy that he could not speak to the children or join in their play. His introversion continued for many weeks. The school, one of the progressive type, believed in allowing children to set their own pace, but even the teachers were baffled by the duration of this boy's isolation. No games or toys enticed him to join the group.

One day I brought paints and brushes into the room. He went up eagerly to the table on which I had placed the materials, examined them, picked up a big brush, and began his first picture. He worked with complete absorption for fully half an hour, making one picture after another and talking quite a bit about what they were meant to be. He was exhilarated by this new activity. Soon it was time for milk and biscuits. He walked up to a little girl and quite boldly asked her to sit with him so they could drink their milk together.

This seems a very simple incident, but in it is the germ of a similar situation that occurs constantly with older people. Where it has not been resolved, it becomes much more serious and complicated. Jimmy had been thrown into a group of children who could do everything well. They seemed to him perfectly happy and self-assured, apparently afraid of nothing. He was afraid of everything—afraid he could not play their games, afraid they would laugh at him. But now all this was changed. He had painted many lovely pictures; he had felt a great throb of pleasure and power. From this achievement he felt himself ready and equal to meet his fellows.

2. Hilda, through her art, changed from a slow and difficult child to a normal and capable one. From the time she entered Walden School at the age of nine, she had been slower than average in her studies.

Her lack of interest was evidenced by inattentiveness in class and by habitual tardiness in the morning. The school psychiatrist, in studying the child's difficulties, attributed them to an emotional blocking resulting from problems in the home. Hilda had attended the school for about a year with no change in her attitude.

One day she came up to the studio and began drawing. She showed ability so quickly that it was quite natural for me to encourage her. Her ideas were original, even subtle; her colour, distinctive; and her work was enriched by deep feeling. As her art improved, she herself blossomed. Because of her intense interest, her energy was channelled for the first time, and she worked long and with great concentration. This new ability to work was in turn transferred to her other studies. She even began to come to school on time. These potential abilities had been latent in her; what I gave was the spark needed to free her energy. The recognition she received from her classmates and other teachers because of her superiority in art contributed much to her happiness.

One of her first pictures was a landscape. It seemed to be divided into two parts. Across the middle was a horizontal line of trees forming an archway in the centre; below that, a lake. The upper part of the picture, containing the sky and trees, was light and promising; the lower part which contained the shore and the water, was closed in and impenetrable. The picture suggested a sharp division in herself; only the archway of trees with the water flowing under them made a connecting link. The rich purple and blue of the water suggested unexplored depths.

Several sides of her nature showed themselves in her painting during the next few years. Sometimes her pictures were morbid. There was a head of a young man pierced by a ray of light which killed him. This probably expressed both a fear of and a wish for destruction. Objectifying this mood, she unconsciously rid herself of it and next turned to a totally different aspect of life. It was a healthy elemental expression—"Negro Head" (Ill. 132), dark and vigorous, filling the canvas. This elemental quality is important, for it indicates an aspect of herself, once trampled on but now expressed.

Through her painting Hilda grew stronger and began to move out of her clouded and depressed state. "Magic Staircase" (Ill. 133), painted

132. NEGRO HEAD. By Hilda at twelve years of age.

when she was twelve, is important in her development. It is the beginning of hope. It pictures a young girl in white, her back turned, long hair flowing to her waist. She is going upstairs. This is in itself significant, symbolizing a rising up out of difficulty. On both sides of the staircase are roofs, towers, and minarets of a fantasy city painted in rose, yellow, and blue. The brilliant colouring portrays her happier state. A new integration of herself is beginning.

By the following spring, when she was thirteen, her work showed still further gain in technical expression and psychical health. "A Hurt Tree" (Ill. 134) was done at this time. The well-expressed sense of space is always the sign of a growing personality.

Hilda's art always had a style and quality of its own; a sardonic tang ran through it. The colours often ranged through the dark purples to olive greens and mustards. I encouraged her own colour harmonies as I considered them a true expression of her type and personality. Later on the preservation of this colour sense contributed much to her success in design.

All through high school Hilda's interest in art continued, and her work with me progressed. After she graduated, she went to Vienna to study textile designing. She received a scholarship at the Kunstgewerbe Schule, an unusual honour to be conferred on an American student, since scholarships were not often given to foreigners. On her return to New York she found work in a design studio. Her designs were purchased by the best manufacturers, including Cheney Brothers. After a successful career as a textile designer, she married. Although Hilda gave up her professional work at the time of her marriage, she has continued to use her artistic talents in her home.

Hilda's story shows step by step how an unhappy and maladjusted

133. MAGIC STAIRCASE
By Hilda at twelve years of age.

134. A HURT TREE. By Hilda at thirteen
years of age.

child was brought to normality and to happiness through the therapeutic
use of art.

3. Ned's mother was a widow with four sons. Ned, the youngest,
was just thirteen. He was shy, sensitive, different from the average
rough-and-tumble boy. He did not even like athletics or enjoy the society
of boys his own age. The mother was under the care of an analyst who
had sent other patients to me. The analyst believed I could help the
boy free himself from too close home ties by an interest in art, and that,
if Ned experienced a sense of achievement in art, he might overcome his
sense of inferiority to other boys.

Ned's environment had been favourable—affectionate home surroundings, good schools with opportunity for all kinds of study. Music

and dancing had developed his feeling for rhythm and harmony and had made him receptive.

He came to me in June after my studio had closed and just before I was to take a vacation. It was an inopportune time—there were only two weeks in which I could try to help him. I wanted to wait until autumn, but his mother urged me to take him then, thinking there would be something gained towards his summer. I finally consented, working in my home.

When Ned first came, I let him draw whatever he wished. I always do this in order to see how the pupil works and what he will do without suggestion of any kind. Ned drew an Indian pueblo with coloured chalks. Somewhat like a photograph or picture postcard, stiff and inhibited, it was done on a rather small scale.

Then I gave him large sheets of paper, explaining the significance of drawing big lines with his whole body. Next I let him experiment in making designs, first out of straight lines, then out of curves. He responded with great freedom and gusto. The room was being dismantled for the summer; a ladder had been left standing. There was no easel. As Ned was fairly tall, I put his board with paper on the chiffonier. When he tried to reach the top, he found he was not quite tall enough. I suggested using the ladder. That appealed to him and excited him. He worked running up and down, reaching out in a way that freed his muscles more thoroughly than any exercises I had given.

When Ned said that he did not know what to do next, I suggested that he again try his original subject of the Indian pueblo. The result was an expansion beyond all expectation. Instead of the little pueblo seen far away, he drew a large, primitive head of an Indian seen at close range and omitted the pueblo entirely. The primitive element in him had surely been uncovered by the elemental quality of the rhythm he had been experiencing. Both the concept and the manner of execution were crude, powerful, and simple, whereas before they had been timid and indefinite. This was not chance, as subsequent work showed.

Ned then did a Negro with his back turned to the spectator, hands uplifted in prayer to a large and gorgeous sun. Rich purple, orange, and rose predominated. Next there was a large head of a woman, very tender and rendered with deep feeling; tulips were in the background.

The colours were blue, green, and violet. The great simplicity and large flowing lines were amazing. During those two weeks Ned did five large, coloured chalk drawings, all in an extremely free, imaginative way, and each quite different from the other.

Then we were separated for a year. Meanwhile Ned received other instruction which caused him to lose both courage and all innate sense of rhythm and fearless use of imagination. When he came back to me, it took a month to rebuild his courage and faith. He could not make even the simplest design of lines and curves with freedom. He was sensitive to criticism, unable to draw from his own source. Nothing I suggested helped. One day I asked, "How would you like to draw a line expressive of some feeling?" He brightened up at this and tried fear, defiance, love, and gaiety. Fear was black and blue, with the lines crawly in character. Defiance was sharply cut, the colours clear red and light green. Love was designated with soft curves and hues of rose and light blue. Gaiety was done in dancing rhythms in orange and black.

After this Ned again did not know what to do. I said, "Suppose you were given a commission to decorate a public room with these ideas, and you had to express them so that the public would understand." He was delighted and translated each of these abstract line drawings into more formal compositions.

When Ned returned to my studio the next summer, we had a talk about what he should paint next. He rejected anything casual.

"I don't want to do just another landscape; it must mean something to me," he said. "I know what I want, the elements—fire and water, earth and air—that would be something I'd like to do! I'll begin with water, because when I heard *La Mer* by Debussy, I saw in my mind the figure of a woman moving upward in a tide of water; the colours were blue and green."

His next effort was "Fire". This was a picture of an elf springing out of the flames. The colours were red, orange, and yellow, with a little sharp green behind the flames, like sulphur from old wood. After that he designed the third picture called "Earth". It showed a section of the planet whirling and blown by the wind, the birth of trees and man and woman on its surface. Unfortunately, the summer ended before he designed the picture illustrating air.

Through these three years of steady interest and continuity of work, Ned developed character and independence. By his own choice of subjects and their development, he learned to know his own wishes and his own mind. A strong, deep love of his work had given him a central interest in life. He became quite happy and free from all sense of inferiority. At last he felt on an equal footing with his companions. His friends and family recognized the change and welcomed it. This adjustment and new direction were just what the analyst had hoped might be achieved.

4. Louise, a retarded child, was also led to growth and orientation through the therapy of art. Doctors and psychiatrists had been consulted about her, and the consensus of their opinion was that she had all her faculties and normal abilities, but was handicapped by a great sense of inferiority caused by constant comparison with her elder sister who was exceptionally brilliant. They also noted an extreme nervous condition and lack of ability to concentrate. It was thought that these symptoms might be an outgrowth of her insecurity.

On the advice of the psychiatrists, the girl had been attending a boarding school, but her mother felt that little progress was being made. As Louise's interest was art, the headmistress suggested to Mrs. B. that Louise might find therapeutic help, as well as satisfaction for her talent, in my school.

Mrs. B. brought Louise when she was sixteen years old. We outlined a course of study which would give her imagination free play to do its healing work and which would, in addition, give her an opportunity to learn techniques in water-colour, oil, lithography, and fresco in order to train her powers of concentration and execution. To supplement her art work, a tutor was engaged at home to help her keep up with her school studies.

When Louise first came to me, she talked constantly to the other students, disturbing them very much. She was unable to concentrate on her work, which appeared chaotic and vague. In her talk she frequently spoke of intimate home affairs. Gradually this condition improved. Her work showed a growing control and a better power of expression. She became concentrated on her work and talked less, often working quietly for hours at a time.

135. CHILDREN AT GAMES. First drawing by Louise at
sixteen years of age.

The stages of her growth over a period of four years can be envisaged by a study of four typical pictures, two of which are reproduced here. "Children at Games" (Ill. 135) was one of the first. It is crude and unformed, showing immaturity for her age.

A second painting done three months later showed more power, form, and movement. The chief fault was bad placing of the group—Louise left an empty foreground. I am convinced from many examples that this inability to include the foreground in the design means inability to meet problems nearest to one.

The third picture is a water-colour. Although the figures are still crudely done, the picture has a real painter's quality. The composition is good—one senses the sea, the sky, the shore, and the people moving

136. Skating. Painting by Louise at eighteen years of age.

on it. Her control has grown as well as her ability to put her images into plastic form.

The fourth picture, "Skating" (Ill. 136), was painted on a gesso panel in tempera. This was done during her third year. It shows distinct improvement—greater sureness, better co-ordination in the whole composition, more life and movement. Notice how rich in character the foreground has become. In fact, the whole spatial conception has broadened.

Louise enjoyed the entire process of learning fresco: preparing the lime, sand, and marble dust; plastering the board; making a careful drawing; tracing it; and making the final painting which had to be done rapidly while the plaster was still damp. I placed Louise with the fresco group because the effort to complete a fresco required concentration.

and I felt sure that her interest in it would help towards its completion. It did mean much to her and assisted in building up her self-confidence.

Along with her artistic development one could see improvement in Louise's adaptation to social life and to her studies and an increase in her general happiness.

Her mother said, "At present it is a joy to me to see her school work marked 'excellent' nearly every time—that tells the story in itself."

ADULTS

In dealing with adults I use the same techniques I have described in the work with children—the free movement, the scribble, the sound and breath exercises—merely adapting them to their less open and less responsive state. Adults go slower and have more resistances than children in trying out these new ways. I have found that stimulation of fantasy is one of the most fruitful methods of eliciting the hidden powers in the adult.

Fantasy may be an instrument for recording deep, unconscious processes which can be clarified when objectified in drawings. The sceptical will doubt its value and regard it as nothing but idle daydreaming. Present-day psychology, however, has given it a place in human development which must be recognized. In his book *Psychological Types*, Dr. C. G. Jung brilliantly states the importance of fantasy:

> Society requires man to specialize, and rates him higher who develops some function extremely well because it is of more use to Society. For the individual, however, the greater development is the development of the self. The treasures of the soul may lie buried in his inferior function. His will is identified with the superior function through habit. It is only by going down with the unconscious where the functions lie side by side, undifferentiated, and by bringing up through fantasy this crude and unused function to light that it may be developed and the possibility of attaching the will to it becomes a reality, not only a wish.

Art is a path through which unused functions may be developed, for through art the hidden wishes and fantasies of the pupil can assert themselves. Jung has given a clear explanation of the way fantasy functions in an artist, showing us why its use is important:

Memories of objects stimulate the artist, set in action his own psychic processes. The objects are acted upon, broken up, changed, and associated with his own individual quality. Thus is brought forth a new presentation of quite another character. The forms are the same, but a new element has entered in and made a new product.

In the modern approach to art, we encourage the introduction of this new element and help the student to give it form. In giving it form the student works as an artist. This takes effort and requires the exercise of will. These two phases, the bringing up of material from the unconscious and the use of the will to develop this material, are analogous to the analytic process. This approach is an important part of the psychological technique I use in teaching art. I study each individual, his personality and his type. From observing his work I usually can judge which are his superior and his inferior functions. Then I proceed to find ways of developing the inferior side, and thereby to balance his work and his character.

Young people are usually quite unaware of these changes taking place, but with adults a realization of a new condition is apparent. They have expressed in different ways the idea that a door has been opened to a new world, and though they may have worked in this fashion only a short period of time, they have gained enduring and increased health and strength.

1. An example of this strengthening influence is found in the experience of a young woman, M.K., who entered one of my teachers' training classes. She had begun life as an artist; the desire to continue art work was very strong. She married, had two children, and, in her need to add to family income, had become a teacher of art in a progressive school. The struggle to keep up both her domestic and professional duties left no time for the artist. She was strained, unhappy, and ailing. In my class she found an opportunity to express her tumult in symbolic pictures. She told me that this work had not only made her happier, but had actually made her well; through the winter she had not once visited a doctor. The really deep creative work she was able to produce brought up the imprisoned, unconscious element. She has since written me from another city to which she moved that this influence has been lasting.

2. Another type may be able to express itself emotionally, but without organization. Then ways must be found for that person, at that time, to become aware of balance and relatedness. R.S.'s story provides an interesting example. This woman was vital and active, highly strung and emotional, but somewhat chaotic. Her work showed all these characteristics. She was, at the moment, finding satisfaction in a series of flower paintings. They were large, decorative, and keyed high in colour. The attention was directed entirely to the flower, very little to the spaces in the paper, which were "non-flower" and which could also have been developed. One day she said, "I've had enough of this, and I don't know what I want to do next. I feel somehow satiated with gorgeous flowers."

I had expected this to happen and was ready for her. "The flower is really a symbol of yourself," I told her, "and your absorption in enjoying the painting of these various flowers in rich colours has been a necessary and genuine experience for you. You really became acquainted with yourself and your needs in doing it. There is a side of you, sensuous and narcissistic, that needed to be expressed and lived through. But do you notice how empty the spaces around the picture are? You might imagine the flower as a symbol of yourself, and the spaces, which could be background, as the rest of the universe. In these paintings you have been unaware of that part of life. The work shows a lack of relatedness, and that is a reflection of the same thing in your life. Perhaps without knowing it and because of your emotional disturbances, you have been rather self-absorbed and not able to give out enough to your family or friends, nor to be aware of their needs. Having refreshed yourself for a long period of expression through much-needed dwelling with sensation in an art form, you now have satiated yourself and are ready for a broader horizon.

"Suppose we take a plant and stand it on the window-sill. In your next picture make your objective the relationship of your plant to space and the objects that fill it—the space in front of the object, the object itself, and the space behind the object—and no matter what part you are working on, don't let yourself focus on that part alone. Always think of it in relation to all the other parts. Then, through this symbol of the plant related to the world, you will become awakened to this effect on yourself. You will subtly transfer your art discovery into the same awareness of human relations, relating yourself to the rest of the world."

R.S. responded with real understanding and enthusiasm, and, during the years that followed, both her life and her work became more meaningful and better organized. R.S. felt that she had channelled her surplus energy—that her art had given her a place in the universe, that she had found a rhythm (an outgo and income as she put it), and that work had become so much a part of her life that it would go on and sustain her no matter what conditions might befall her.

Even more dramatic illustrations of the therapeutic value of fantasy are found in those cases sent me by physicians and analysts in which drawing from the unconscious is definitely used for the purpose of healing. This collaboration with the analyst is possible because my work does not cut across the patient's transference to the analyst. I function as the creative teacher, perceiving the meaning of the pupil's work, but leaving the analysis to the psychiatrist.

My approach to a patient is not very different from that which I use towards an ordinary student in art, except that the emphasis is placed on expression of fantasy with a minimum of time spent on technical proficiency. The rhythmic repetition of lines in a well-balanced position calms the patient, converting tumult and tension to peace and relaxation. The scribble stirs his fantasy, and thus the hidden tale evolves.

3. V.L., a woman of forty-five, had suffered from a nervous condition. One of her symptoms was a severe depression in which she felt an abject inferiority. She had remained in that state for some time. In her art she found a new avenue of release from her suffering. The drawings selected show clearly the gradual lifting of the burden and the beginning of a new outlook.

She responded unusually well and produced a great deal of work. She not only had a great number of images to work from, but also wrote about each one. The drawings lifted her out of her depression. I reproduce one set of her sketches, with her own comments which explain her motivation and delicate execution:

"A Universe" (Ill. 137)—black, austere, revengeful. Man the inchworm, drawing himself up by his own length—along the desert way. Fear—abasement—menace!

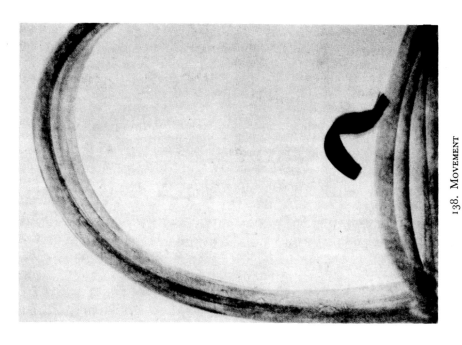

138. MOVEMENT

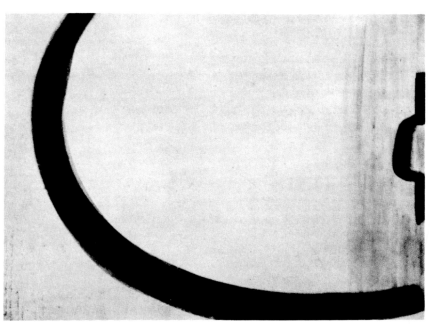

137. A UNIVERSE

"Movement" (Ill. 138)—labour—heaviness. Curved ground indicates coming heights and depths (rhythms).

"The Arc Changes" (Ill. 139). The small figure becomes more upright, the past follows. Uphill road indicates steadier movement.

"The Arc More Beneficent" (Ill. 140)—suggestion of hill and valley, ground has been covered. Figure more upright and also takes more definite shape. Arc has flavour of rainbow.

She continued this work through the winter. By the spring her problems were clarified and her depression left her.

4. A man of about fifty, wealthy, and retired, A.R. was an entirely different type from the last example. He had had a nervous breakdown caused by the emotional shock of discovering his wife's infidelity. At the time he came to me he had partly recovered and was going through an analysis.

He arrived with his trained nurse. After one lesson I saw she was interested in drawing, too, so I let her work at the same time. I could see that this gave the hour added zest for A.R. also. The record I made of his lessons reveals in just what way this work helped him.

LESSON I

1. Free movements in black and white rhythm.

2. Used green chalk, drew design with right hand. It showed a centre and pattern.

3. Took green chalk in each hand. Made loops half-way down picture on each side, then reversed loops. He said, "I don't know why I reversed it; I didn't intend to, but something just made me. It's quite fun to see what will come out."

I replied, "It is good to find out that movement as well as the mind can be a guide."

4. Made other free designs with apparent enjoyment.

LESSON II

1. He had an idea at once. He was an engineer, and it came from his knowledge of that profession. "I want to draw the area we trace by a subordinate roller, rolling around," he said. He made the interlacing curves and then filled them in, using green and orange. Then he

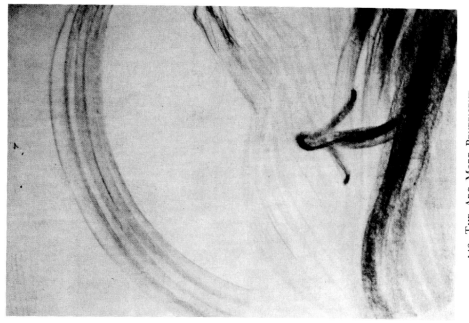

140. The Arc More Beneficent

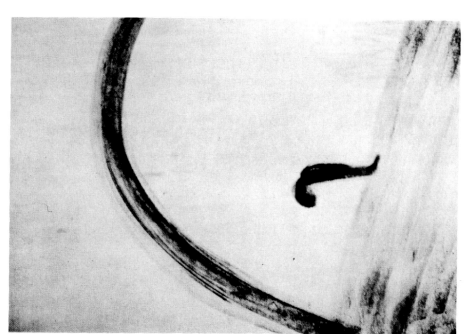

139. The Arc Changes

commented, "It's funny how a colour can change a mood. I came in very gloomy—I saw a man killed on the way down here. I picked up green and orange chalks and I was changed!"

2. Made a more exact design with crossing lines making squares and diagonals, with small curves fitting in. "This should really be done with a compass and T-square," he said. I answered, "It depends on your object. Are you doing it for the sake of an exact drawing, or are you doing it for the movement and strength and beauty you can put into it so that you yourself will change and find rest and peace in your work?" He smiled, showing he understood, but said nothing.

LESSON III

1. He swung certain movements, starting from bottom of paper and moving up and outward. He said, "It makes me want to do a tree."

2. He went ahead and drew a rather crude tree with a house behind it; he said it was his own house.

3. We talked over how he could do better, and he made another study of a house and tree which was much better drawn—longer concentration than on any other drawing.

LESSON IV

1. Came in saying he felt tired and did not know what to draw. I said, "Let's talk a bit. Until now you have taken your start from rhythmic movement: why not start from feeling? Let yourself recall any strong feelings and see if they suggest any images." He got up and went to work. He took "rage" as his theme, making a jagged smear of red and then partly hiding it with black. At the bottom he drew a small black pistol. With the completion of this picture, out poured the story of his rage and humiliation.

He said, "I was thinking of a very dirty dog—a man I was advised to shoot through the belly. I very nearly did. He has broken up three or four homes already, a conscienceless fellow." Tears sprang to his eyes, then he looked at his picture and continued. "The red is rage, a zigzag, and the black is depression superimposed on it."

Then he spoke more fully of his state of conflict. He told me that he really wanted his wife back, yet had rejected her and that he was in constant torment.

We then talked of analysis, and he said he didn't see how it would help him settle his problem. I told him I thought analysis led to the discovery of one's own soul, that relation within oneself to one's soul was greater than any human relation, and that the integration that came from it gave one power to order one's life. In his case he would either let his wife go because he would be strong enough to have overcome his need for her, or he would be able to win her back. But whatever the outcome, he would not remain in torment. The picture comforted him.

2. He next made a large blue circle, containing a yellow five-pointed star and a red centre. The symbolism is obvious, but may be interpreted differently by different people. The large blue circle is man in a spiritual state, the yellow star may be hope, or light, and the red centre, a new vitality. A.R.'s whole mood had changed. He was at peace for the time being; he had at least had a glimpse of how he might rise beyond his conflict.

3. Drew a picture of his own living-room, with his nurse in an orange dress reclining on the sofa reading. There was a window and a view could be seen through it. The picture suggested serenity and quiet.

LESSON V

He said he would like to work from an object. He saw a bowl of flowers in the room and spent the whole evening painting them. I helped him on problems of arrangement and colour. He seemed to enjoy the work and stayed quite late.

LESSON VI

This time he said, as he came in, "I want to paint a ship. You know I like sailing. I know quite a lot about boats." The painting developed into a strong, fresh piece of work. The ship was in full sail under a sunny sky and on a sea of blue swells. A ship in full sail on a blue day seemed to suggest new health and power.

LESSON VII

Last time he had mentioned a desire to work from life, so I had engaged a model for this lesson. A.R. did surprisingly well for so new a student.

The work from the model continued to interest him, giving him an increasingly absorbing problem to deal with. For the remaining lessons, until we separated for the summer, he continued to work from life.

His analysis proceeded well, and his art continued to give him an extremely satisfying occupation. Eventually he and his wife were divorced, and he has since remarried happily.

5. J.V. was a man of forty-nine, a failure. He was an illegitimate child whose parents had married after his birth. They were Germans, living in Germany. His home life had been unhappy, his parents having quarrelled constantly. He felt that his impulses to help in the household had been crushed, and that his natural love of beauty had been trampled upon. He married a woman whom he could not please or satisfy. His mother, a stronger character than his wife, contrived to break up the marriage. J.V. knew other women intimately, but without real respect; none measured up to his mother. He was brought up in the hotel business, but had never made a success of it. Discouraged, he had taken to drink and even to drugs.

At the time he came to me, he was living apart from his wife. She had a business of her own in the country, whereas he lived in town; he went home week-ends to audit her books in order to earn enough to live on and to bolster his self-respect. To gain a further prop he attended an art school which attempted to stimulate the students to creative work through the hearing of music. The study proved useless and J.V. gained neither clarification nor understanding from the teacher. He had been ill, unable to function at all, and had moved to a men's boarding house, walking in the park to pass his time. He had sunk to a very low ebb.

I drew from him painfully that his mother had tried to keep him like a child, never permitting him to live his own life, and that his father had further crushed him by terrorizing him. In my work with him I planned to elicit these past memories in his unconscious drawings and then to reawaken that time in his boyhood when he still harboured hope

of accomplishing things. In this way, I would be using art as a means
of re-establishing a connection with himself. Perhaps he might then be
able to rid himself of the mother image, grow up, and become a man.
Then he might conceivably establish a new relation with his wife or, if
that were not possible, orientate himself in the world of affairs. I give below
excerpts from notes I made of J.V.'s studies with me. The most important
parts of our conversations discussing his background and work are quoted
verbatim. The rest is briefly summarized.

FIRST LESSON

He showed me a portfolio of his work from the art school he had
attended. The work was weak and sentimental, lacking in any decided
form, colour, or design, and very empty. I could see at a glance that
the work had little relation to his rather strong masculine personality.
The kind of expression he used was borrowed from paintings he had
seen and was influenced by insipid teachings. I told him this frankly,
at the same time encouraging him by saying that I was sure he had
better stuff in him and that we would try to bring it out. I asked him
to put aside for the moment his ambitions to make a good picture which
"he could hang on the wall" and instead approach drawing and painting
from a new angle so that his individual self would emerge and guide
him. He listened with intense eagerness, and indicated that his mind
welcomed new ideas and new approaches.

He began with liberating exercises which took some time. They were
followed by scribbles. He shows an incredibly fertile imagination in the
pictures he visualized in the scribble. (As he progressed, he liked this
method of release so well that he used it throughout. The associations,
too, were spontaneous and extremely vivid; in the course of his studies
they revealed the whole story of his life. I have rarely had a student
produce so many images from the past which issued from associated
memories, nor had one who could articulate his thoughts and feelings
about them so clearly.)

His first drawing was very dramatic. It is called "Death" (Ill. 141),
and depicts a man standing over a prostrate figure of a woman and
killing her. He said of the drawing: "I'm not sure what it means, but
it is a conquering of a part of myself. You brought out my strength."

141. DEATH

It appeared to me to be an extremely rapid uncovering of a deep
inner problem. It is too early to analyse its meaning, but it may have
one of several implications. Perhaps he is attacking the weak side of
himself, or perhaps the mother image has been raised from his unconscious and he is trying to rid himself of it. The story he told of his life
indicates how destructive his mother was towards him; he probably
harbours very resentful feelings against her.

SECOND LESSON

He began by talking about his past. He spoke freely of the fighting
between his parents, of his mother's domination, of his fear of his father,

and of his own failure in life. While he was talking, I was considering how best to begin. It occurred to me that this was a case in which a return to early memories might prove cathartic and cleansing to a soul so burdened with sorrow and despair. I asked him how he would like to return to his youth, to the time before he was crushed, back to his beginning. The idea appealed to him strongly. He made a scribble which he called "Nature" (Ill. 142). He said about it: "First when I gazed at my scribble, I saw a female form carrying an embryo. She was headless and blue in colour. It was my mother with myself within. Then I saw my father's head rising behind it. There was a crown of spikes on his head; he had a devilish aspect. I saw him in black and red." The picture contains a very revealing story. One cannot help but observe its powerfully primitive quality. The colours express the same feeling of this birth fantasy.

Immediately after this picture J.V. produced something dramatically opposite. In the scribble which he titled "Innocence: Rebirth" (Ill. 143), he saw a simple, primitive animal form. He was uncertain just what animal, "but it was young and innocent". He used pale yellow to depict the animal and pale green for the background. It was very fresh, suggesting a child's expression of spring. Suddenly he picked up a piece of heavy black chalk and outlined the animal, thus destroying much of its simple purity. He was talking to himself as he drew and said, "This is pure and childish, the way a boy would try to draw a cat or any animal, nothing to do with sex. I think it is a rabbit and a bull combined in one. A bull-headed creature would not mind things the way I do. A rabbit runs away from danger and responsibility."

I commented on what he had done and said, "As you were drawing swiftly in pale yellow and green the animal suggested one new-born with long thin legs and a big head not quite awake. I thought perhaps it was a symbol of your present new state, just appearing after your birth fantasy. Then you suddenly put this black line around it and it lost this tender, childlike simplicity and was reduced to a harsh poster-like drawing." (I noticed he appeared different when he was drawing the black line. Before he had looked very serene and happy, later he frowned.) "Can you tell me why you put that black line in? Did it come from the same place the yellow and green came from?" I asked.

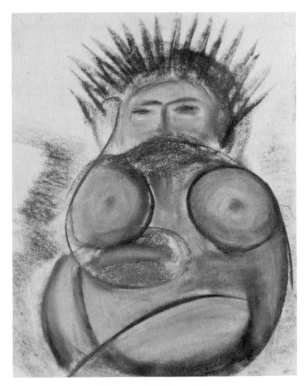

142. NATURE: A BIRTH FANTASY

His answer was, "I put in the black line because I thought the picture wasn't definite enough, and I ought to do something to help it. The yellow and green came from here" (he touched himself in the abdomen) "and the black came from my head trying to fix it."

I replied, "You see, at this stage, you want to keep your head out of it. We're just trying to let the material come through play and imagination. Later on you can use your head again when you want to organize this material, but first we must get the material up."

The lesson continued. He seemed to have tremendous energy; he drew four more scribbles, and each signified something out of the past which had meaning for him.

The next was a cat with a large terrifying head; the colours were yellow, crimson, and black. He said of it, "Fear came up. That's my father's face, a devil. My father used to frighten me. He would put a towel over his head, make noises, and pop out from the closet door. It made me hysterical, and that amused him."

The next he called "Childish Curiosity Unsatisfied". It was a drawing of a headless female figure bent over as if to look at her own organs. The colours were strong blue and red. As he drew, J.V. commented, "Sinister-looking thing, isn't it? It's interesting that the thing has no head. The head could be seen at any time, so there was no curiosity about it."

For his next scribble he took a piece of red chalk, using it together with white. It became a snow scene in Switzerland: he was on a slide and a young girl danced before him in the sun with an object between them. He called it "Dividing Wedge". He talked animatedly about this

143. INNOCENCE: REBIRTH

picture and said, "The soft pink colour reminded me of twilight in winter in the snow in Switzerland. I was about eighteen at the time. This is me on the right, and the young girl on the left is just blossoming forth. Something comes between, something ugly—mother again. First vision of an innocent love affair of a young boy. The girl is capering around with her arms lifted up. The ugly thing which comes between looks like a womb."

I asked him, "Did your mother interfere with your girl?"

"Yes," he replied. "It was an innocent love affair in Switzerland. I had a package of love letters in a trunk. I came home unexpectedly and found my mother rummaging around in the trunk and reading them. There was a big fight between us. She always tried to put something between me and everything I had to do with women."

This drawing revealed the mother's jealousy and destructiveness towards his love interests.

He told me a little about his background. His father hated his home; he had been an apprentice with his mother's father in a photographer's shop. His mother didn't really care for his father, but had taken pity on him and let him make love to her. Soon after she became pregnant. The man tried to escape, but was forced to marry the girl. "I was everything to my mother, but what she gave me was smother love, not mother love. I never knew what real love was, constantly torn between my mother and my father. A child wants to look up to both, but each one pulled down the other to me when one was absent. I was young and wanted to get out. I did at sixteen. I was always looking for something that I couldn't find where I happened to be. I remember once I had a birthday party, with cake and everything, but I sneaked away from it and went to a movie and then wandered around the streets looking for something. Perhaps I've found it now at forty-nine. I've always had the feeling I never amounted to anything."

THIRD LESSON

In this lesson J.V. drew only three pictures. The first was titled "The Swan". He said about this: "It's a swan, an aggressive kind of bird. When I was a little child in Wiesbaden, I remember a lake in the park. A big German soldier was walking with a girl. He began to tease the swan to show off. The swan came out of the water and ran after him, and as the soldier tried to run away, he stumbled and fell down, looking very silly; so I had a memory of a swan attacking. I also have been scared by geese. I was chased by them and fell down on the cobblestones in the street."

I answered, "It would seem from this association that you are bringing up the aggressive side of yourself, as symbolized by the swan. And as that is your need, I should say it's a healthy picture."

The second picture, which he titled "Hot Head", was done on black paper, with the left hand. He used yellow, crimson, and brown chalks. It was a picture of the aggressive, masculine German type; it could easily be a symbolic portrait of his father. About this picture J.V. remarked, "That could be Hitler himself, also probably the same type of soldier I talked about before. It might be a type of authority, or just my father —he spelled authority. He was a strict disciplinarian. Just looking at the picture arouses fear in me; the way his jaws are set is enough to scare you." He clipped his words when he talked to me. "I definitely had a fear of my father and have hated authority ever since."

I suggested, "Let your fears come up. Make as many fantasies of fear as you wish."

This episode was followed by his third picture, which he called "Dominant Vitality". It was done from a scribble, with red and green chalks on black paper.

J.V. said, "When I first looked at the scribble it seemed like a boy prostrate, whipped by an old man. I turned it another way and it looked lovely, just the way it is."

I replied, "You don't need to touch it if you don't want to. Learn to listen to the voice inside yourself and be your own authority. If you became that in art, you will be able to transfer it to living. When you do look at the scribble, don't look *at* it, look *through* it to a great distance."

J.V. commented, "No, I think it isn't finished. Now it looks like a grasshopper." (He went on with red and green chalk.) "I think it is now complete. It looks like the larva of a beetle, just come out of the egg, soft now, without much shape. Powerful hind legs, by means of which he can propel himself. There is no fear in this picture. He's eager to go. All he wants is a chance to start."

I had previously suggested his trying to work with the left hand, and now asked him, "How do you like working with the left hand?"

"I like it much better. I used to be left-handed until my father beat it out of me. He almost cut off my hand one day."

His reference to the trouble he had with his father over being left-handed came out quite by chance, but it may throw a light on some of his suffering.

(We are learning now that it is valuable to use the hand which comes naturally to us, that arbitrarily to force a left-handed person to become right-handed retards his growth, forces him to an unnatural usage, and creates a sense of inferiority because *his* way has been condemned. Part of J.V.'s trouble may have been caused by his father's refusal to allow him to use the hand which seemed most natural to him.

Sir James Frazer, in *The Golden Bough*, speaks of the religious symbolism involved in priests holding their emblems in the right hand (for example, Osiris) and the priestesses holding theirs in the left (for example, Isis). Some present-day psychologists claim that the right side symbolizes the masculine, and the left side the feminine. In my personal experience I have found many gifted children to be left-handed. Among the many great artists who have been left-handed are Leonardo and Michael Angelo. Perhaps these persons have bi-sexual natures.

FOURTH LESSON

His first picture he called "The Devil". It was done in red, orange, and eggplant on black paper, with the left hand. J.V. talked a long time about this drawing and said, "It started to be kind of a sea-lion. Then it turned into a clown trying to make him do a trick. The clown changed into a devil, but a devil won't scare an old sea-lion who is strong and with one flick of his tail can take care of the old devil that is after him. Here is a case of fearlessness. It's just a big bugaboo that doesn't amount to much. The devil reminds me of a figure in a Punch and Judy show I played with when I was a child. Jack-in-the-box is meant to frighten people, but isn't dangerous. I had an uncle who made the puppets for the Punch and Judy show. I wanted to help him make them, but he wouldn't let me. I think if I had had some guidance in those days I might have developed myself. I wrote little plays. As many as twenty-five kids in the neighbourhood came in. I was stage manager and printed my tickets and sold them for one cent each, but everything I tried to do someone put a damper on. The owner of the house wouldn't allow children in the house and he stopped it. It was *authority* again that I was afraid of."

I explained to him: "Yes, it was authority. But authority is always there, in some form or another. You see, we can't put all the blame on the landlord or the parent. Each of us has to assert his own individuality and find a way to overcome unfair restriction, in spite of authority, if we want to do a thing hard enough. For instance, in this case, you might have found an empty lot where you could do your plays if you had had enough desire to do so. What you have to do now is to learn to develop this strength within yourself. You must find a way to carry out your will in spite of authority. Become your own authority, that's a form of growing up." He absorbed what I had just said, and then continued:

"I always said to myself, 'What's the use?' Now I feel there's something there. Maybe I could do something about it, and give myself a chance to come out. One reason why I gave up social intercourse with other people was because I never could assert myself. When I speak to people they say, 'What?' as if I were talking to myself. I don't know whether it's because I don't pronounce correctly, but people always look at me and ask me to repeat. Other people say things and seem to have authority with what they say, but always when I go into a grocery store, I can't attract the attention of the clerk. The others all get ahead of me, and I don't want to get mad at the clerk because then I'd just get into another argument. I am always getting into arguments, but I think you have touched the trouble now.

"The way these thoughts in my system come out in my drawing is very strange. If I sat down with a paper and pencil I never could get them out."

"This work, you see, is bringing material from your unconscious," I told him. "If you sat down to write your thoughts, it would be from the conscious."

He questioned, "Well, it seems to be going very well. Do you think I'll be all set by June?"

My answer to him was, "A thing like this takes time. It's like a gradual growth and, also, it's something which is never really finished. You may be in a little better shape by June, but that's all I can say."

"When I left last time," he said, "I felt as if I was walking on clouds. Several times while I was here, I could feel myself give a big sigh of relief as if some 'strain was disengaged right here" (touching himself in the solar plexus). "Something has been clutching me there all the time."

"I understand," I said to him. "That is a nerve centre, and when you are nervous, there is great tension there. I can show you some exercises to help rest you." (These eased his tension and refreshed him.)

J.V. continued, "Another difficulty of mine is that I get confused. You need a good memory in business. My memory is terrible—plays me tricks. In the hotel business, one of the main things is a good memory for names and faces. It is as if I hated everybody, didn't care for the people I had to wait on—lacked control."

I then suggested, "You evidently were in conflict over your business, and your distaste for it helped you forget. Consciously you were trying to run this business, but unconsciously you were in protest."

J.V. rambled on. "My whole life has been blighted—I haven't known what it was all about. I'm just beginning to see. In the picture the seal is strength with no brains to guide it. I want to abuse it and use military methods on it. I see now I have been cruel to myself. I have to show myself a new kindness. I have abused a child, beaten it up—done that to my unconscious. I must make peace with it, then it will serve me. It's as if I had a big dog, a big animal, and had beaten it up. The more I did it, the more obstinate it got. I never understood it, I don't speak its language. 'I' is only one-tenth of my being. The other is submerged. I can't do anything with it. I have only known that little 'I'—pinpoint 'I'. In school we were taught that all intelligence was in a skull-box. My wife says that I have a wonderful intelligence, but do not know what to do with it."

"So, you see, you have another kind of intelligence."

"But aren't there four kinds?" he questioned. "Thinking, day-dreaming, rationalization, and creative thinking? I was born to be creative in my thinking, not to be a clerk and do index filing. I was not meant to do that thing."

"You have other potentialities," I answered. "You are trying to develop them now. We suffer in proportion to our unused functions, and you have suffered because you haven't used your possibilities."

"That's certainly true," he said.

"Have you ever thought about your intentions?"

"Yes," he replied. "I don't understand that other part of myself; it is hammering at me all the time, but it doesn't come through—like a wall between, it doesn't come through. There are certain ideas that come out of my head in daydream fashion—you don't pay any attention, don't react to them. Most of the time I am using what I call 'intelligence' arguing about things. If I had listened to that little voice, I would have saved myself a lot of trouble. The voice is like radio waves, only I don't seem able to tune in on them. This sort of thing happens to me. Last Friday I had a feeling come over me about the possibility of an automobile accident, so, crossing the streets, I said to myself, 'I must be very careful.' Also on Monday and Tuesday I thought a great deal about Dr. H., so much so that during an intermission at school I called up his office. They told me he was up in Boston, that his daughter had just been killed in an automobile accident. So that must have been the one that I was getting through my intuition. It shows there's something in my brain besides a skull-box, but I have never been able to use it, and don't quite trust it."

"Perhaps you can learn something from this, that there really is intuition, and that if you listen to it and strengthen your faith in it, it may help to change your life," I replied.

He said, "As a child I know I was psychic, but I didn't pay any attention to it—I listened to Mamma instead of my own voice. I need outside people to tell me things. This afternoon we are getting at what has been my confusion all my life. I have been fighting myself all my life and in conflict I gave up."

"Conflict throws you into confusion, and you have to make a choice. We grow by making decisions, choosing things for ourselves," I explained.

"That's right," he said. "All along others have decided for me, Mamma bought my underwear, my wife bought my ties. Somehow the right choice overpowered me. I always felt it wouldn't be perfect, so I'd leave it for someone else to do. Unless it was perfect, it wasn't worth while bothering about. If I can't get perfection, it isn't worth trying to do anything."

I countered with, "People sometimes make a mistake about holding to this idea of perfection. It can become sterile rather than creative. It is better to think of the purpose of growth as being from the imperfect to the perfect, or from the young and frail and unformed to the mature, rich in its colour and form and perfection. If you have that point of view you are willing to do crude, simple things first. After all, there is arrogance in imagining you are so powerful you can be perfect at the first try. Life is not built that way."

(During these lessons he had been producing an amazing stream of drawings from his repressed life. The incredible fact about the lessons was the way in which he could express himself so freely. With only a little guidance or clarification from me he could go on and perceive the meaning in his drawings and let them recall to him his past experiences, the hurts and mishandlings that had brought about his present condition. Following these revelations a hope was born in him that he might make a new life for himself. His last lesson follows.)

FIFTH LESSON

He called his first picture "Face About". It was a strong black scribble on small white paper with added touches of blue, rose, and yellow-orange.

J.V. commented, "If that isn't crazy, I don't know what it is. Looks like a fellow crouching. Face is where his rear end ought to be. I would be facing the past instead of forward—living in the past. He hasn't any mouth. Mouth is the means of expression, and yet I like something about the colours. Perhaps he's just a clown and can't be taken seriously. At least he's well defined, wrong as far as drawing is concerned, but definite clean-cut outlines. Is it a realization of something getting clearer in mind, that I have really been turned the wrong way round, that I have to make a face-about? Does that make sense?"

His second picture was titled "Sowing the Seeds". A scribble of a woman kneeling, it was done in rose and blue chalks on small white paper.

His third picture, "Taking the Plunge" (Ill. 144), was the brown figure of a man diving into a blue ocean.

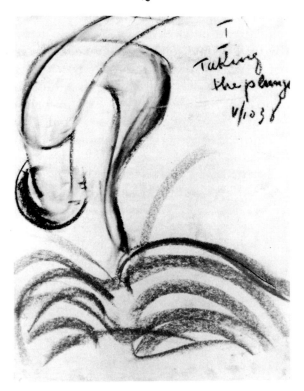

144. TAKING THE PLUNGE

About this J.V. said, "Well, I guess that's what I'm doing now."
I answered, "I'm glad you're ready."

"Taking the Plunge" is an important picture signifying the man's willingness to go on at any cost. It was the last drawing he made before he left me.

Now J.V. had to make a decision. He was undecided what to do next. His wife and some friends were motoring out West and had asked him to go with them. He considered going, thinking it would give him an opportunity for painting. On the other hand, he felt a strong pull to return to Germany, to revisit his old home, and perhaps to try the hotel business again. He said he had some connections there who had offered to help him find work. He finally made his decision to go West and give himself one more chance in America, both to find work and to see whether he and his wife could get along.

On his return to New York he came to see me again. He looked well, but said the trip had been a disappointment; he had not found work and he had painted only a little as they travelled a great deal. The problem of his marriage was settled—he and his wife had decided to separate. Now he was ready to go back to Germany to see whether he could rehabilitate himself there. He was finally and completely through with America and his marriage.

A few months later I had a postcard from Germany. He was happier, he wrote, than he had ever been, had found friends and work, and was earning a satisfactory living. This was just before the war. How much his days with me contributed to his new orientation I cannot state. I have recounted his story as it appeared from beneath the surface, bit by bit. Possibly his art experience and the thoughts which came to him as he worked and talked, may have clarified his problems and enabled him to choose a new way of life.

What J.V. and the others have been realizing has been stated in a vigorous challenge for us all by Stephen Spender.[1]

The felt life in the work of art is only intense, and often painful, because it actually touches the life of deep and terrible experience. Without this experience, art would simply express a frictionless tendency towards a vacuous perfection. But in true art there is a real conflict of life, a real breaking up and melting down of intractable material, feelings and sensations which seem incapable of expression until they have been thus transformed. A work of art doesn't say, "I am life, I offer you the opportunity of becoming me." On the contrary, it says, "This is what life is like. It is even realer, less to be evaded, than you thought. But I offer you an example of acceptance and understanding. Now, go back and live!"

[1] *Partisan Review*, Mar.–Apr., 1940. "September Journal."

CHAPTER XXV

Mario—Renewal through New Use of Breath and Sound

THE story of Mario is given last because it offers the most dramatic illustration of the value and influence of art in the development of the child.

The Counseling Centre for Gifted Children announced a competition for four scholarships to be given the most promising contestants. Hundreds applied. Among them came Mario, a nine-year-old boy of Italian descent. He was slender, dark, and very shy.

He brought with him some little sketches he had made at school. In them I saw evidence of imagination, a strong sense of life, people in movement, and an ability to draw a whole scene. For example, in a drawing called "The Flag Goes By" (Ill. 145), he drew not only the main subject of the soldiers marching and carrying the flag, but also the street, the houses, and the crowd of onlookers. His demonstration of this space-time sense, which I hold is of utmost significance, caused me to take an interest and consider him in the contest.

Dressed in his best blue suit, Mario came to the test directly from his first Communion. Naturally, he was quite excited over these two events in the same day. The test consisted of three parts. First, the pupil was told to choose his own subject and draw it in the way he was used to working. This was followed by liberating exercises of breath and movement. The third part was drawing the same subject again. This procedure would reveal how much the pupil had absorbed, and had used, the liberating exercises. It would measure his receptivity to them.

Mario's choice was the subject of "Communion" (Ill. 146). His mind and heart were filled with the new experience, and he put much feeling into his pictures. The first drawing was careless and vague, and although the second one was more positive and a bit clearer, it was still

339

145. The Flag Goes By. Brought from home by Mario at nine years of age.

unsatisfactory. The extremely mussy and hesitant quality in all the work rather prejudiced me against him, so in my first round of selections I rejected him.

When I again went over the work of all the children, I noticed one sketch of his I had previously passed by. It was "The Pirate" (Ill. 147). A pirate was suspended outside a ship; all the paints on his seat were falling off into space while he, with great concentration, went on painting a skull and crossbones on the side. I was struck with the strange situation in the picture, with the intensity of the man's expression. In the drawing of the head I saw such great ability that I was sufficiently interested to go over Mario's work again. There was something decidedly original and penetrating, indefinable but arresting, in his style. Perhaps the vagueness and indecision in his drawings was caused by fear or by a feeling of insecurity. I decided, after all, that he should receive one of the scholarships. He was with us for eight years. The choice was justified.

In the beginning, Mario had a quiet, scared way of working. He seemed always to expect to be scolded. He was very unsociable, seldom talking to the other children or enjoying himself in childish ways. He behaved a little like an animal that has been hurt and is unnaturally timid. His greatest manifest difficulty was his inability to complete a picture. He always enjoyed starting a drawing and never lacked ideas. As soon as he came into the studio, he would take off his coat, go up to the easel, and plunge right in. After a time, however, his interest would flag. The picture was never as good as he wanted. Disappointed, he

146. COMMUNION
First picture by Mario at nine years of age.

147. THE PIRATE. By Mario at nine years of age.

would quietly slip the picture into the waste-basket before I could help him overcome the difficulty and thus enable him to carry the picture further. He preferred to make a new beginning.

There were times, however, when I reached him while he was still struggling. Before he could destroy the picture, we would discuss the problem. I told him he must learn to solve the problem in this particular picture because, if he ran away from it here, he would meet it in a new shape in the next picture. I reminded him he still had the original image in his mind and could return to that for fresh inspiration. Slowly the idea penetrated, and he began to make use of it. His interest span and concentration have grown, and, with each successive year, this difficulty grows less.

During our talks, Mario told me how much he cared about his painting and how he feared that for economic reasons he would not be able to continue his work as he grew up. (He must have heard this at home.) I tried to present a picture of a road he could travel, explaining that his creative ability might be related to some form of commercial art by which he could earn a living and still remain true to himself in his expression. But, I told him, the first step in that career must be the ability to complete a picture even if it were not as nearly perfect as he would like. All this helped him.

A number of his pictures have been selected to illustrate the phases he passed through.

First, there is "Street Fight" (Ill. 148), done after about four months' work in the class. It is an early drawing chosen to show how he began to develop action, courage, and power. While the drawing is crude, it will be interesting to contrast it with his later development.

148. STREET FIGHT. By Mario at nine years of age.

149. GIRAFFES. By Mario at ten years of age.

150. An Indian. By Mario at ten years of age.

Mario loves animals and has a gift for interpreting them. "Camels" and "Giraffes" (Ill. 149) are two of his animal drawings. Both show a side of his nature quite different from his expressions of aggression.

The next two pictures were done about a year later. The first is called "An Indian" (Ill. 150). It is strong, but not well drawn, and seemed to me to come from some conventional school programme— perhaps the study of American history. I talked to him about finding subjects for his work from his own life, his experiences, imaginings, or feelings. When I mentioned some common experiences, such as situations in which we feel love, hate, anger, or fear, he stopped me there and pounced on fear. He said, "I could do plenty of pictures of fear."

I asked him whether he would draw one of these ideas, and he instantly said, "Yes." This drawing he named "Fear: the Graveyard at

151. FEAR: THE GRAVEYARD AT MIDNIGHT. By Mario at ten years of age.

Midnight" (Ill. 151). He said, "It's night, and the spirits have arrived from the grave. There are a spirit and something like a vampire walking around the graveyard. Here are the tombstones and the graves; down here are skulls, and up above are bats flying. It's midnight in the cemetery."

In the drawing, the picture grew too black and thus lost some of its eerie light. I showed him the possibilities of retrieving it by use of eraser and chamois. He caught on quickly and found again the desired quality.

This pair of drawings demonstrates that when real feeling is evoked, the work deepens. The necessary expression is found because spirit creates its own form. The tragic quality of the picture gives us a glimpse into the child's soul. He uses the death principle to kill something that is hurting him, and he uses the creative principle to lift himself out of his pain. He must have experienced living terrors and then objectified his struggle in his art in which he creates light for himself.

This exposure of hidden fears was the beginning of a sequence of pictures exhibiting aggression and cruelty. These all indicated a great terror of life, caused by we know not what incidents or words which had frightened him and had made him afraid of the future. The young cannot conceive the world outside, and if security in the home is shaken their whole structure topples.

The next picture Mario called "Cruelty: Man Beating a Horse" (Ill. 152). It is another expression of suffering, cruelty, and injustice. He started right in without saying a word. When I came back, he had a fine sketch of a rearing horse. I asked him what the picture was going to be. He replied, "There is a wagon behind the horse and it is tipped over with everything falling out." (Recall the picture of the pirate and the pots of paint falling down also.) "The driver was drunk. He made the wagon tip over, but he blamed it on the horse. He was drinking in the wagon, and there were bottles all around. He was mad with the horse and started hitting him, and the horse started bleeding."

About that time the circus came to town. It occurred to me that a little fun might be a good thing for Mario, so I invited him to go with me. He was delighted at the prospect. When the day came, we started out happily. First, we went to lunch. We talked of many things. Mario

152. Cruelty: Man Beating a Horse. By Mario at eleven years of age.

was interested in politics, world affairs, and sports, knew a great deal about the war situation in Europe, and had his opinions about everything. When discussing sports, I asked him whether there was anything he especially longed to have. I hoped that by engaging in some sport he would have opportunity to play more with other boys.

In a flash he answered, "Oh, yes, a baseball and mitt."

"What kind of mitt?" I asked.

"A first baseman's mitt," he said at once, at the same time punching his left fist into his right hand to demonstrate its use.

"Perhaps we can find one after the circus," I said.

All the way up to Madison Square Garden, he kept telling me about the performers we were going to see. He knew them all by

153. THE LION TAMER. By Mario at eleven years of age.

Finally, after he had seen enough, we went out to the street, and he said, "I want to tell you, Mrs. Cane, I had the best time I ever had in my life this afternoon." Then he turned and said abruptly, "Oh, there's a sports shop!" So we went into Davega's, and he got just what he wanted—a good first baseman's mitt and one fine baseball. He was terribly happy and said, "Gee, I wonder what my father'll say about this!"

When I took him to the subway, Mario said, "You know, the glove is almost better than the circus."

Undoubtedly a change came over him after our day together. He became more friendly and gradually began participating in the life of the group. His drawings still dealt with calamitous subjects, but were produced with more ease and fluency. The torrent had to be poured out to cleanse him before he could build anew.

The week following the circus he made several drawings from memory. In one, "The Lion Tamer" (Ill. 153), his interpretation is again on the cruel side—the tamer brandishes his whip over the cowering lions.

We were approaching the end of the term. The war was absorbing the interest of many in the class. Mario's expression of it may have had some significance from his own life. He illustrated a scene in war— "Agony: Wounded" (Ill. 154)—one soldier helping a fallen comrade. His drawing grew more direct and fearless; his comprehension of the figure increased. This war picture concluded the spring of that year.

In the following autumn when the class resumed, Mario was still drawing destructive subjects. Among them were a leopard approaching a village at night, waiting for his prey, and a bound captive about to be beheaded, with the executioner holding an axe uplifted and the priest waiting for the victim. There was even a murder, the victim lying on the ground with a knife in his back. He called this drawing "Guilt" (Ill. 155).

During the Christmas holidays I had looked over the work done in the autumn and was dissatisfied. The general impression was poverty in colour. I decided to try to refresh Mario by using the simple approach I employ with little children. I said, "Let's go over to the table where the coloured chalks are laid out and select the one colour which speaks to you most strongly, the one you want most. Hold the chalk you have

154. AGONY: WOUNDED
By Mario at eleven years of age.

chosen in your hand, feel it, and know it. Now pass it over all the other colours. Wait until the chalk in your hand asks for the one it wants most.''

Thus we find colours belonging to each child's own colour field. The first is his key colour; the second, its stimulant or complement. If a child works for a time in his own colour field, he establishes for ever his own colour sense and can expand from there.

Mario chose a strong bright green and clear yellow. He then made a drawing of a landscape in black chalk—a hillside with ferns and trees, beyond that a yellow valley and distant hill of green. The whole was a fine bright picture of an outdoor mood of summer. In the next, he depicted rocks in yellow, orange, brown, and green. This had light and vigour. Afterwards he dropped colour for a while and made some pencil drawings. These were not important enough to record. Because of his continued return to black and white, I thought it wise to let him experiment with sound and breath in order to stimulate his colour sense.

In my various experiments with releasing the creative powers, I have found that letting the child breathe deeply and make simple vowel sounds as he breathes in and out, will have a direct bearing on his productive capacity. The decarbonizing of the lungs by exhaling and the recharging by new oxygen intake increase the blood circulation, clear the head, and supply new energy. This sounding of vowels becomes a chant. The child enjoys this exercise and, if he keeps his eyes closed, the breathing, singing, and chanting excite his colour vision; desire to express what he sees follows. Thus, form is born in a new way. We have this cycle: breath, sound, and movement producing new energy and inspiring colour vision; vision evoking desire; and desire put forth into action creating form. Darkness of the paper is as helpful to the creative birth as the darkness in the earth is to the seed. Art should not imitate nature, but should learn from its process.

When Mario returned to the studio, a small piece of black paper was there ready for him. He went straight to the coloured chalks and swiftly chose deep rose and pale yellow. He made at once a design, "The Heart" (Pl. XXI), a sound picture from "AH". Totally different from anything he had ever done before, it is a sketch of a heart-shaped form done in the deep rose-red, encircled by a line of clear yellow. The colours used are expressive of what had just happened to him. The rich red is the new dynamic force; the yellow symbolizes light which filtered in when his arms were raised; his sounds brought new inspiration.

This was followed by another abstraction, similar to the first, but stronger, with a blue circle added. The colour blue symbolizes feeling, and in this instance adds the inner quality of Mario's own spirit after the inrush of strength and light.

Immediately after this, he asked for a large piece of paper and did a simple landscape of hills and trees. "It is the feeling of spring," he said. "I'm trying to use my chalks to show the soft feeling, not hard like in my drawings." The colours were delicate shades of yellow and green.

This picture was a tentative, somewhat timid try-out of his new approach, but the next picture was truly a new step. He calls it "The

155. GUILT. By Mario at eleven years of age.

Bluebird Guarding Its Eggs" (Pl. XXII). It is a full and beautiful expression of his new life, a new step in his work. The colours used are the same rich blue, rose, and clear yellow of the abstractions; he has added brown for the branches and white for the eggs. Brown is the colour of birth, and white of new life. The eggs symbolize the new life, and the watchfulness of the mother bird expresses protection and love. This is a masterly composition. He had never done anything to compare with it before. The design is fine; the colour is expressive and powerful, and his new life breathes through it. The sequence that follows is stirring.

The fish was done in coloured chalk on black paper from the sound "OH". The colour and movement are extremely beautiful. Mario was beginning to feel rhythm in himself; he was a part of the moving water and the growing grasses.

Next came a sketch seen in the mind while chanting to the sound of "AH". He called it "Man Dancing in Flames". It evidently expresses some of the new emotion awakened in him through his singing and colour association. As he looked at his sketch new thoughts came to him and he did a larger picture of two men dancing before the fire. He called it "Pagan Rites: Men Dancing before the Fire God" (Pl. XXIII). The little sketch doubtless depicts himself come alive with the feeling of the dance and the warmth of fire. Then as the theme evolved it became a ceremonial rite. The figures are dancing and throwing gold upon the flames to their god. This is really a pagan religious picture which has come out of himself from his singing. The beauty and freedom of this in comparison with the darkness and cringing fear in the Communion picture graphically reveal the change in the boy.

"Abstract Form" was inspired by a chanting of the "OH-OH" sound, accompanied by swinging movements with rounded forms. This picture shows the real origin of abstract art derived from the movement, breath, and sound of one's own body. Mario knew there is light and line in art, but now he became aware of a basic colour world and attained a new depth of colour consciousness within himself.

This picture was immediately followed by "The Cave Man" (Ill. 156), one of the most powerful and impressive things that I have ever seen a pupil do. I think it is great art. The brown line represents man; the yellow outline, the force outside himself or God; the heavenly blue

XXI. THE HEART. Sound picture drawn after
chanting "AH". By Mario at twelve years of age.

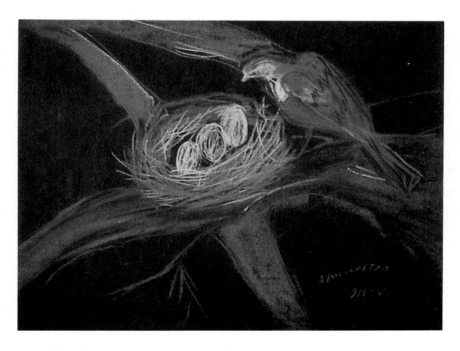

XXII. THE BLUEBIRD GUARDING ITS EGGS. By Mario at twelve years of age.

XXIII. Pagan Rites: Men Dancing before the Fire God
Sound picture. By Mario at twelve years of age.

156. THE CAVE MAN. By Mario at twelve years of age.

157. STATUE OF APHRODITE AT NIGHT. By Mario at
thirteen years of age.

behind the man represents emotion—it is the blue of ultimate things.
It is as if the picture said, "I have grown to man's estate." Mario actually
wrote on the back, "A lonely cave man—his friends deserted him; he
sits and broods." The year before, he wanted to behead everything, now
Mario saw himself a true man in relation to the universe.

Done in black and white, "Statue of Aphrodite at Night" (Ill. 157),
depicts with classic purity and essential vigour the kneeling figure of a
woman. It is truly plastic in form, as was the last picture. It has great
beauty and dignity. Mario had now discovered the feminine form of
ideal beauty for him. The woman he produced was a dream woman,
comparable to the man he had found. Her gentleness is a counterpart
to the strength of the cave man. The fact that he selected Aphrodite as
his ideal woman has real significance. She was the goddess of love,
beauty, and life. At this moment of his awakening she was the unconscious
symbol of these things for the growing boy.

Some months before, he had produced a drawing of a totally different type of woman, "A Tough Woman" (Ill. 158). It was his first expression of sex and revealed a rather low idea, extremely sensual and tough. The hair is a sharp yellow and the lips red—probably the impression he had received in the streets or from the movies. Now, having gone through an inner contact with deeper sources, he unconsciously produced this higher type of woman.

"Man Working" (Ill. 159) is a picture of a labourer bent over, lifting a very heavy bar. It seemed that Mario had completed a cycle. First, he cleansed himself of his fears and aggressive impulses through expression; next, he found his own colour key and harmonies through breath and sound; then he discovered his primitive ideas of man, woman, and

158. A TOUGH WOMAN. By Mario at twelve years of age.

159. MAN WORKING. By Mario at thirteen years of
age. Last picture of this series.

God and found himself in relation to the universe. Now he returned to
take up the burden of living with new strength.

The next phase of his work found him interested in studying different
types of men. He made portrait sketches from memory of many people
seen in the streets, subways, and buses. Some of the sketches were "The
Bum" (Ill. 160), "The Businessman" (Ill. 161), "The Young Student"
(Ill. 162), and "The Schoolmaster" (Ill. 163). These drawings show a
new maturity.

The next year, when Mario was sixteen, he returned to his interest
in religion. This time he drew in coloured chalks the picture, "The
Temptation" (Ill. 164). He wrote about this:

160. THE BUM. By Mario at fifteen years of age.

161. THE BUSINESSMAN. By Mario at fifteen years of age.

162. THE YOUNG STUDENT. By Mario at fifteen years of age.

163. THE SCHOOLMASTER. By Mario at fifteen years of age.

This scene was taken from the Bible. It is supposed to show how the people of that time after crucifying Christ were lured by the devil. The devil is the man perched up on the small cliff. The men struggled for the gold he showed them, and many died in the attempt to get it. None of the men finally got the gold as the devil disappeared.

As the winter progressed, he developed his interest in black-and-white drawing, concentrating more on the idea of illustration. The pictures called "The Barber Shop" (Ill. 165) and "The Wise Man" (Ill. 166) are good examples. The latter is a great advance over any previous work and holds promise of his future growth. Again he showed progress in technique and human insight.

Mario is now about to graduate from high school. In the evenings he is taking a course in illustration at Pratt Institute in Brooklyn. His present plan is to become an illustrator.

Writing of his plans for the future, he says:

My immediate interest is to work towards book illustration in the magazine field. I prefer working in black and white, and especially like to draw people because I deal with them every day and naturally like to transpose them on paper. I think I am influenced by Daumier, and I don't care much for modern art. Working in the Saturday class has helped me to acquire freedom in my work. Now at Pratt I am learning more detailed technique in the use of mass, line, black and white, and so on. I think this school will help me a great deal. Sometimes when I draw I get many ideas, and these ideas confuse me and complicate my drawing, but recently I see more clearly what I want to do than formerly.

Here, then, is a living example that art is not an escape from life, as was once erroneously claimed by Freud, but a solution of problems conditioned by parents or created by the child himself through his own misunderstanding of life. A child sees only one phase of existence at a time; he cannot see ways out of his dilemmas. If his future is threatened, he sees it as final tragedy.

But Mario has found a solution. He has taken the painful thing out of his life through its expression in art and has found new health in body, soul, and mind. If this can be done for him, it can be done for many. Art may some day become our soundest therapy. For through art expression man finds his own pattern within himself and subsequently his pattern in relation to his fellow men.

164. THE TEMPTATION. By Mario at sixteen years of age.

165. THE BARBER SHOP. By Mario at seventeen years of age.

166. THE WISE MAN. By Mario at seventeen years of age.

Summary

THE fundamental issue presented in this book is how best to develop the "Artist in Each of Us". The concept is as follows: no amount of direct technical training in drawing or painting can compare in value with the ability to alter the conditions within the artist. He is the instrument through which the art is produced. It follows that the art can be no better than the instrument.

The chief value of creative experience for the child lies in its power to release his emotions and ideas, give them form, and through this activity to develop and integrate him as a human being. In creative work all of his functions come into play; and the teacher's part is to see that they actually do function. Thus, instead of judging the drawing or painting as a product to be corrected or improved, the teacher uses the drawing as an index of the child's state and tries to improve that, knowing that if the child is fully alive, his work will be.

Is his body free, and are his movements rhythmic? Are his feelings governing his work or are they inhibited? Is his imagination awake and active, or is it dormant? The teacher must learn how to release him, physically, emotionally, and spiritually.

With this point of view our task has been to study the child as a whole, and to try to observe under just what conditions he creates best; secondly, to consider what our attitude should be towards him; thirdly, to help him function fully in physical, emotional, and spiritual aspects of his being in order that he may become happy and whole and creative —an integrated human being.

In this indirect approach to the teaching of art, the student's body is liberated, his emotions expressed, his consciousness deepened, and his horizons widened. This spiritual awakening will create its own form. As a result, his art changes miraculously and to an immeasurable degree quite beyond our powers to achieve by direct teaching.

This sums up our attitude towards the potential artist in the student.

An issue of equal importance in this educational problem is the role of the teacher. In this case it concerns the artist in the teacher which exists dormantly, but is neglected ignominiously. In the meagre role assigned to the teachers in schools, economically and socially, they have little opportunity for leisure and self-development. We must realize that one cannot pour from an empty cup and that to become true guardians of our children's souls, teachers need time to cultivate their own.

It is difficult to see just how this change can be brought about, how this great injustice to teachers is to be altered. Not until we value wisdom more than power and ease will the demand for fairer treatment and consideration of the teacher's needs be recognized and dealt with adequately.

In this new attitude to the potential artist in each of us, which is growing everywhere, we should find a new attitude towards the teacher who needs the same kind of liberation and nourishment.

The teacher is the embodiment of the democratic principle: it is his duty, his chief assignment to develop the individuality of each pupil, to cherish and inspire the human spirit. In this proud role, he becomes the guardian of a deeper culture, a truer democracy.

COMMENTS BY STUDENTS AND COLLEAGUES OF FLORENCE CANE

FLORENCE Cane was one of those rare beings who brought out the best in each individual she had contact with. First as a young student and later (1950-52) as a young teacher associated with her, I found Florence to be always encouraging, always positive, provocative, and inspiring. It seemed as if she had a secret knowledge of your potential, of your talent and abilities, as if she believed in you more than you believed in yourself, knew you better than you knew yourself, and knew how to bring forth and help you develop that potential. Because she believed, you believed too. Her encouragement gave you courage.

Nothing was imposed from without; her method was the antithesis of academicism in art teaching. She believed implicitly that organic and unconscious processes were at the heart of creative production; that the power in a work comes from within and the structure of a work is formed by this process. All her methods were ways of allowing the intuitive and the unconscious to emerge and of giving them free play. She knew this was the source and had faith that once it was opened up everything would follow naturally.

Florence was a seminal figure in my life and a dear friend. She was my first art teacher and the first to give me the encouragement as well as the opportunity to teach. Subsequently, my own approach to painting and to teaching have in part been inspired by her example.

In rereading her book I am impressed by how her personality seems to breathe on every page, how her intelligence and humanity come through. As valid as I believe her theories and methods to be (and I am certain they can still raise important questions and open eyes today amongst art educators, if only they will take them as seriously as some art therapists do), I nevertheless feel she is larger than her formulations. She of course wanted to believe that her ideas could be passed on, but I have my doubts. No matter how well-intentioned one is, there is always the danger of academicism when one is following precepts rather than discovering them for oneself. The intuition and presence of a great spirit cannot be simulated, only emulated. She was after all, for those lucky enough to have known her, one of a kind.

STEVEN GILBERT
Painter and Teacher of Painting
The Maryland Institute, College of Art
New York, May 1983

WHEN I came to the Walden School, I was twelve years old. My first painting was an oil—a Dutch street scene. I carefully painted each wooden shoe, full skirt, white bonnet—all in rather dreary colors. Florence must have watched me for some time before she sat down with me to talk about what I was doing. This was her method. She didn't touch what we did, suggest how else to draw, or another color to use. She would discuss what might be the reason for the problem. She knew when to intervene and when to sit by. In this case the Dutch painting was put aside in favor of some large, beautifully colored chalks and a large sheet of paper. Florence suggested I might try making a design using my whole arm, not just my fingers.

Florence Cane describes a later experience of mine on pages 100-103 of this book; her account almost exactly matches my memory. I think the story illustrates her gift as a teacher—it lay in this ability to reach one, to in some inner way free one's wish to do—and help release one's ideas. She did not impose a model to follow from the outside or a proper way to render an object. She encouraged us to find our own way, and because of her approach my ideas were connected to *me*.

Now many years later, teaching contemporary dance, those early experiences with Florence come back to me. In one of my classes the students listen to music; then they draw their feeling of the music. To help them use the whole body in making the shapes, I use the exercises Florence used with us long ago. It works.

This fall I asked some third-year students who were learning to teach dance to children to read an article Florence had published many years ago. It was interesting how fresh and stimulating her ideas still are. Perhaps, I think a little ruefully, it would be better if her ideas did not have to remind us of those truths which were once at the forefront and are now too often forgotten.

JANE DUDLEY, Teacher
London School of Contemporary Dance
London, May 1983

WE teachers at the Walden School came into Florence's studio like children (I was thirty years old), wide-eyed children entering a fantasy setting of easels, stools, canvases, paint boxes, brushes, pots, fruits, flowers, textiles. Under a kind of generous mothering, Florence opened the way and we moved on until we found our own relation to line, space, color. Student became painter. Painter became artist when the scarlet cyclamen blossom of the composed still life on the table became the miracle-flame on the canvas. We came into awareness of the artist in each of us. As teachers we would use this awareness to open the way for our students into their own creativeness.

BERTA RANTZ, Former Teacher
Director of the High School
The Walden School
Walnut Creek, California, March 1983

ALTHOUGH I was a completely untalented student in Florence Cane's high school art class at the Walden School, I was treated—as were all students—like a serious artist. From her I learned to look at objects, noting not only their shape and color but also how light, shadow, and perspective changed the way they looked. Without actually saying so she conveyed the impression that she expected you to produce a painting worthy of consideration. Her serious, respectful discussion of a finished piece of work somehow caused the student to look at pictures ever after with an appreciation of the intention, the problems, and the success of the artist.

RIVA ROBINSON
Retired Teacher and Counselor
New York City High Schools
New York, May 1983

WHEN I started teaching dance at the Walden School, I joined one of Florence Cane's painting classes. My first painting was, to my surprise, rather formal and realistic—and Florence was quick to contrast it with my free, rhythmic body movement in dance.

This was an important lesson for me. Her methods made me realize how fundamental free movement is to painting as well as to dance. It was a wonderful experience that was visible at once in my next painting.

ELIZABETH DELZA
Teacher of Dance
New York, May 1983